Vigilantes in Gold Rush San Francisco

VIGILANTES IN GOLD RUSH SAN FRANCISCO

♦

Robert M. Senkewicz, S. J.

STANFORD UNIVERSITY PRESS
Stanford, California 1985

Stanford University Press
Stanford, California

Printed in the United States of America

CIP data appear at the end of the book

Published with the assistance of the Edgar M. Kahn Memorial Fund

Sources of illustrations: pp. xii–xiii, 91, 95, 101, courtesy of the Bancroft Library; pp. 92, 93 (top), 96–100, courtesy of the California State Library; p. 93 (bottom), courtesy of the Wells Fargo Bank History Department; p. 94, courtesy of the International Museum of Photography at George Eastman House; p. 102, copy in private collection of Lyndon Farwell, a descendant of James Farwell, one of the 1856 vigilantes.
Endpaper illustration: The hanging of John Jenkins on the night of June 10, by the San Francisco Vigilance Committee of 1851. An 1891 drawing by A. Castaigne after a contemporary lithograph; published in *The Century Magazine* 43, no. 1 (Nov. 1891): 137.

For my mother
and
my father

Preface

Although I hope it is not too noticeable, this book began as a doctoral dissertation. As a graduate student at Stanford, I wanted to write about a nineteenth-century American city and I did not want to have to travel too far for the research. That eccentric combination reduced the number of potential urban sites to one. Professor Don Fehrenbacher agreed to direct the work. I was delighted when he allowed that the last word on the San Francisco vigilance committees had perhaps not been written, but a trifle wary when he told me that he was planning to spend that next year at William and Mary. I had already heard too many horror stories from friends around the country about the perils of trying to maintain a long-distance working relationship with a dissertation director!

I need not have worried. Professor Fehrenbacher must have used up scores of typewriter ribbons and spent a small fortune on postage encouraging me, deflating my more outrageous meanderings with well-aimed barbs, and editing my prose—all with never more than a week's time elapsing between my sending him a letter or chapter and receiving a response. American historians, who know how much time and energy he put into preparing the late David Potter's notes and essays for publication, are well aware of Don Fehrenbacher's generosity and commitment. I experienced those qualities as a graduate student. Even though I have mercifully not inflicted the present manuscript on him, I want to thank him for teaching me by example how selfless an academic mentor can be.

I do not know how most people feel when they finish dissertations, but after I finished mine, I wanted to put as much psychological distance as possible between myself and the San Francisco vigilantes. Circumstances helped. I studied for three years at the Jesuit School of Theology at Berkeley and then went to teach, first humanities and then history, at the University of

Santa Clara. For the first few years as a teacher I prepared the seemingly infinite number of new courses that are so familiar to beginning faculty members at undergraduate institutions. To this day, I have never taught one course or seminar centered on San Francisco or on vigilantes. I would like to think that both my students and I have benefited from the omission.

Earlier versions of material that appears in this book were published in the *Pacific Historian* (Fall 1979) and the *Southern California Quarterly* (Winter 1979). I wish to thank the editors of both for permission to use that material here. I presented a paper on gold rush San Francisco at the 1978 meeting of the American Catholic Historical Association. I thank Professor Richard Maxwell Brown, commentator at that session, for suggestions he made at that time. No one but me, of course, is responsible for any errors in the book.

Before I began to research this project, I had never thought of librarians as members of a helping profession, but I certainly do so now. The staffs of the Bancroft Library at the University of California, Berkeley, the California Historical Society in San Francisco, the Huntington Library in San Marino, the California State Library in Sacramento, the Beinecke and Sterling libraries at Yale University, the New York Historical Society in New York, and the Nevada Historical Society in Reno could give lessons in competent listening and patience to, say, priests.

At Santa Clara, I received a summer research grant from the president, William Rewak, and secretarial assistance from the office of the then academic vice-president, William Donnelly. I thank them both. Two colleagues in the history department, Gerald McKevitt and Mary McDougall Gordon, offered constant advice and support over the years. I first began to write the present manuscript while I was teaching for a year at Old College in Reno. I thank John Leary, its founder and president, for much support.

At Stanford University Press, I consider myself privileged to have had Shirley Taylor assigned as editor. The times I read her blue-penciled suggestions and wondered why I could not have put it like that in the first place are too numerous to recount.

My greatest debt is to my extended family, the Jesuit Community at Santa Clara. Over the last eight years, as young teacher, prodigal son, and advancing-to-middle-age partner, I have always received much more from each of them than I have been able to give. For four of the past five years, I have shared a small house a block from campus with six of them. Dan Germann, Paul Locatelli, Gerry McKevitt, John Privett, Jim Reites, and Manny Velasquez, Marthas all, are overjoyed that the book is finally done so that this Mary can get back to mopping the kitchen.

R.M.S.

Contents

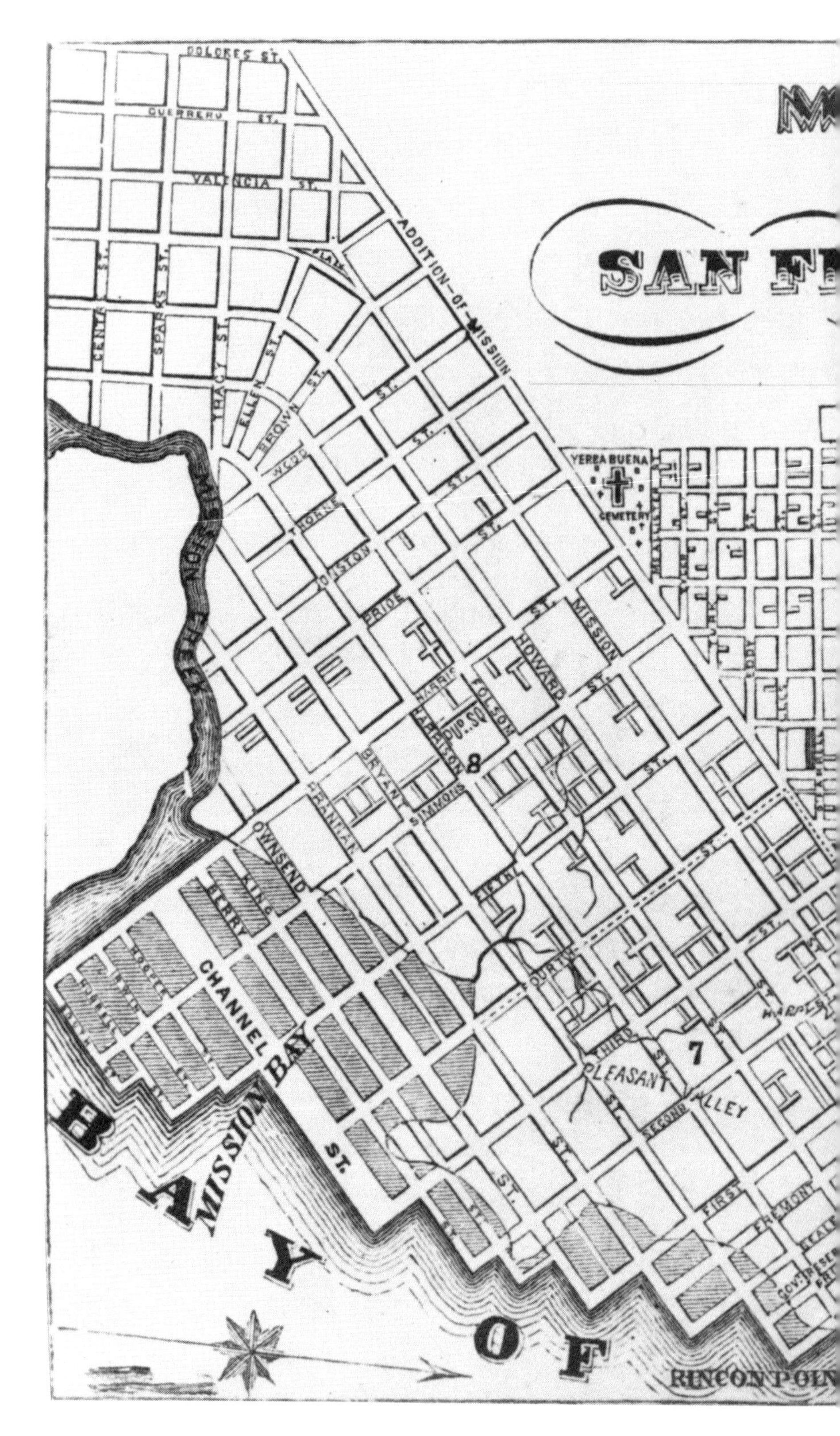
DOLORES ST.
GUERRERO ST.
VALENCIA ST.
SPARKS ST.
TRACY ST.
ELLEN ST.
BROWN ST.
ADDITION OF MISSION
YERBA BUENA
CEMETERY
MISSION
HOWARD
FOLSOM
HARRISON
BRYANT
BRANNAN
SIMMONS
8
KING
BERRY
CHANNEL
MISSION BAY
FIFTH
FOURTH
THIRD
PLEASANT VALLEY
7
SECOND
FIRST
FREMONT
B
A
Y
OF

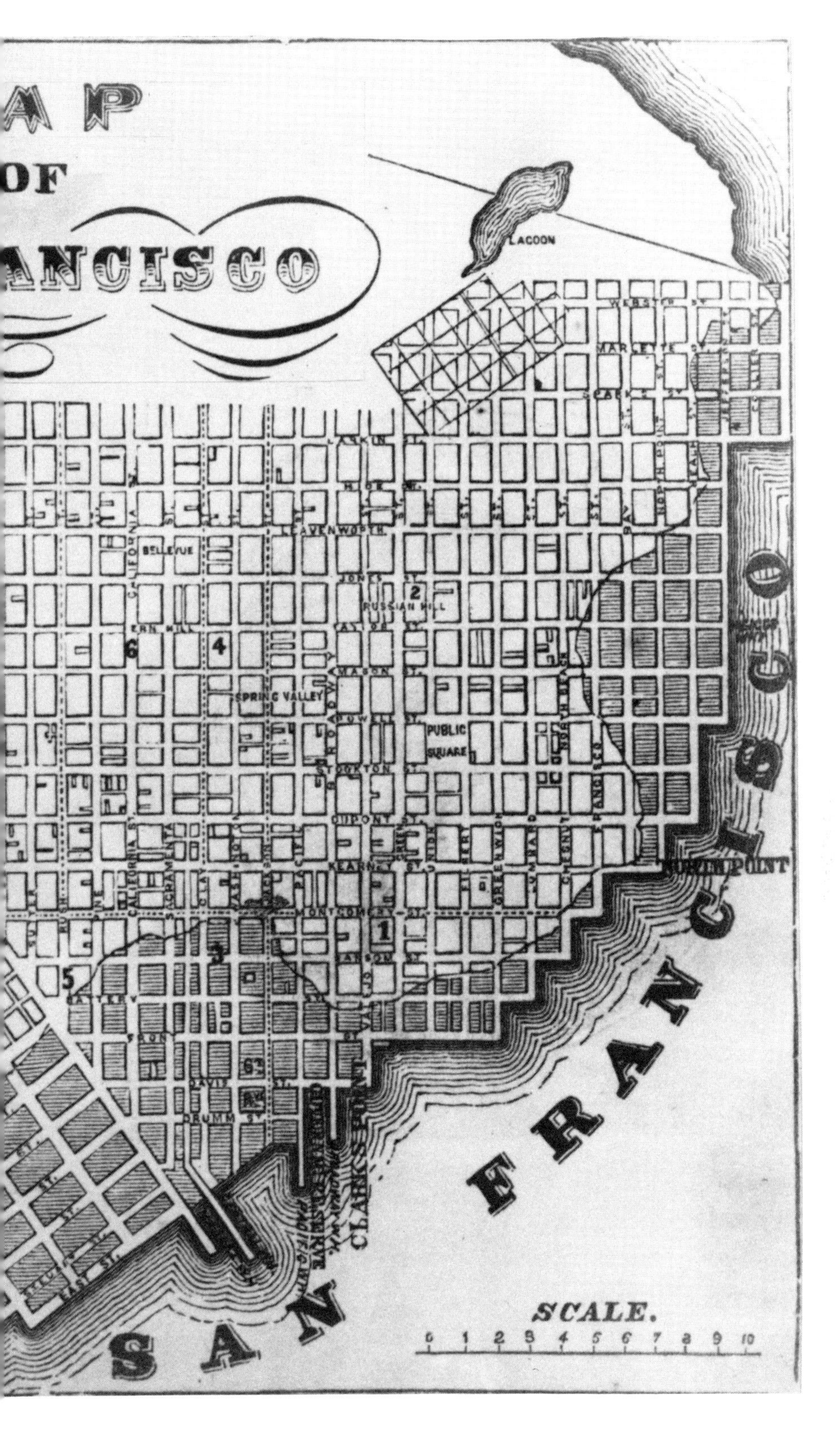

OF
LAGOON
LARKIN ST.
LEAVENWORTH
BELLEVUE
JONES ST.
RUSSIAN HILL
SPRING VALLEY
MASON ST.
POWELL ST.
PUBLIC
SQUARE
STOCKTON ST.
DUPONT ST.
KEARNEY ST.
MONTGOMERY ST.
SANSOM ST.
BATTERY
DAVIS ST.
DRUMM ST.
CLARK'S POINT
NORTH POINT
SAN FRANCISCO
SCALE.
0 1 2 3 4 5 6 7 8 9 10

Map (*overleaf*): San Francisco in 1854. The shaded area is land filled in from the bay. Bold numbers indicate the location of the wards.

Vigilantes in Gold Rush San Francisco

CHAPTER 1

THE ARRIVALS

And as men migrated from the east, they found a plain in the land of Shinar and settled there. . . . Then they said, "Come, let us build ourselves a city, and a tower with its top in the heavens, and let us make a name for ourselves."

—Genesis 11: 2, 4

♦

I suppose that there is plenty of news to write about here, but I do not know what it is, for such things that would set cities and towns and states in an uproar scarcely attract a passing notice here.

—Laborer Milton Hall,
writing from San Francisco, June 27, 1854

♦

This land of strangers, where nothing but the merciless grasp of the money getter greets you on every side. . . . There are no men of leisure here, all are in a race.

—Businessman William K. Weston,
writing from San Francisco, April 28, 1851

♦

All California is only a sort of theater, where everything goes ahead on the high pressure principle. You can't stand still if you would, and the consequence is that you are whirled around and about, until you are apt to get dizzy.

—Lawyer Joseph B. Crockett,
writing from San Francisco, May 1, 1854

♦

These men left their first country to improve their condition; they quit their second to ameliorate it still more; fortune awaits them everywhere, but not happiness. The desire of prosperity has become an ardent and restless passion in their minds, which grows by what it feeds on. *—Alexis de Tocqueville*

♦ I ♦

Four events shaped the memory of many gold rush San Franciscans. Their content was robbery and killing, and their themes were outrage, patience, and vengeance.

Around eight o'clock on the evening of February 19, 1851, a man entered the store of C. J. Jansen and Co. on the corner of Montgomery and Washington streets. The store was in the midst of the gold rush port's business district, only a block from the bustling waterfront and another block from Portsmouth Square, the heart of the city's commercial area. The man asked Jansen, who was preparing to close shop and then eat the late dinner that was standard fare for the harried merchants of the town, for a dozen blankets. This was not an unusual request: the man could well have been a miner outfitting himself for a summer of panning in the Mother Lode country. Nights tended to be cool in the foothills of the Sierra Nevada. Jansen began automatically counting out the blankets for the customer. As he was doing so, he may have noticed another man entering the store.

The customer stopped Jansen as he was counting and told him that he wanted white blankets, not colored ones. This was an unusual request, for the miners generally asked for blankets that did not show dirt. The last thing Jansen remembered was stooping down to get the white blankets.

When he came to, he was on the floor with a heavy throbbing in his head. He managed to crawl to the door and shout for help. His prospective dinner partner, auctioneer Theodore Payne, came from his own office across the way. He discovered that Jansen had been beaten on the head. About $2,000 was missing from his desk. Payne immediately called the police. When they arrived, Jansen described for them, as best he could, the appearance of the assailants.

The next day, the police separately arrested two men who fitted the descriptions. Both were Australians. One, who gave his name as Robert Windred, had been arrested during a pickup card game along the waterfront. The other called himself

Thomas Berdue. But "Berdue" bore an uncanny resemblance to James Stuart, wanted for murder in the interior of the state. Both men were taken to jail. A crowd, angry at the robbery and excited that the notorious Stuart was in custody, gathered outside the jail. The press, both reflecting and whipping up public sentiment, began to call for blood. "We deprecate Lynch Law," intoned one paper, "but the outraged public will appeal to that unless some far more efficient measures be adopted in other quarters."

On Saturday morning, February 22, the two prisoners were taken to the rooms in which Jansen was recovering from the attack. Although Jansen said he could not swear to it, he agreed that the prisoners were the same men who had been in the store. Word of the identification spread through the crowd, which had gathered again, and mutterings that the two should be lynched began to circulate. Some people passed around a printed handbill that stated bluntly, "Let each man be his own executioner," and urged a public meeting for the next day at Portsmouth Square. The crowd followed the police and the prisoners to the City Hall, where the arraignment was to take place. As many as could jammed into the courtroom, and over a thousand remained outside. After the court proceedings were finished, some members of the crowd made an unorganized attempt to storm the building and seize the prisoners. The police and a militia company, the Washington Guards, whose headquarters were next door and who had been put on alert, managed to repel the mob, but it proved impossible to get the prisoners through the crowd back to the jail. So they were stashed in the basement of a nearby hotel, while part of the crowd remained outside to ensure that they were not secreted away.

The next day, Sunday, a mass of people, estimated at about five to six thousand, crammed into the Plaza. Mayor John Geary spoke to the crowd and urged them to leave the prisoners to the authorities. He assured the assembly that the trial would take place soon, and he said that those who were interested in justice should present themselves for jury duty at that time. Then a young commission merchant, William T. Coleman, got the crowd's attention. No one had confidence in the courts, he told them, and he recommended the formation of a people's court to try the prisoners immediately. His speech was greeted with loud cheers, and the leaders of the crowd rushed into the building. The mayor and the police, powerless before such overwhelming odds, withdrew.

Inside, the throng chose three of its members as judges, empaneled a jury of its own composition, appointed Coleman as prosecutor, and agreed to the requests of three lawyers that they be allowed to serve as defense attorneys. The trial was held that afternoon, but the amateur Coleman was outclassed by the professional attorneys. By exploiting the uncertainties of the situation, especially the fact that Jansen was not entirely lucid and his identification of the prisoners therefore suspect, the defense managed to deadlock the de facto jury, with nine voting for conviction and three for acquittal. When the verdict was announced to the crowd outside, a few men yelled out that the prisoners should be hanged anyway. But it was already late in the afternoon, and most people were getting tired. So the crowd drifted off. The prisoners were returned to the legal authorities, who tried and convicted both of them.

On Tuesday evening, June 10, 1851, George Virgin left his shipping office near the aptly named Long Wharf, which stretched almost a half-mile into the bay from the foot of Commercial Street. Virgin was going to check on the sailing time of one of the vessels he dealt with. As he was returning to his office, he saw a man hastily rowing away from the wharf in a small dinghy. In the same dinghy he also noticed his office safe! Virgin's shouts attracted the attention of other merchants and boatmen, who took out after the thief. The man in the dinghy managed to pitch the safe overboard just before he was apprehended.

As a group of merchants prepared to take the thief—whose name was John Jenkins—to the police station, one of them, commission merchant George Schenck, had a better idea. Schenck had joined a secret vigilance committee only a few days earlier. He suggested bringing Jenkins before the vigilantes, who had their headquarters in a group of vacant offices on the corner of Bush and Sansome streets, in the building that also housed Sam Brannan's real estate brokerage. The other merchants agreed with Schenck, and they took Jenkins to the offices. A committee meeting had just adjourned, and several of the members were still present.

The sight of a live Australian thief stirred up the vigilantes, who so far had not done very much except draw up a long constitution and give themselves secret numbers. George Oakes, who had been one of the organizers of the committee, was also a foreman of Empire Engine Co. No. 1. He went out and rang the firebell, the prearranged signal for the vigilantes to assemble. When about thirty men had arrived, a trial was at once called in order, with Schenck as the prosecutor and Brannan as the chief judge. No one seemed to think that there was any need for a defense attorney.

Around eleven that night, the vigilante court found Jenkins guilty of theft and sentenced him to death by hanging. By this time a crowd of curiosity seekers had gathered outside and was buzzing with rumors. Brannan came out and harangued them about the inadequacies of the law and told them that he and some others had decided that the time had come to take the law into their own hands. At half-past one, Jenkins was led by gun-toting vigilantes to Portsmouth Square. A rope was thrown over the beam of the old adobe customs house and a noose was strung at one end of it. The noose was placed around Jenkins's neck; affecting indifference, he continued to smoke a cigar.

Then there was a moment's hesitation, but it was broken by Brannan's cry, "Every lover of liberty and good order lay hold of this rope!" A group of men responded by grabbing the rope. They jerked it down, broke Jenkins's neck, and lifted him off the ground. After a while they tied the rope to a post and kept Jenkins strung up all night. At dawn they allowed the coroner to cut him down.

William Richardson had been a United States marshal for the Northern District of California for over two years, and he knew his way around San Francisco. On Thursday, November 15, 1855, he accompanied his new wife and a woman friend of hers to the New American Theater, where a group called the Amazing Ravels was offering a pantomime entitled "Nicodemus, or the Unfortunate Fisherman." During the performance, the women complained to Richardson that a man in the pit of the theater was constantly turning around and leering at them. They pointed him out, and the marshal left his seat, went to the offending man, and told him to stop. The man replied that he was not directing his glances at Richardson's wife or her friend, but at the woman behind them, Arabella

Ryan, the live-in companion of gambler Charles Cora. When Richardson returned to his seat and told the women what was happening, they apparently made some arch and audible comments about the low kind of woman that was being let into the theater nowadays and wondering just what Belle Cora, as she was better known, knew about culture anyway! The women asked to have her removed, but the management soothed things down and the performance continued.

Later that evening, after he had escorted the two women home, Richardson stopped off at the Blue Wing, a downtown saloon frequented by politicians, for a few drinks. As he was leaving after midnight, Charles Cora, on his own way into the saloon, passed him and joked about the incident in the theater. Richardson followed Cora back inside, but a friend of his, future Congressman Joseph McKibben, persuaded him to forget it and go home to get some sleep instead.

Two days later, after a few rounds of drinks at another saloon, the Court Exchange, Richardson began to brood once more about the incident in the theater. Ignoring the advice of his friends, he went back to the Blue Wing and found Cora. He told Cora that the two of them needed to have a chat, and they went out for a walk around the block. The conversation seemed to go well for a time, but outside Fox and O'Connor's, a wholesale liquor store near the corner of Clay and Leidesdorff streets, they stopped and the exchange heated up. Suddenly Cora pulled out a derringer and shot. Richardson, both hands in his pockets (Cora claimed that Richardson had guns in both pockets and was preparing to shoot him), fell mortally wounded into Cora's arms. Cora held him for a minute and then let him slump to the ground.

Cora was immediately arrested. Someone started ringing a firebell, which had been the signal for the 1851 vigilantes to gather. A crowd collected in front of the Oriental Hotel. Sam Brannan addressed it and urged, in his typically extravagant fashion, that Cora be strung up immediately. But it was not to be a night for lynching, and the crowd drifted away.

The newly started *Daily Evening Bulletin* leaped into the fray. The editor, James King, wrote column after column in which he claimed that Cora would be allowed to escape or that the jury which would judge his guilt or innocence would be stacked or bribed. On November 20, King wrote, "If the jury which tries Cora is packed, either *hang the sheriff* or drive him out of town and make him resign. If Billy Mulligan [a jail-keeper] lets his friend Cora escape, *hang Billy Mulligan* or drive him into banishment." Two days later King entitled another editorial simply "Hang the Sheriff."

Cora's trial ended in a deadlocked jury in January and he remained in jail awaiting another trial. But King began his piece the next day, "Hung be the heavens with black!" He went on, "Rejoice ye gamblers and harlots! rejoice with exceeding gladness! Assemble in your dens of infamy tonight and let the costly wine flow freely, and let the welkin ring with your shouts of joy! . . . We want no vigilance committee if it can be avoided, but we do want to see the murderer punished for his crimes."

James Patrick Casey was a member of the San Francisco County Board of Supervisors and editor of a small paper called the *Sunday Times*. Like many men who had come to the Pacific Coast in the 1850's, Casey wanted to put his past behind him. He had good reason for desiring to do so, for that past had included a stay in an infamous New York prison. But habits are not easily abandoned, and Casey's career in San Francisco was turbulent. He had been embroiled in a number of controversies, including an 1855 shoot-out with John Bagley in a dispute over a local Democratic primary.

On May 9, 1856, as part of a controversy involving patronage at the Customs House, an anonymous letter to the *Bulletin* argued that Bagley, because he had tried to kill Casey, was unfit for public office. Two days later, the *Sunday Times* published another anonymous letter in which it was claimed that *Bulletin* editor King was currently attacking the United States marshal because his brother Tom had been an unsuccessful aspirant for that position after the death of Richardson. Tom King denied the charge, and over the next few days he periodically accosted Casey in the street and demanded to know the name of the author of the anonymous letter. Casey refused to make the name public, and on May 14 James King reacted by attacking the Supervisor:

It does not matter how bad a man Casey had been, or how much benefit it might be to the public to have him out of the way, we cannot accord to any one citizen the right to kill him, or even beat him without justifiable provocation. The fact that Casey has been an inmate of

Sing Sing prison in New York, is no offence against the laws of this state; nor is the fact of his having stuffed himself through the ballot-box, as elected to the board of supervisors from a district where it is said he was not even a candidate, any justification for Mr. Bagley to shoot Casey however richly the latter may deserve to have his neck stretched for such fraud on the people.

The *Bulletin* hit the streets about three in the afternoon. Soon after that, Casey stormed into James King's office and screamed that he did not like to see his past raked up. King merely asked Casey if the allegations in the editorial were true or not, and ordered him out. As he was leaving, Casey declared that he would continue to publish whatever he wanted to in his paper. King retorted that that was fine with him, since he never bothered to read Casey's paper anyway. With that, Casey left. About an hour later, as King was walking home from work, Casey shot him.

The next morning a notice appeared in the newspapers: "The members of the Vigilance Committee in good standing will please meet at No. 105½ Sacramento Street, this day, Thursday, 15th instant, at nine o'clock A.M. By order of the COMMITTEE OF THIRTEEN." Within a week, both Casey and Cora had been hanged by the vigilantes.[1]

◆ II ◆

There were two large vigilance committees in the first decade of San Francisco's history. The 1856 committee ultimately enrolled between six thousand and eight thousand men and was the largest such extralegal movement in American history. An earlier vigilance committee in 1851 enlisted approximately seven hundred men. Compared with other instances of American vigilantism, neither San Francisco committee was particularly murderous. Each hanged four persons and forced another forty to fifty to leave the city for a time. The number of deaths was less than the thirty persons killed by a vigilance committee in Virginia City, Montana, between 1863 and 1865, or the thirty-five persons killed by vigilantes in the northern and eastern part of the same state some twenty years later. However, since San Francisco vigilantism took place in a city of some 50,000 persons, its activities were closely recorded in the press of that city and also in the press of the eastern cities that shipped goods to California. San Francisco vigilantism was a highly publicized as well as a highly dramatic phenomenon.[2]

This dramatic quality has proved to be both a blessing and a curse. On the positive side, the vigilantes ensured that the gold rush city would never have to recover its history. San Francisco generally remembered its vigilantes. The tale of Judge Lynch persisted through the succeeding decades. When, for instance, Robert Louis Stevenson visited the city in the late nineteenth century, his description of William Tell Coleman, who had led the 1856 effort, as the "lion of the vigilantes" served to connect the residents of the city to their past. Even today, accounts of the committees with such breezy titles as "The Reign of the Vigilantes" turn up regularly in the popular or semipopular journals.[3] Unlike some historians, I think that that is good. A historical memory that might at points be exaggerated or inaccurate is better than no historical memory at all.

The vigilantes and their actions were so dramatic, however, that they set the terms for the genuine historical writing that narrated and interpreted them. Beginning in 1866 with the publication of Franklin Tuthill's *History of California*, the vigilantes' own justification for their behavior was accepted as the correct version of what happened between 1851 and 1856, and why. Anti-vigilante protests and skeptical commentaries were forgotten or (like Sherman's *Memoirs*) jeered at. The vigilantes had to act, it was said, because San Francisco was in the grip of lawless criminals and corrupt politicians. Josiah Royce revised this interpretation somewhat in his *California* (1886), by making the whole city guilty—of apathy and public carelessness. So vigilante activity became the action of "honest men" in restoring a sensible public spirit. John Nugent, editor of the anti-vigilante *Herald*, had called the vigilantes in 1856 a "mercantile junta." Royce admitted the business caste of the vigilantes without serious consideration of what that meant.

Hubert Howe Bancroft, in 1887, took a similarly apologetic approach in *Popular Tribunals* and even dedicated the second volume to the archvigilante himself, William T. Coleman. With only a few dissenting voices, this was the general historical view until the beginning of the third decade of the twentieth century, and even for some years after the publication in 1921 of Mary Floyd Williams's exhaustive work on the 1851 vigilance committee. Indeed, it was not until 1936 that Williams's dissenting views on the "constructive" work of the committee began to gain followers, when Stanton Coblentz ventured to say that the vigilantes perhaps did "more harm than good." Even as late as 1956 one historian was still praising the "nobility of motive and restraint" of the vigilantes.

Skeptics and critics have now become numerous, either in fiction (Walter Van Tilburg Clark's powerful 1940 novel, *The Ox-Bow Incident*, certainly indicated a shift in the popular consciousness) or in straight historical appraisals. William Henry Ellison, in *A Self-Governing Dominion* (1950), condemned the 1856 committee lock, stock, and barrel. Ellison's thoroughgoing reappraisal of the imitative approach that had been more or less standard for almost a century introduced a new wave of historians who have found the vigilantes to be violators of civil rights and defiant of the legal system.

Stimulated by Richard Maxwell Brown's pioneering work, a number of historians have carefully investigated the makeup of the committees and the background in which they grew to prominence. Kevin Starr, in particular, has paid some attention to the religious bias of the committees, and others, notably Roger Lotchin and Peter Decker, have done a great deal to clarify the merchant-businessman character of the vigilantes, and to emphasize the intense moral fervor that characterized their acts.*

But we must come back, I think, to San Francisco itself. Some of the analytical writers, in their zeal to relate the urbanization of San Francisco to larger social processes at work in the whole country in the 1840's and 1850's, have tended to become a bit too removed from the texture of life as it was lived then and there. They neglect the picture the San Franciscans drew of themselves. Granted that that picture had been too highly colored by contemporary would-be historians and a century or so of imitators; still, it is a picture that cannot be turned to the wall, for it helps us to understand why the vigilantes acted as they did. I think that there is a great deal to be learned in studying gold rush San Francisco without bothering to pretend, as the imitative historians often did, that it was especially good, especially bad, or especially different. To appreci-

*The reader who is interested in a fuller discussion of the historiography of the San Francisco vigilantes may refer to the Appendix, pp. 203–31.

ate this, we need simply to reflect on three things: first, what San Francisco was; second, why it was founded; and third, whom it did not have.

First, San Francisco was a city. As such, it was a peculiarly apt expression of American life during the late antebellum period. The two decades between 1840 and 1860 witnessed the greatest proportional increase in city dwellers that the United States has ever seen. The percentage of Americans living in what the census bureau defined as "urban territory" almost doubled during those twenty years: from 11 percent in 1840, the figure reached nearly 20 percent in 1860.[4]

San Francisco was also a Western city; it was at the core of the westward movement. Our national surge to the west was never an exclusively agricultural phenomenon. The frontier was urban at the beginning; only secondarily was it rural. The wilderness was hacked into forts and towns and cities before it was transformed into a network of family farms. The genuinely representative figure of the frontier was not the sturdy and independent yeoman. It was rather the propagandist, the urban booster, trumpeting to the land the glories of Chicago or Cincinnati or Omaha or Denver. As a western antebellum city, San Francisco was, despite its extremely remote location, in the mainstream of the America that was careening toward civil war. More than that: it was the *last* major antebellum western city, and we might find in its experience signposts pointing the way to the postwar urban future.[5]

Second, San Francisco, in common with its eighteenth-century predecessors along the Atlantic Coast, was founded for commerce. But unlike its predecessors, San Francisco was founded at a time when commerce and trade, pursued for frankly individual gain, enjoyed a secure place at the summit of approved national activities. Some historians of colonial America argue that in prerevolutionary America, commerce was regarded in many quarters as dirty and illegitimate, that it was seen as corrupting of disinterested virtue, and that the personal acquisitiveness that it demanded and fostered was condemned as corrosive of community. Such a time, if indeed it ever really existed, was long gone by the 1840's.[6]

As a natural result, in the city by the bay a relentlessly grid pattern of streets and thoroughfares was imposed on a landscape that was anything but hospitable to right angles. One early San Franciscan complained, "Nature so formed the site of this city that no one could mistake where she intended the streets to run," but the lament was both misplaced and irrelevant. The grid plan was the plan of trade; it gave the businessmen of the city the maximum amount of space for their commercial establishments and the easiest method of access for the greatest number of firms. The San Francisco complaint was as ineffectual as William Cullen Bryant's earlier one that "commerce" was "devouring inch by inch" the city's harbor. In New York, San Francisco, and everywhere else in America, commerce was king. In laying out the grid pattern of city after city, commerce simply affirmed the contours of the moral landscape it had created. When early San Franciscans started calling their city the "emporium of the Pacific," they paid homage to the rules of the universe they so gladly inhabited.[7]

Third, the population of gold rush San Francisco was extraordinarily one-dimensional. The city was overwhelmingly populated by young, adult, white males. The 1852 state census reported that women accounted for only 18 percent of the population; even if that figure was a bit low, the general trend it indicated was certainly present. All through the gold rush period, the typical San Franciscan never lived in a family group.[8]

There were also few Indians; the Spanish had done the job of turning populated land into virgin land before the *gringos* arrived on the scene. As Americans, the inhabitants of early San Francisco regularly indulged in the rhetoric of racial superiority. But their remarks had no edge to them, for a hatchet in the skull did not lurk around the next bend in the road. So an editor could blithely sniff about the California natives, "It will not take many interviews with the leaders of these acorn eaters to cure the most romantic of all previous ideas of 'lords of the forest,' 'nature's noblemen' and similar appellations which have been applied to the Indian." His sentence, and all the others like it, made no practical difference in the life of the city.[9]

The city was primarily of European stock. Of the non-Europeans, the Chinese were the most numerous, though the precise number of them who lived in San Francisco at any point in the 1850's is uncertain. The contemporary *Annals of San Francisco* estimated that in 1852 there were "three to four thousand" Chinese in the city. That would make them from 8 to 11 percent of the population. A figure of 10 percent in the early part of the decade would probably be reasonably accurate. In 1860 the federal census counted 2,719 Chinese in San Francisco, or only 5 percent of the population. Overall, then, a decent guess would be that for all of the 1850's the Chinese accounted for less than 10 percent of the city's population. But most of California's Chinese were not in San Francisco. In 1852 the state authorities made a rough estimate that around 25,000 Chinese lived in the entire state, which would have meant that San Francisco had between 12 and 16 percent of the total. By the end of the decade, the city accounted for only 8 percent of all the Chinese in the state. For the gold rush period as a whole, a fair estimate would be that nine out of every ten Chinese in California lived in the interior of the state.

With its predominantly white, male, European-descended population, the city could fashion and repeat stereotypes to its heart's content. It would not have to reap any whirlwind for twenty years. Someone could write that Chinese women were "among the filthiest and most abandoned of their sex," and the young men of San Francisco could chuckle, indulge in fantasies, or think whatever they wanted, all to the same insignificant effect. An editor could crack that a Chinese conversation "sounds like a gobbling of turkey cocks intermingled with the drawing of numerous corks," and life would go on as if he had never penned the sentence. Someone else could offer the opinion that the Chinese "keep up a chattering that would do honor to a whole barnyard of fowls," and those who thought that was clever could snicker enthusiastically over their morning coffee without consequence.[10]

Demographically, San Francisco was not a typical American city, but imaginatively it was everything that young, white, masculine America dreamed. San Francisco was West; San Francisco was easy riches; San Francisco was excitement; San Francisco was gold. The city was a playland for the nineteenth-century American mind.

♦ III ♦

Its beginnings as an American city were pedestrian enough. In 1846 elements of the United States Navy, without having to fire a shot, occupied the Mexican village of Yerba Buena. Nestled in a cove on the eastern shore of a California peninsula, south of the strait John C. Frémont had christened the Golden Gate, the village contained scarcely two hundred persons, reported living in "22 shanties, 31 frame houses and 26 adobe buildings."[11]

Yerba Buena was not a typical Mexican pueblo. Most of the California settlements that had been encouraged by the Mexican government in the 1830's and 1840's were composed of small farmers working the tracts they had received as grants from the authorities, but Yerba Buena was populated mainly by Yankee and European traders, attracted by its location on the western shore of San Francisco Bay. Two navigable rivers, which meandered through the large valley to the east from their separate sources in the mountains a hundred miles away from the village, emptied into the bay. From Yerba Buena, a trader had access to a large part of the interior.

The American occupation affected the character of this trading center in diverse ways. A newspaper, the *California Star*, appeared in January 1847, and a few months later a private school opened its doors. The population grew rapidly. In January 1847, the *Star* reported that the number of people in Yerba Buena had increased from the 200 of 1846 to a bit more than 300. In June, the military authorities conducted a census that recorded 459 inhabitants in the town. In March 1848, a school census counted a total population of 812. In two years the population had quadrupled.

The discovery of gold along the American River in 1848 changed the town into a city. San Francisco was estimated to contain 2,000 persons in February 1849 and to have housed 5,000 by the end of that year. In May 1850, one traveler estimated that there were 40,000 people in or near the city. At the beginning of 1851, the *Daily Alta California* estimated 23,000. In a state census taken in 1852, the population of San Francisco was counted as 36,151. A contemporary annalist argued that this figure was too low; his own estimate, perhaps inflated by a measure of civic pride, was on the order of 42,000. One recent and careful estimate has arrived at the figure of 56,000 people in San Francisco in 1856. Whatever the precise figures may have been, the pattern was clear enough: the rapid population growth that had followed the American occupation was sustained by the gold rush. In ten years, the population of San Francisco increased at least two hundred fold.[12]

The gold rush also affected the physical character of the town.

Tents and shanties multiplied all around the cove, and the construction of more permanent buildings soon commenced. Besides supplying needed shelter, this building activity provided a ready source of employment for those who had neither the patience nor the inclination to pan for gold. In addition, a feverish construction of wharves out into the bay was initiated to accommodate the increasing number of ships. By the end of 1850, twelve such structures had been completed. The city built and owned several of them, but most were privately built and maintained.[13]

If goods were to be moved, streets had to be graded and made firm, especially around the waterfront. At first, brushwood, tree limbs, and empty crates were thrown into the mud, but this method of road construction soon outlived its limited usefulness. "I saw a man try to cross Montgomery Street, the greatest business street in the town, where there were no bushes laid down or boards to walk on," one resident reported in early 1850. "He was about half drunk or he would not have attempted it. . . . He floundered in up to his waist, then up to his neck, and had not some person thrown him a rope, he would have drowned." By the end of 1850, seven streets had been graded and nine were graced by sewers. These operations cost over half a million dollars, with the city paying one-third and the owners of the adjoining property two-thirds of the cost.[14]

Besides the building of houses, streets, and wharves, there was one other important type of construction activity during these years. The owners of property fronting the cove often dumped debris such as old crates, trees, and even parts of derelict ships into what was, at low tide, a mud flat. The debris was then covered with dirt, and thus the shoreline was extended out into what had been the water. This work was more time-consuming and expensive than building a wharf, but it was also quite profitable. By 1849 the public sale of shorefront lots, which the new owners could then fill in, had become a principal source of public revenue.[15]

The American occupation and the gold rush did not change everything, however, for there were continuities that stretched from before the American occupation to after the gold rush. The most striking of these was the town's commercial orientation, which was responsible for its name being changed from Yerba Buena to San Francisco. In 1847, two Yankee traders, Robert G. Semple and Thomas O. Larkin, hatched a plan to lay out a town on the eastern shore of the bay and name it Francesca, ostensibly in honor of the wife of Mariano Vallejo. The object of the scheme was to take advantage of the well-known name of the bay, San Francisco, and thus have the merchandise that was sent from the East to "San Francisco" landed at the town of Francesca. When the traders at Yerba Buena learned of the scheme, they immediately petitioned the military authorities to change the name of Yerba Buena to San Francisco. The change was effected, and the renamed Yerba Buena remained the central unloading point for California goods. This position proved of inestimable value when gold was discovered the very next year.[16]

The political environment of San Francisco was somewhat confused before the gold rush and remained so for a time after it had begun. The earliest Americans attempted to adapt the Mexican forms of government to their own use. Thus, Americans filled the office of *alcalde* (a combination executive and judicial official) and sat on the *ayuntamiento* (town council). Through the years 1847–49, a series of elections and counter-elections was held by rival groups, and at one time the city had, as a result, two sets of officials, neither of which was recognized by the other or by the military governor. The political situation was stabilized to a degree in 1849 when John Geary, a Democratic postmaster from Pittsburgh, gained wide support in the city and from the military governor and was elected alcalde.

In 1850, San Francisco was incorporated by the de facto state legislature. From then until 1856, the mayor was elected at large, and a town council, which consisted of two boards (aldermen and assistant aldermen), was elected on a ward basis. However, since many of those arriving at San Francisco spent only half the year in the city and the other half at the diggings, city politics was shifting and confused. What organization there was tended to develop at the ward level.[17]

♦ IV ♦

Those who populated this city came from all over the world, but their moods and their visions more often than not coincided. They were excited and they were confident. When they arrived at San Francisco, they were enthusiastic. Their correspondence demonstrates a kind of breathlessness and a self-conscious sense of enormous astonishment. They insisted that they had disembarked at a place that was, above all, different. For some, the difference was in the very air itself. "To think of the mercury for weeks below zero!" one newly arrived Easterner marveled. "I have not seen it at this city below the freezing point! Why does not everyone who lives north of the Mason-Dixon line start at once for California?" A few months later he was still amazed: "I don't see how a man can be sick in such a country. There is more fresh air here than in any other place I ever saw."[18]

The place was also wild and exotic. "Whether it should be called a villa, a brothel, or a Babylon, I am at a loss to determine," an Italian priest confessed. Another recent arrival wrote to relatives back home, "This is the hardest place I was ever in, and I have been told the same by those who have lived here for years. They say that even the ministers who come out to preach the gospel countenance what a street sweeper would be ashamed of." A few months later he reflected, "I have seen how different men are when they are freed from the restraints of society from what they appear to be under its influence. I have seen worse characters than I supposed ever existed except in imagination." The gold rush port, the arrivals often claimed, would be unrecognizable to their correspondents. "You would be surprised to see what a city San Francisco is," Harvey Lamb wrote to his mother. "Cleveland can't hold a candle to it." The present inhabitants of San Francisco would doubtless have agreed with Lamb, as they would also have with Andrew Jackson Davis, who wrote in 1854, "I feel that I am in the Center of the world."[19]

A storekeeper, certain that his readers had never seen anything like the city, wrote, probably exaggerating, "I can count eight languages that I have heard spoken in the store this morning." Another man put it more whimsically. He imagined that he was home in the East, and that small children were coming up to him and asking for pennies. His fantasy reaction was, "A cent? What is that, my child? Children play with dollars in California." Convinced that he himself had changed radically during his San Francisco stay, he excused another comment in a letter by remarking, "I write this for your eye only . . . Californians are apt to speak plainly."[20]

San Francisco was a place, they asserted, where everything was lived at a faster pace. A lawyer wrote, "Everything goes ahead on the high pressure principle. You can't stand still if you would, and the consequence is that you are whirled around and about, until you are apt to become dizzy." Another resident declared, "There are no men of leisure here, all are in a race." Buildings seemed to sprout up at a miraculous tempo. "It is an everyday occurrence here," said one man, "to pass one night by a vacant lot and the next day to find a two story house built, a large assortment of goods moved in and a wholesale store in full operation." He concluded, "You don't believe all this—but it is true." And miracles were not confined to buildings. An age that worshipped statistics only slightly less than ours saw in population growth the assurance of the future prosperity of the state. Speaking of children, one resident claimed, "One lady in the valley of the city has had four pairs, and ready again! Maybe two more. Hurrah for California!"[21]

Sentiments like these are liberally sprinkled through the correspondence of the gold rush period. Taken as a whole, they seem to indicate an insistence that San Francisco was a city set apart from the rest of the country, that eastern readers would not be at home there, that society along the Pacific was fundamentally different from society along the Atlantic.

The difference, they thought, consisted largely in the benevolence of the environment. These men had set out for California to strike it rich, and they settled in San Francisco because they confidently fancied themselves shrewd business operators. They were, in fact, hustlers. Their minds endlessly scheming, they were confident that they would be able to pocket the gold the miners were digging.[22]

Though they had to travel light, most of these hustlers brought with them rather heavy expectations. They traveled across the country or around the Cape with an almost limitless optimism and a blind faith that, whatever had been their pasts, they could prosper along the Pacific. As early as 1846 one resident wrote enthusiastically about "the busy stir of American industry" that, he predicted, would soon transform California and aid those bold enough to seize the moment. For the next decade, thousands of entrepreneurs, confident that the pot of gold would stir in their favor, streamed into San Francisco.[23]

In 1853 one recent arrival reported, "Men start for this country with bright expectations that they will be the fortunate ones . . . the extent of their magnificent castles knows no bounds." This estimate of the general mentality of the immigrants was quite accurate. "If one has moderate capital, he can make money fast," was the typically optimistic appraisal of one '49er. "Unless some great misfortune overtakes us," predicted another man the next year, "we can hardly fail of making money." Another individual was confident that San Francisco would be gracious to him. "My destiny was not to a fortune in Iowa," he wrote, "but this is a country where I can conquer destiny and subdue fate." He went on, "If God spares my life, I will show them [his Iowa friends] and the world that I have the ability to make a mark in the world."[24]

This optimism did not die easily. After two and a half years in San Francisco, for instance, Charles Daniell had still not made his fortune. He then went into a retail partnership with someone named Johnson and wrote home, "Our business prospects are very flattering. We have the best facilities for doing a large amount of business of any house in our line, and there seems to be no reason why we should not, after we get fairly established, take a lead." Unfortunately for him, the firm did not take any lead and it was swept quietly into the crowded bin of San Francisco failures.[25]

Again, the father of Roger Sherman Baldwin suggested, after his son had been in San Francisco for two years without making his pile, that the young man might want to consider returning home. The son's reply was at once instructive and pathetic. "If I supposed that I could make my way at home," he pleaded, "I should never have come to California." So he stayed, clinging desperately to the receding dream. He speculated in this and that, all to no avail. He finally headed for the interior of the state and settled in Ophir, which was, he assured his mother, "the most moral town in the mines." He invested in a water project and dabbled in mining claims, but nothing worked out. Finally, his fortune forever unmade, he was thrown from a horse and died.[26]

The variety of ways in which people like these sought to get ahead in San Francisco was legion. Perhaps glances at one of the city's most prominent merchants, one of its most extensive landholders, and its most famous politician might serve to render a bit more concrete the methods of attempted personal advancement that flourished in the city by the bay.

William Tell Coleman, who lived long enough and amassed enough wealth to be able to purchase apotheosis from Hubert Howe Bancroft, was the son of a moderately prominent Kentucky legislator and a distant relative of George Washington.

After a boyhood spent on a farm, he headed west and worked at a number of occupations through the upper Mississippi valley—mainly at odd jobs on an Illinois railroad for which an uncle of his was an engineer. He was later involved in insurance and lumber businesses in St. Louis, where he managed to get a degree from the fledgling St. Louis University and studied law. After college, he managed a plantation in Louisiana and supervised lumbering operations in Wisconsin.[27]

In the spring of 1849 he decided to join the gold rush and headed overland for California. Reaching Sacramento, he calculated that investing in property was a more profitable enterprise than breaking one's back in the diggings. He bought a lot, advertised himself as a carpenter, and built a few houses. He was so successful at this venture that people started contracting with him for construction beyond his abilities. Rather than erecting structures that he feared might collapse in the face of the first good wind, he collected some provisions and went to the mines with something of a traveling general store. As long as he was at the diggings, he decided to try his luck, but three days of panning reconvinced him that there must be a better way of making a living. So he headed for San Francisco at the beginning of 1850, determined to become a merchant.

In the early days of the port of San Francisco, while Atlantic-Pacific commercial contacts were still being organized, many of the ships that called at the port were at the complete disposition of the vessel's captain, who had a personal stake in the commercial success of the voyage. A few shrewd deals enabled Coleman to make a name for himself among the captains of the Pacific vessels. Before long he was a leading importer. In 1852 he completed his social arrival by marrying the daughter of Daniel Page, a former mayor of St. Louis and one of the founders of the banking house of Page, Bacon, and Co.

Joseph Libby Folsom was not a jack-of-all-trades like Coleman, but he also became rich. He was born in New Hampshire and received an appointment to West Point through the good graces of Congressman Franklin Pierce. After his commissioning, he spent a few years fighting the Seminoles in Florida and then returned to West Point as an instructor in infantry tactics. When the Mexican War broke out, he got an appointment as quartermaster for a regiment of New York volunteers.

When Folsom arrived in California, he divided his time between being quartermaster, serving as Collector of the port of

San Francisco, and gobbling up choice lots in the town. At the death of William Leidesdorff, a black Danish trader who had accumulated forty-one lots by March 1848, Folsom traveled to the Virgin Islands and sought out Leidesdorff's relatives. Feigning grief, he informed them of their loss and commiserated with them on their lack of financial security. Out of pure friendship, he offered to pay them $50,000 for what he said were some worthless mud-filled lots that Leidesdorff had bought along the cove at Yerba Buena. They gratefully accepted this generous offer, and, at one stroke, Folsom became one of the largest landowners in the city. When the relatives discovered that Folsom had deceived them about the value of the lots, they filed suit. The litigation, which contributed to the uncertainty of land titles in San Francisco, dragged on past Folsom's own death in January 1856.[28]

For *David Colbert Broderick*, business was not commerce or land, but it was nevertheless rewarding. He was one of California's first professional politicians. He was born in the nation's capital in 1820. His father, Thomas, an Irish stonecutter, had been recruited to come to the United States to work on the construction of the public buildings in Washington, including the rising Capitol building. After finishing his work in Washington, Thomas Broderick took his family to New York, where the current construction assured him steady work.[29]

In New York, David tried stonecutting for a while, but he soon gave it up to open a tavern catering to Irish laborers. He also joined a volunteer fire company and was elected its foreman before he reached the age of twenty-one. Although apparently not a member of the Tammany Society, he did have contacts with the political operators of New York and obtained a minor post at the Customs House. He was a member of the convention that revised the New York City charter in 1846, and during the convention revealed himself as a man of clear Locofoco sympathies, which were not shared by a majority of the delegates. He received the Democratic nomination for Congress in 1846 but lost the election when the late entry of a nativist candidate cut into his vote. Broderick remained active in city politics, but without any great success. In 1849, at the urging of John D. Stevenson, who had raised a company in New York to fight in the Mexican War and then stayed in California after the cessation of hostilities, he headed for the land of gold.

When Broderick arrived in San Francisco, an illness that he

had acquired while crossing Central America prevented his going to the diggings, so he turned his already considerable organizational abilities to the San Francisco political scene. In view of the fires that were ravaging the young city, he grasped the political possibilities of the volunteer fire company. He was instrumental in organizing the first such group in San Francisco, the Empire Engine Co. No. 1. This move served its purposes, for he was soon elected to the California Senate.

In the Senate, he helped draft the charter incorporating San Francisco, and it is probably more than a coincidence that the political forms of the new city bore a remarkable resemblance to those of the New York with which Broderick was so familiar.

In 1851, the resignation of Governor Peter Burnett necessitated a reshuffling of top state officials, and Broderick was elected president of the Senate. Already he had advanced higher in California than in New York, and he quickly set his sights upon the United States Senate. A good part of the political history of the state during the 1850's can be written simply by narrating his attempts to secure the election of a legislature that would send him to the Senate. This finally happened in 1857.

Broderick, a man of Locofoco and free-soil sympathies, in the legislature opposed such measures as a foreign miners' tax, a bill forbidding the immigration of free blacks into California, and a state fugitive slave law, but in his private affairs he was not exactly on the other man's side. As soon as he arrived in San Francisco, he and a friend went into the assaying business. Since California did not yet have a mint, coin was in scarce supply. Broderick's firm minted private coins, which contained less gold than their face value. The difference was pocketed by the firm, and Broderick invested his share in real estate. While in the legislature, he carefully shepherded these investments, always leading the opposition to bills that might have tended to undermine his legal title to the land and water lots he had purchased.

• V •

Besides their wealth and their prominence, these three men had something else in common: during their California careers, they all invested in land. Coleman dabbled for a time, but real estate was a principal source of wealth for both Folsom and Broderick. This desire for real estate demonstrates probably better than anything else the close relationship that existed in San Francisco and every other antebellum American city between business and politics.

With his eye for detail and his penchant for organization, lawyer and future governor Henry Haight, in a letter to his father in 1850, outlined the various types of land arrangements that had structured real estate holdings in the city over the preceding years. Haight noted that there were two types of land grants that stemmed from the Mexican period. First, he said, San Francisco contained "lots granted by the alcalde of the pueblo with the condition always inserted in the grant that the grantee shall enclose with a fence and build a house. These grants are of fifty varas square [a *vara* was thirty-three and one-third inches] and a hundred varas square and are mostly in the center of the city." The background to these grants was that the Mexican government, like most governments, had attempted to use its land as an instrument of national policy. Since an overriding national need was population, the government, in laws of 1824 and 1828, attempted to induce immigration with offers of land. Liberal tracts were granted, but under legal conditions that were designed to ensure the achievement of the government's primary goal, an increase in population. The grantee was required to live on the land and to improve it and was forbidden to mortgage it, sell it, or transfer possession in mortmain to the Church. Finally, the grantee was required, at least nominally, to become a Mexican citizen and a Catholic.[30]

These general provisions applied to lands within the jurisdiction of a pueblo such as Yerba Buena, which received four square leagues of land for distribution. The lots granted by the pueblo authorities had to be improved within a year of the grant, and the prohibition against absentee ownership meant that legally a person could not own more than one lot.

Another type of Mexican grant, Haight reported, consisted of "lots on the edge of the bay, for salting and curing hides." Yerba Buena was a coastal pueblo, and therefore its lands came under the provisions of a law that reserved to the governor of the province the disposition of the lands immediately adjacent to the high water mark. In 1835 the governor exercised this power by forbidding the granting of any land within two hundred varas of the beach. In 1839 the pueblo was surveyed and the lines were run, with the beach property reserved for government use.[31]

Since Yerba Buena was populated by traders, the land itself possessed little inherent value. Rather, the location of any particular lot determined its worth: the closer to the beach, the more valuable it was for commercial purposes. During the Mexican period, according to Bruno Fritzsche, only sixty-four lots were granted. Even though it was, strictly speaking, illegal, twelve lots changed hands in one fashion or another during these years. The coming of the Americans brought a quick end to this leisurely pace of land transactions: "Within the first twenty months of United States' administration, the number of grants rose to 844."[32]

Haight identified other types of grants and sales that dated from after the American conquest. One type was "private grants from the alcalde under the military regime subsequent to the conquest of the country." He went on to observe, "These grants were made, many of them in fact, to the alcalde himself, the grantee being a man of straw. They were made indiscriminately, often, in fact, for a trifle and to persons already large holders of real estate." Haight was referring here to the years immediately after 1846, when the laws and governmental forms of Mexico still held sway in the city, and Americans simply filled the Mexican offices. Under Mexican law, the alcalde filled out the deeds to the granted lands. The only charge was a registration fee of about twelve to sixteen dollars per deed. The American alcaldes and ayuntamientos swiftly repealed the prohibition against multiple ownership of lots, and just as swiftly began granting lots to themselves and their friends, all for nothing more than the nominal registration fee. They also ordered another survey of the town. This second survey increased the number and size of the available lots, and the lots were quickly disposed of.[33]

Haight also noted that there had been "grants of water lots . . . on the flats between the high water mark and the city limits, which east of the city makes an area of several acres, a great part bare at low tide." In March 1847, the military governor, Stephen Watts Kearny, granted the town the right to sell some of the beach and waterfront lots, with the understanding that the money from the sales would be used to finance harbor improvements. Since the Mexican governor had specifically reserved these lands and the laws of Mexico were still technically in force, it was not clear just where Kearny was getting this authority, and doubts were publicly expressed about the legitimacy of the sales; but they took place anyway. Water lots were of course more valuable for commerce than lots farther inland, and some of these were divided, with a single lot split into three new ones. A batch of these was sold at a public auction in September 1847. One of the many disputes about land followed. The alcalde demanded that the purchaser pay him for deeds for each of the new lots. Some purchasers, aggrieved over the extra expenses, retorted that those who bought three of the new lots that had formed one of the old lots ought to be allowed to cover the whole transaction with just one deed. For perhaps the first time in the history of San Francisco, but hardly the last, the complaint of "official extortion" was voiced. Then, as more often than not during the succeeding years, this cry was raised by one set of operators who had been outwitted by another. The splitting of the water lots continued, despite the protests of speculators like Joseph L. Folsom, and additional sales were held in 1848 and 1850.[34]

Finally there were the grants that Haight and others in the city referred to as "the Colton grants." The background to these grants was that one of the Mexican positions filled by the Americans was that of *prefect*. This officer had general supervisory power over the other officials and could appoint a few minor officials, such as justice of the peace. In 1849 the prefect, Horace Hawes, appointed G. Q. Colton to the office of justice of the peace. Colton promptly claimed authority, under Mexican law, to make land grants and proceeded to do so. For a fee of $100, anyone could go to Colton and buy a deed to a piece of property in the town. Even though some of the lots that Colton granted had already been granted away by the alcaldes or sold at the Kearny sales, Colton did a brisk business in grants, since his interpretation of Mexican law was especially welcome to those who had not been on the inside during the time of the alcalde grants. After busying himself at deed-writing for a time, Colton pocketed the fee money and went to the East, never to return.

Hawes, meanwhile, in an effort to undermine the legitimacy of the alcalde and the ayuntamiento, asked them for an audit of the grants they had made. He probably suspected that they would refuse to place on the public record the fact that they had been so extensively involved in land transactions for their own personal gain. He was correct: the ayuntamiento declared the Colton grants void and formally petitioned Governor Burnett to remove Hawes as prefect. Hawes sent the governor a report of his own, which accused the ayuntamiento of corruption, but the governor then ordered that all sales and grants be stopped until the matter could be cleared up. Hawes published his report, listing the members of the ayuntamiento who had accumulated lots in town, and the ayuntamiento then formally accused Hawes of corruption for the Colton grants. The governor finally decided to end the matter by siding with the ayuntamiento and suspending Hawes. The alcalde grantees had won the first round. Their property appeared to be safe, while the Colton-granted property was temporarily consigned to a legal limbo.[35]

The matter was soon taken to court, where the alcalde grantees received a series of legal rebuffs: in 1850, a superior court decided that neither Kearny nor the American alcaldes had the power to sell any beach or water lots, since these had been reserved by the Mexican authorities. In 1851, the state Supreme Court ruled that American alcaldes and ayuntamientos had not possessed the right to grant *any* land. At one stroke, the alcalde grants, which included the substantial holdings of such opportunistic tycoons as Folsom, Sam Brannan, Talbot Green, W. D. M. Howard, and Rodman M. Price, were voided.

The Supreme Court decision was handed down in January 1851, and everyone concerned immediately rushed off to the legislature, which was meeting in San Jose. The object was to induce the state to renounce all rights to and interest in the contested property. The land would then obviously belong to the city, which could accordingly legalize whatever grants it wanted to. The alcalde grantees reached the legislators first and, by filling their stomachs, quenching their thirsts, and lining their pockets, obtained passage of the First Water Lot Act. By the terms of this statute, the state renounced all interest in the San Francisco beach property and land in return for 25 percent of the amount received from all real estate sales in the city.[36]

The Colton grantees were not far behind, however, with their own food, drink, and bribes, and their efforts were rewarded with the passage of the Second Water Lot Act. By this act, the state offered to forego the 25 percent provision of the first act if the city would specifically confirm the Colton grants. (The common council voted to accept the offer, but the mayor vetoed it.) But despite the determined efforts of Broderick, who was apparently associated with the Colton grantees, the next session of the legislature refused to repeal the First Water Lot Act. Combined with the city's refusal to accept the terms of the Second Act, this meant that the alcalde grantees were victorious. Their triumph was confirmed in 1853, when the state Supreme Court reversed itself and upheld the alcalde grants.[37]

The alcalde grantees were soon challenged by Broderick and the new Democratic Governor John Bigler, in what was known as the Extension project. The roots of this scheme went back to 1850, when Hawes and the ayuntamiento were snapping at each other. In an attempt to deflate the charges of corruption that were swirling about them, the members of the ayuntamiento decided to stop the sales of land for a time and let things settle down. But since land sales had been the main source of public revenue, some other method had to be found to finance the necessary public improvements, especially the paving and grading of streets.

Scrip, bearing an interest of 3 percent a month, was issued in July 1850 and periodically thereafter. By the spring of 1851, the municipal debt was over one million dollars, and something had to be done. The legislature, spurred by Broderick, passed an act for funding the debt of San Francisco and establishing a five-member Commission of the Funded Debt to oversee the operation. Creditors of the city were invited to exchange scrip for city stock that carried an annual 10 percent interest and was under the control of the newly established commission. The surety of payment was intended to compensate for the reduction of interest.[38]

Most city creditors welcomed the funding and exchanged their scrip for the stock, but some did not, and one of those, Dr. Peter Smith, took the city to court. Smith had contracted with the city in 1850 to care for the indigent sick. He had been paid in scrip, which he now sued to recover at full value, together with the accrued interest. He won a series of suits in the lower courts, and the sheriff prepared to sell some property, mainly beach lots, to raise money to satisfy the claim. But the

Commissioners of the Funded Debt published a notice contesting the legality of the sales, advising the public not to participate, and expressing confidence that the sales would be thrown out by the higher courts. (They were not.) As a result, the sales were sparsely attended, partly because of the stand of the commission and partly because a vigilance committee was operating at the time and holding the forefront of attention. Those who did attend worked together to hold down the bids, and the result was that the sale did not raise enough money to satisfy the Smith claim. More sales had to be organized, and the "Peter Smith" buyers soon held a large amount of waterfront property.[39]

At this point the sales intersected the affair of the alcalde grants. One feature of the First Water Lot Act had been to establish a "permanent" water line, which was located in such a way as to maximize the value of the alcalde-granted property. This was the act that Broderick had pushed to have repealed by the 1852 legislature. Broderick had made something of a killing for himself at the Peter Smith sales, and the repeal of the act would have worked in favor of the Peter Smith holders. If the "permanent" water line were abolished, the alcalde property, which was adjusted to it, would have depreciated, and property farther out along the beach, where the Peter Smith sales had been, would have appreciated.[40]

At the beginning of the 1853 session of the legislature, Bigler proposed that the state should repeal the 1851 Water Acts, take over the waterfront itself, and extend the "permanent" line two hundred yards out into the bay. He argued that from the sales of this property the state could retire its own debt. The Peter Smith holders would have benefited from the change in the line. The alcalde grantees were of course opposed to any repeal. As one San Francisco merchant wrote, "If this [the Extension project] is carried through, it will make Montgomery Street a long way uptown and will affect the prices of real estate all over the town." The alcalde holders mounted an impressive show of force, and, after bitter debate in the press and in the legislature, the bill was defeated in the Senate, when the Lieutenant-Governor cast the deciding vote against it. After more than five years, the alcalde holders were finally secure in their titles.[41]

In those five years, much else had happened, however. In San Francisco as in other antebellum cities in the West, what happened tended to revolve around three interrelated issues: business, politics, and religion. Before San Francisco was well settled, the developing merchant group came to the position that at least some of their problems could be solved by violence against one of the minorities in the city. When the results of that violence, the 1851 vigilance committee, proved ephemeral, the merchants decided that in order to effect the ill-defined changes they thought they wanted, they would have to enter politics. The most successful door into the political arena, to their minds, was labeled "religion," specifically anti-popery. Business, politics, and religion thus came together in 1856 to form the largest vigilante movement the United States had ever seen.

CHAPTER 2

THE HUSTLERS

And the whole congregation murmured against Moses and Aaron in the wilderness, and said to them, "Would that we had died by the hand of the Lord in the land of Egypt, when we sat by the fleshpots and ate bread to the full; for you have brought us out into this wilderness to kill this whole assembly with hunger."

—*Exodus 16: 2–3*

♦

How sadly disappointed people are when they arrive here, they all form a very wrong idea of this place, about making a fortune in a hurry . . . they will be sorry if they ever set their feet upon this place.

—*Laborer Milton Hall, writing from San Francisco, April 25, 1852*

♦

There are not a dozen men in the town I would trust for five hundred dollars.

—*Businessman Robert S. Lammot, writing from San Francisco, January 14, 1851*

♦

I know of no country, indeed, where the love of money has taken a stronger hold on the affections of men.

—*Alexis de Tocqueville*

◆ I ◆

When any product that is in demand is suddenly available in large quantities, ordinary people begin to see visions of fabulous wealth, theirs for the seizing. The result is a "rush," as people swarm into the region where the product can be produced. Such a rush, the gold rush of 1849, was the main reason for the growth of San Francisco. That many Americans were willing to rush for gold surprised no one at the time, for this was a society in which, as Edward Pessen has said, "Wealth appears to have been the surest sign of social, as well as economic, position." Their unquestioned belief that their civilization was superior to that of the decadent Spanish did not prevent the gringos in the late 1840's and early 1850's from moving after the gold with a single-mindedness and an intensity that would have been the envy of an earlier generation of *conquistadores*.[1]

Those who set their sights squarely on the object of the rush, be it gold, silver, or tobacco, rarely find themselves as fully rewarded as they had dreamed. During the tobacco boom in Jamestown in the 1620's, for instance, ordinary tobacco growers did not reap tremendous profits. Riches were reserved to another group of men: those who set their sights not on the object of the rush but on the rushers themselves. If you could control what the rushers needed—in the case of Jamestown, food and field hands—you could make money. And so it was in California. An occasional miner might strike it relatively rich, of course, but if he wanted to keep his newly acquired money, he really had only one choice: to get out of California fast. Otherwise, his gold would end up in the accounts of a San Francisco or Sacramento merchant. Philip D. Armour, to cite one example, accumulated some money at the mines, and then took the first boat back to Chicago. There he sank the gold into what eventually became a highly successful meat-packing operation.[2]

So, for most of the '49ers the rewarding rush was not the gold rush. In San Francisco, the profitable rush was a more hidden and secondary rush, the rush of the hustlers. The needs of the conquistadores at the mines were the basic ones of food, shelter, and clothing. When word began to trickle back to the East that miners would pay fifty cents just to have their shirts washed, that lumber bought for $10 per thousand feet was fetching $300 per thousand, that prefabricated houses costing only $300 were commanding $2,800, and that flour was going at phenomenal prices, sharp young men, determined to pocket what the miners were panning, swarmed into the city by the bay. San Francisco was, in Gunther Barth's felicitous phrase, an "instant city," and an instant city was, above all, an emporium for its hinterland. An 1853 resident described San Francisco, not inaccurately, as "a conglomeration of pagans, Mahommedans, Mormons, Jews, and Christians—all worshipping mammon."[3]

In a rush to take advantage of a boom, the winners often tended to be those who simply showed up first. This had been the case in other western American cities. In Chicago in 1836, for example, when the population of the town was less than 4,000, over a million dollars' worth of goods was sold. Land values skyrocketed—one paper claimed that property was increasing "one hundred per cent per DAY." This was doubtless a great exaggeration, but it had a kernel of truth to it, and those who had managed to get there in time did quite well for themselves. As Bessie L. Pierce put it, "Prosperity was, indeed, on all sides." So, if you wanted to capitalize on the gold rush, you had to get to San Francisco pretty quickly. Many did. By the fall of 1849, a British captain commented, "Merchants are doing a large amount of business who have only just commenced mercantile transactions." But you also had to get there with something to sell. Accordingly, the hustlers scrambled in the East before they scrambled to the West.[4]

Edward T. Hosmer was rather typical of this breed. Almost as soon as he heard about the gold discoveries, he left his home in upstate New York and went to New York City, by way of Albany, contacting friends of his father and gathering a cargo to take to San Francisco. He also made arrangements with a commission merchant in New York to send him goods on a regular basis after he reached California. When he arrived in San Francisco, he carefully toured the city, seeking persons from New York with whom he might be able to establish a business relationship. By the end of 1849 he reported in a letter to his parents, "The firm of Hosmer and Co. is A-No. 1 here . . . goods are ordered from New York to the care of *Hosmer and Co.* by a number of our friends."[5]

Alfred A. Dibblee was a New England version of the same sort of entrepreneur. In Boston he collected assorted merchandise from friends of the family and established permanent lines of communication between San Francisco and Massachusetts. When he arrived at San Francisco, he met a man named Chicester, a brother-in-law of William Harbeck, a substantial Boston shipper. The two formed a partnership, and after Chicester retired from the business, Dibblee arranged to retain the Harbeck account. This, together with his own Boston relationship, afforded him a decent business. By the end of the decade he was president of the San Francisco Chamber of Commerce.[6]

Other traders also joined the rush. Frederick W. Macondray, for example, had spent much of the 1820's commanding a vessel on the Boston–China route and much of the 1830's as manager of a receiving storeship in the Orient. When he decided to go to California at the end of the 1840's, he was able to draw on these experiences and contacts, and he quickly established himself as one of San Francisco's leading importers of goods from Boston and China.[7]

Down in Delaware, Robert S. Lammot, whose stepsister had married into the Du Pont family, heard about the gold in California, looked into the mirror, and saw the Du Ponts' prosperous and respected western agent. But first he had to show them that he could manage a business on his own. So he headed straight for Philadelphia. "It is my wish now," he wrote Alfred Du Pont, "to get from some of the Philadelphia merchants consignments of flour, provisions, or anything else they might be disposed to send to San Francisco, in order to give me a start in business when I arrive there."[8]

♦ II ♦

Once you got yourself established as a merchant, it was imperative that you kept your eastern suppliers accurately informed of the needs of the California market and the peculiarities of the California trade. This could take up a tremendous amount of time and energy, for there was an enormous number of relevant details to pass along. For example, since ships going around South America encountered virtually every kind of weather, goods bound for California had to be packed very carefully to avoid breakage or damage from seepage in the hold of a vessel: damaged goods, of course, had to be sold at lower prices. Even before the gold rush began, the Army Quartermaster at San Francisco had advised his superiors in Washington that good packing was a matter of "first importance," and his anxieties were echoed in many other letters out of the gold rush port.[9]

The weather and economy of the Golden State combined to produce a regional peculiarity of the California trade with which merchants on both the East and West coasts had to reckon. An 1855 newspaper put the matter in a nutshell, observing, "The major part of our business is done in the spring and the fall." For along the Pacific slope the winters tended to be wet and the summers dry, and the mining of gold depended on this seasonal pattern. Good mining in the interior of the state demanded a high level of water in the streams and rivers; otherwise panning for gold proved too difficult. A dry winter meant poor mining, and poor mining meant bad business for the San Francisco commission merchants who had imported goods into California. So as the fall passed into winter, merchants and miners would anxiously scan the heavens. "The miners," a San Francisco merchant wrote in 1851, "are waiting for rain, which is very much wanted." Should dry weather persist into January, anxiety would be the tone of the market. As one resident wrote in January 1855, "Business is pretty dull of all kinds. We have had very little rain as yet, as we must have it to give things a start." Conversely, a rainy winter was enough to lift the spirits of a San Francisco importer and stimulate him to send cheery advices to his supplier.[10]

After the rains ended in the spring, the miners were anxious to head for the diggings to take advantage of the swollen condition of the streams and rivers. So they wanted to provision themselves as quickly as possible. The result was that large quantities of goods had to be shipped to the interior in the space of a few weeks, as soon as the trails that served as roads dried up.

During the summer, when the miners were scattered through the hills and difficult to reach, the San Francisco trade generally slackened and the city's merchants awaited the end of the mining season. When the streams dried up and riverbeds could no longer be worked, the miners trickled back to the larger towns and cities. They had gold to spend—at least some of them did—and the fall trade commenced. This had to be done before the rains began and storms rendered the roads impassible. If a merchant had a stock of goods on the road when the rains came, he could suffer a large loss. In January 1853, for instance, a lawyer reported that even though "the whole country had been flooded," one merchant tried to ship $25,000 worth of potatoes and lost them all. In the fall, then, as in the spring, large shipments were made from San Francisco in the space of a few weeks and then the volume of trade contracted as quickly as it had expanded.[11]

Even though these weather patterns were constant in the broad sense—it did not rain for extended periods during the summer and it did rain fairly often during the winter—they were not reliable enough to serve as a base for specific business projections. The spring trade might begin in February, as it did in 1850 and 1851, or it might not begin until the end of March, as was the case in 1853. Weather compounded the uncertainty of doing business in San Francisco.

It takes time and experience to establish a stable network of commercial intelligence and, as their experience with the weather demonstrated, the San Francisco merchants were especially short on both. They also had to come to grips with the unpredictability of demand and the problem of trying to anticipate needs a year hence. Mostly, they gambled on a burgeoning market. Letters sent to the East soon after the discovery of gold all urged their suppliers to send as much as they could as soon as they could. William Sherman's advice to his brother John was typical. "If you can, even when you receive this," he wrote, "despatch a cargo of assorted articles ready for immediate consumption or use, you can realize more than a hundred percent." The letters that one Boston shipper received the next year showed how quickly things could change. One shipper was cautioned, in a letter written in March 1850 by a dealer named Henry F. Teschenmacher, "It would be impossible to say what kind of cargo would sell well in six months from now, as vessels are expected from all parts of the world." Scarcely a month later, the same shipper was told by another correspondent, "A cargo well assorted to consist primarily of eatables and houses and furniture will pay a good profit." With such conflicting estimates, no shipper could be very certain about what to do. But with fortunes to be made, there was no point in being cautious: the shipper usually gambled and sent whatever he could—knowing that, across the street, his competitor, having the same conflicting appraisals from his own correspondents, was probably doing the same thing, as were all shippers in Boston, New York, Philadelphia, New Orleans, and Baltimore.[12]

There were too many hustlers, too many people trying to establish importing or wholesale or retail businesses in San Francisco, to fill the need. Even though the market quickly became a specialized one, every merchant was gambling; and since they worked on a commission basis, unsold stock was a real burden. A contemporary described the situation at the end of 1851: "The old stores, where so recently all things from a needle to an anchor could be obtained, were nearly extinct; and separate classes of retail shops and wholesale warehouses were now the order of business." One merchant remarked in 1853, "When I see the number of stores in our line of business—many more than there ought to be—I feel a great hesitation in proposing to start another," but he opened a new hardware store anyway, and two months later was complaining, "Our business has been rather dull." During the same year, another merchant remarked to his supplier that barley was not going to rise in price, for "there are too many dealers in this article." As still another resident observed, "Every branch of business is overdone." All these merchants were busy sending out reports and requests to suppliers in the eastern United States, Europe, Chile, China, and Hawaii. Inevitably, oversupply became the basic condition of the market through the 1850's. In fact, the artificially high prices of early 1849 were already on their way down when the goods ordered in that year finally arrived in San Francisco. By the summer of the same year an observer noted, "There is no stable price for anything. The merchants trade on the principle to get all they can for everything." And they found that they could generally get less than they liked.[13]

The major papers of the city, which reflected the views of the leading merchants who were their advertisers, constantly moaned about the overabundance of stocks. The remark of an 1851 paper was typical: "The amount of goods selling today is considerable; yet the supply of most articles seems to be adequate to the demand, and it is only when an article which is in demand becomes scarce that an extra price can be obtained."[14]

The actual supply of any item of merchandise in the market was not the only thing that could cause prices to tumble. Rumor of another shipment could turn the trick. In January 1853, for example, "On receipt of word that a large stock of flour was on its way from Chile, flour immediately took a downward turn." The shrewd importer did his best to sell his stock as soon as possible rather than be caught with an oversupply when a clipper sailed in loaded with more of the same item. In 1852, for instance, Henry Bainbridge closed a deal to sell some rice that was just arriving in the port. Because of an error in unloading the ship, he did not receive the rice immediately, and by the time he finally tracked it down, more rice had arrived and "materially deteriorated the price." His deal fell through, and the unfortunate Bainbridge was left literally holding the bags.[15]

Everyone complained about this permanent condition of oversupply, which one merchant called "the inflation of an overdone business." As early as the summer of 1849, a visitor reported, "The city is so full of goods that they have no place to put them and the streets are full." A disappointed Robert Lammot had to tell the Du Ponts, "For the past year there has been very little demand for powder in relation to the supply." In July 1850 one merchant wrote, "Lumber is very low. It will not pay first cost after expenses"; and in March 1851 a lawyer observed, "Business is very dull, considering what the merchants expected the spring trade to bring. . . . We are so overstocked with goods that unless new markets are opened the depression must continue for some time." During the same month, the *Alta* issued a complaint that San Francisco merchants were to reiterate often during succeeding years: "Before, we could not get adequate supplies from all sources; now we find our markets broken down with merchandise from the eastern states." A ship captain who had arrived in the city early in 1851 wrote, "I found on my arrival the market to be extremely dull . . . the whole country is full of goods and large arrivals are expected. All kinds of trade are so very uncertain and fluctuating that for my own part I put no reliance on any hope of great improvement."[16]

Even after a fire had devastated large sections of the city in May, Macondray and Co. cautioned its suppliers not to jump to conclusions and send a lot of building materials. The firm warned that the 15 to 20 percent jump in prices that had occurred after the fire might prove to be only temporary: "Whether this advance will be maintained is a matter of some doubt, as the market was previously very heavily overstocked. . . . We would caution our friends against being hurried into renewed shipments until more accurate information can be obtained." The company was correct in its judgment, for even though there was much rebuilding to be done, the price of lumber did not rise appreciably after the fire. Matters looked a bit better in a few areas of trade. Samuel Weston, who had earlier complained to his father that nothing he had was selling except shovels, reported that the market was slightly better for other types of hardware after the fire, but that that was about all.[17]

Business remained in the same depressed state throughout 1851. One merchant grumbled, "There is enough lumber to last for five years, and though many fortunes have been lost by shipping it here (for very few shipments that have arrived here for a year past have paid expenses, let alone first costs) yet it is still sent in the hope of a raise." Sales became so infrequent in the middle of the summer that Macondray and Co. was forced to adopt the expensive expedient of returning some of the tea it had received from China. One merchant groaned that "business is good for nothing in San Francisco."[18]

Nonetheless, shipments to California continued. In September 1851 one paper noted with great exasperation, "We have had large arrivals today, and looking at their manifests we are astonished to see large quantities on them with which we are and have been overstocked for more than six months past. . . . No one need wonder at large losses on these goods." An anonymous correspondent took out his frustrations, and no doubt those of many merchants, by sending a satirical letter to the *Herald* in which he "advised" eastern suppliers to send immediately "five hundred assorted cargoes, as the supply on the market is not sufficient for more than fifteen months." He continued, "Any article quoted at high prices, the consumption of which is limited, should be shipped in large quantities, in order to compete with the host of other shippers."[19]

During 1852 there was a brief respite, due in part to complaints of this sort and also to a short but sharp economic downturn in the East. In February, business was reported as "dull," but the next month Robert Lammot wrote his father, "There is a better show of good prices than I have known for two years. The market is more steady and settled." By May, Roger Baldwin observed, "Business is brisk, money plenty, an immense immigration pouring in. Everybody seems to feel that the prosperity of California is a fixed fact, and as most people are making money more or less, a very general air of satisfaction prevails." In July, a merchant wrote gleefully, "We are now head over ears in business. Receiving goods from three vessels all at once and making very respectable sales at the same time." In September, one paper spoke of "limited supplies" and "exorbitant speculator prices." And at the end of November, one laborer writing from San Francisco to his wife complained about "the high price of provisions."[20]

The year 1852 was the only good year the city's importers were to experience, however. By the time news of higher prices in California had reached the East, the 1851 slump was over, and shippers immediately responded with a greater volume of goods, hoping to capitalize on what appeared from that great distance to be an expanding market in San Francisco. By 1853, goods of all sorts were once again flowing into the city, with the inevitable consequences of overstocking and lower prices.

Early in 1853, one San Francisco commission house reported to a dealer in Chile that barley was abundant at San Francisco and that shipments from Chile would result in losses "unless the price improves soon." The news that a large shipment of flour was on the way created a temporary panic, as holders frantically tried to unload their stocks before the fleet arrived. By the end of March, merchants were advising suppliers of Chilean flour that "Chile produce can be sold only for a loss" and were recommending "great caution in making shipments for some months to come." "Amid all this business and bustle," William Sherman observed, "there is more poverty than in New York. Not a day without distressed individuals asking for money."[21]

The word "dull" now began to appear with depressing regularity in business correspondence. "Times are exceedingly dull for business just now," Charles Daniell lamented at the end of April 1853. In June he complained that "the market is overloaded with all kinds of goods. People at home have been shipping as though this were a place of three million instead of

300,000. . . . It will take a long time to work off the present glut." Flour recovered a bit in July, encouraging the advice that "flour now on the way will pay a handsome profit to the importer," but that situation did not last long. By the middle of August, one firm that had recommended shipments earlier in the summer was forced to recant; in September it had to admit to considerable difficulty in selling the barley it had ordered.[22]

To make matters worse, early reports indicated that the harvest in the interior of the state was going to be a good one and that home-grown wheat might be able to supply a large part of the winter demand; and these reports were followed by news from Australia about lower prices there, which ruled it out as a place to dump any surplus from California. The usual fall trade took place, and although the volume involved was fairly respectable, the market prices for sellers were disappointing. "Large sales are being made daily," one dealer reported, "but at very low prices." In November one observer reported, "Business is dull . . . San Francisco is overstocked with goods of almost every description. The wholesale auctioneers are crying daily 'going, going, gone' for whole invoices and cargoes of goods." In December, Lammot surveyed the preceding year gloomily. "Business is generally very dull," he sighed, "and prices of all kinds of merchandise are exceedingly low."[23]

The situation did not improve as the decade wore on. Though the frustrated merchants did not know it, gold production had peaked in 1853. For the rest of the decade, fewer miners with less gold would mean declining business opportunities. In January 1854, as a sign of the coming age, a number of smaller importers, caught with huge inventories, failed. By March, business was reported "as dull as it can be," and requests were made "not to send either flour or barley here, unless there should be an actual failure of crops here, which is not likely to happen." By May, merchants were complaining of "the tightness of the money market." The next month, a teamster, whose own livelihood was tied up with the general state of the market, complained, "We don't need supplies here of scarce anything." The real estate market began to slump also. "Times continue miserably dull," Sherman lamented in July. "Real estate is unsaleable, and rents have declined." In November, noting the constant indebtedness of the major mercantile houses, one man commented, "It is simply overtrading. . . . The country has been so overcrammed with goods. . . . We now have a sufficient stock of many articles to supply us for many years."[24]

The market was apparently so glutted that even a curtailing of shipments, which occurred in late 1854, could have little effect. The house of Grogan and Lent predicted in October 1854 that even though there had been "an almost total cessation of shipments here," prices would probably not improve for a few months; then, they hoped, "some articles will become scarce." At the end of the year, a disconsolate merchant lamented, "During the past two years, our business has been getting worse and worse. To save our eastern consignors from losses, we have held on to their goods at a continued expense to ourselves, in a vain hope of improvement in our market." But hope continued to be in vain. By February and March of the next year, dealers in Chile were being advised in increasingly shrill terms not to send any more flour, since, for what must have been the umpteenth time, "whilst goods continue to arrive in large quantities, prices must give way." A lawyer observed, "Times are excessively gloomy here . . . no one doing well except the lawyers." The overabundance of goods, combined with the bank failures of 1855, led one San Francisco commission merchant to report, "The whole country is for sale."[25]

The business depression could be aggravated by unforeseen circumstances. In August 1855, some holders of sugar, despairing of the low prices, thought they might do better by putting the sugar up for auction. In the middle of the auction, a boat loaded with sugar arrived in port. Bidding fell off, and the unlucky owners of the sugar had to call off the sale.[26]

All in all, the importers had a precarious time. By 1856, all the importers in the city had more goods on hand than they could sell without sustaining losses. In January, the *Chronicle* exploded against "the insane adventures here . . . of eastern shippers," but such tirades did little good. The paper saw small reason to hope that there would be enough demand from the interior of the state to realize profits on trade unless and until shipments from the East entirely ceased. And the shippers seemed to be working more furiously than ever. In March, the *Herald* observed with disgust, "Whereas ordinarily we have not been in the habit of receiving two clippers a week, now we have half a dozen a day." Surveying the scene at the end of the month, a third paper found no reason for cheer: "The truth is that with very few exceptions we are overstocked with imported merchandise, and some fifteen or twenty ships are known to be within a few days' sail of us, which will quite rationally account for the existing dull state of business . . . and it is quite as rational to believe that there will be no improvement until the heavy stocks are worked off."[27]

All this created a mercantile stalemate, with sellers unwilling to sell at the prices offered and buyers unwilling to buy, since they were convinced the prices would go down even more: "The country buyers, influenced apparently by the excessive importations of the past three or four weeks, have been very quiet, whilst many of the importers and commission merchants have been equally unwilling to submit their stocks for the reduced rates." To depress things even further, there were rumors of peace in Europe. If this came to pass, one merchant wrote, "No doubt there will be a general tumble in prices all over the world." As the editor of the *Herald* sarcastically reminded his eastern readers—such as they were—"the people residing in California do not wear more clothing or consume more food than any other civilized people." But the caution was not enough: by the beginning of May, it was reported, "Flour and wheat arriving quite freely from Oregon, and the price going down."[28]

◆ III ◆

Americans like to think of themselves as a pragmatic people. Inside each American, it is said, lurks a clever jack-of-all-trades. When things get rough, we roll up our sleeves, use a little Yankee ingenuity, and solve the problem. The pioneer merchants of San Francisco, for all their Yankee ingenuity, seemed unable to solve anything. They certainly recognized their problem. In letter after letter, they complained about their main difficulty, which was of course evident to one and all: the glutted market. And they tried to resolve that problem in four different yet complementary ways. None worked.

The first way was the simplest. Since the goods the merchants held represented a cost to them, they had to try and cut other costs. The easiest way to do that would have been to cut out the middleman. Following the usual pattern of wholesale merchants in the United States, the San Francisco importer did not sell directly to a merchant from the interior of the state, from Sacramento, Stockton, or Marysville, but rather sold in bulk to a specialist, the jobber, who in turn sold the goods to the country merchant. This division of labor apparently arose spontaneously, since keeping in touch with shippers in Boston, New York, or Philadelphia was a full-time job. Maintaining contact with merchants in the interior also took considerable time, and thus the demands of commerce in San Francisco led to the same type of mercantile specialization that had developed in the East and Midwest.[29]

Since the jobber took a commission on the goods he sold, the price the country merchant paid for the material was increased accordingly. This meant that the country merchant wanted to buy when the price was low. Cutting the jobber out of the transaction altogether would have been one way of enabling the country merchant to buy at lower prices while at the same time assuring the importer of an adequate commission. Yet this method of sale directly to the country merchant was never widely attempted, for it proved too complicated. During the 1853 fall trade, for instance, some importers tried to sell flour directly to the country merchants. But the importers soon discovered that they themselves would have to replace the jobbers in extending credit to the country. Since they did not know the country merchants well enough to calculate which of them were good risks and which were not, they quickly drew back from their attempt. The complexities that had produced the importer-jobber specialization in the first place proved compelling enough to offset the monetary advantages of trying to dispense with the traditional pattern.[30]

When the merchants were forced to accept the jobbers, they had to try their second option, to attempt to outwit them. Their interests were at odds, of course: the importer was anxious to sell to the jobber at high prices and thus increase his own commission, whereas the jobber wanted to buy at low prices and sell at high ones, to maximize *his* profit. Much of the business history of gold rush San Francisco could be told simply by relating the maneuvers of these two sets of merchants against each other. Generally, when the importers preferred not to sell, they were besieged by jobbers anxious to buy, and so it went back and forth in a kind of dance. If the importers (or jobbers) took one step forward, the jobbers (or importers) took one step back.

Almost from the start of the gold rush flurry, importers began taking the risk of holding goods when prices sank too low for what they considered a good profit. They reasoned that if no further supplies arrived in the immediate future and the demand for the particular article became acute, the jobbers would be forced to "enter the market" and buy at whatever price the importers asked. The risk lay in holding goods too long, because if a shipment of the article arrived, the jobbers had the advantage. The importers had to get rid of their stock, at whatever price they could get, before the new shipment entered the market and depressed prices still more. As early as 1849, the captain of H.M.S. *Inconstant*, on a visit to San Francisco, noted this propensity of importers to hold until the last possible moment. He wrote to his superiors, "Merchants in anticipation of a rise consequent upon a sudden influx of gold hunters and of from thirty to forty thousand immigrants who have lately crossed the mountains and who are reported to be in great distress have commenced to decline parting with their provisions at the present rates." Sometimes merchants would refuse to unload their ships in an attempt to hide an increase of supplies from the jobbers. If you were trying to sell a jobber some flour, it was certainly not in your interest that he know that a ship loaded with it had just sailed in.[31]

These stalling tactics became a commonplace of commercial life in the gold rush metropolis. Importers tried as best they could to weigh both the season and the volume of goods in and approaching San Francisco, and transacted business according to these calculations. In February 1851, when the opening of the spring trade was not far off, one paper reported, "We find the regular traders are unwilling to force off their stocks of saleable goods, believing that as we are drawing near the opening of the spring trade they will be amply repaid for their loss of time." The importers were gambling, in other words, that the opening of the spring trade would precede the arrival of further amounts of large supplies. The same strategy was employed the following spring. A merchant related, "There seems to be a feeling among the first class merchants here to hold their goods at a figure which will cover first costs and expenses, adding a fair living profit, whether there is a demand for them or not."[32]

But the strategy that worked well in 1852, the only good

year for the importers, was far less successful in 1853 and succeeding years, when the volume of imports grew so huge. In February 1853, while admitting "No one can make a calculation on this market," Alexander B. Grogan wrote his supplier that he had decided to hold the flour he had received rather than force it on the market at a certain loss. Two months later, after the opening of spring trade, the market had not improved: "The 3,000 bags of barley are still on board the storeship *Eleanor*," Grogan reported, "and we shall take advantage of the first favorable change in the market to realize it with as little loss as possible." Food was not the only item subject to this uncertainty, for two weeks later the same merchant wrote the same supplier that he was still being "forced to hold your axes."[33]

The circumstances had not changed by the time the 1854 spring trade rolled around. In late March of 1854, one newspaper observed, "Importers, confident of an advance in rates, are unwilling to sell at present prices." Two months later the same paper offered a more hopeful picture for the future but conceded that importers were still in the process of holding substantial parts of their goods:

> Importers, acting under advices received per last mail, which have occasioned much confidence in our market, are holding at higher rates than are at present obtainable, but must be acceded to by dealers should there be a reaction in business. Should shipments to California continue moderate and in conformity to advices from our well established and respectable merchants, the time will come when consignors will realize, if not great, then at least fair remuneration for their investments.[34]

The time did not come in 1854, and an identical situation developed the next year. As early as January, it was reported in the press, "The bulk of the provisions received per late arrivals, which had not been sold previously to arrival, are going into store, consignees feeling unwilling to accept present rates." At the end of February, partly because of a run on the city's banks and partly because of general conditions, one merchant wrote, "None of the importers has made a sale in two weeks." By April, some of the importers had stopped selling anything at all. "If they had continued to offer goods on the market," one paper explained, "prices must continue to fall to zero." This condition, resulting from the glut of goods, continued into the summer. The *Chronicle* reported in June, "'Holders' idea of the value of goods have rather got beyond those of buyers, and we may look for a lull in operations until further arrivals take place from the Atlantic ports." During the summer, importers continued to hold, placing their increasingly slim hopes upon a strong fall trade:

> As a general thing, consignees of goods not sold to arrive have made no effort to place them today, it being evident that to make sales to any great extent for many descriptions of goods, concessions in prices would have to be made to the buyers, and there is a strong impression that a material improvement must take place in connection with a revival of the country trade, so consignees have mostly adopted the expedient of storing.[35]

Thus it was normal for importers to hold back their goods from the market when they did not think that they would receive what they considered reasonable prices for them. On the other side of the coin, it was equally normal for the jobbers to refuse to buy when they thought that the importers were asking exorbitant prices. The jobbers would simply wait for the fleet, hoping that it would bring a huge supply of the item in dispute and send prices sliding.

This strategy was noted in early 1853, in regard to a fleet that was then overdue from China. The *Alta* said that there was "much speculation" on the cargo the fleet was carrying and that buyers were holding back, banking on lower prices after the fleet arrived. In March, one importer wrote, "We have not had a single enquiry from any of the jobbers" for axes, since "the hardware dealers are all overstocked." In April, the *Chronicle*, whose commercial columns were often written from the standpoint of the jobbers (as the *Herald*'s were written from the standpoint of the auctioneers and the *Alta*'s from the standpoint of the importers), reported that jobbing sales to the country were running ahead of the sales made by the importers to the jobbers, "for the reason that the jobbers have strictly limited their purchases to their actual wants from day to day." In other words, the jobbers were shunning what they considered to be inflated prices by buying only what they needed to satisfy the rock-bottom demand.[36]

A similar situation obtained during the 1855 fall trade. The jobbers were getting more and more into the habit of buying the merest necessities rather than buying in bulk. The *Chron-*

icle summed up the matter in November: "The jobbers appear to be out of the market as buyers, and the reason is that their stocks are generally ample to meet all the trade they are doing at present with the country, and, as a number of vessels from the Atlantic ports are now due, they prefer taking the chances of buying lower when the vessels may get in."[37]

The instability of their relationships with the jobbers led the importers down the slippery road to their third option. This was for a group of them to try to corner the market in any particular commodity and hold out until the jobbers agreed to pay what the importers demanded. This was not an original idea. Merchants' cartels were rapidly becoming something of a national tradition. The commercial life of Chicago in the 1840's, for instance, was punctuated with many of these "speculative flurries." In San Francisco, the press reported on these speculations the way the modern press reports sporting events, with the focus always on winners and losers (and there were generally more of the latter than of the former). These constant speculations bear vivid witness to how far antebellum America had come from the days when there was, on paper at least, such a thing as the common good, and when an attempt to corner the market was illegal.[38]

Speculations were attempted most often in flour, such as in the winter of 1852–53 and also in July 1853, when a group of dealers and importers managed to run up the price, only to be defeated by the volume of imports that arrived by the end of the summer. Many other such instances were mentioned in the commercial correspondence of the period and in the business sections of the press. In January 1854, for example, a group of speculators worked up the price of coffee, only to suffer great losses by the end of the month. In the summer of that same year, a group of flour merchants tried to put themselves in a strong position for the upcoming fall trade. The *Chronicle* reported that holders of Chilean flour had "formed a combination" to try to avoid heavy losses in the fall; it pointed out that holders of American flour had tried the same thing not long before, and their efforts had failed, as the price of American flour had declined.[39]

There was a simple reason why these speculations so seldom worked. Cartels require both a limited amount of the item hoarded and a limited number of people dealing in it. In San

Francisco in the 1850's, there were too many hustlers, pushing too many imports, and the victory was not always to the stronger importers, those with better credit ratings in San Francisco and the East and with more capital and assets than their competitors. These "stronger" importers could hold on to goods and sustain losses for a time, in the hope of future profit; but the "weaker" importers, who needed cash, any cash, to remit to their suppliers and could not afford to wait beyond a week or two, were more easily tempted to break the cartel and sell at whatever price they could get. Their actions lowered the price that the stronger importers could command, and the stronger importers then had to try and form larger cartels, so that they could control practically all the available stocks of an item. But this merely transferred the same problem to another level, for the new combination was only as strong as its weakest member. As one paper put it:

> Experience in this market has amply demonstrated the fact that with a six months' stock of any staple article in the hands of a hundred different holders, prices cannot be maintained at a standard covering the cost of production or manufacture. Chiefly for the reason that one-third to one-half the number of operators have not the means to hold for a sufficient length of time, but are obliged prematurely to realize, in order to raise money, and thereby break down the market. This result to speculation without any proper basis has been witnessed again and again.[40]

Such advice, though it seemed reasonable, did not have a noticeable effect on the way in which business was transacted at the gold rush port. Even though one of the larger importers wrote early in 1855, "Business is daily becoming more regulated, and soon will be confined to the capitalists"—by which he presumably meant the large dealers like himself—speculations continued. Indeed, in the same letter, this aspiring capitalist reported such operations in coffee and sugar. A year earlier, Edwin M. Lewis, who had arrived in San Francisco with a letter of recommendation from a former local real estate tycoon, Rodman M. Price, wrote Price that the man whom he had presented the letter to "wished immediately to give me a chance of speculation in Chile flour"—certainly a dubious favor! The speculative spirit was not confined to wheeler-dealer types. Teamster Thomas T. Seward wrote to his wife, "I came here to make something, and I mean to, if I don't lose it again in speculation. I have had two rather bad ones, the pigs and some machinery for polishing steel," but he declared that he had taken the pledge not to speculate again.[41]

The only successful speculation that involved large quantities was the flour speculation that occurred in the winter of 1852–53, when a combination managed to obtain a corner on flour and keep the price up for several months. Though the San Francisco press said little about it, a good many people grasped the connection between the successful speculation and the shortages of flour in the interior of the state. When reports began to reach the city of a lack of food in the cold and rainy mining areas over the winter, Roger Baldwin wrote home of the common belief that the city's merchants were primarily responsible for the suffering: "I know not what punishment would be too severe for the hard-hearted speculators who . . . have been enabled to keep for so long a time the staple articles of provision up to famine prices. At no time has there been a real scarcity in our market, but while our warehouses were groaning with their weight of flour and pork, none could be procured by the upcountry traders except at the most exorbitant of rates."[42]

If speculations failed, as they often did, the merchants were left with their fourth option: dumping their stocks on the market at whatever price they could command. This was certainly not what they had envisioned when they came round the Horn with dreams of making a fortune, but it was at least a way of remitting *some* money to their suppliers. It was the final blow, but it was the only way out, as the *Chronicle* observed in an article in January 1855: "In a market circumstanced like ours, acting almost solely as a medium of local supply, it follows that the moment the supply demand is satisfied for the time, a cessation of legitimate transactions must ensue, as there are always parties interested in operations who are compelled to realize in order to meet their engagements, they are obliged to force the market, and a decline in prices results."[43]

The market fluctuation was a regular phenomenon in San Francisco, corresponding to fluctuations in the spring and fall trade. During the spring of 1851, the *Alta* remarked, "We find goods pressed on the market in larger quantities than the wants of trade can compass this season." During the fall of 1853, the same paper reported, "Holders, either on necessity or on instructions from correspondents abroad, have pressed sales, and there is a decline in prices." When a cargo of flour arrived the next month, it was immediately dumped on the market, because the importers were already holding so much flour that no one wanted to hold more. The price of flour began to fall, and by January 1854 the movement was general. A merchant described the situation: "The importers are offering goods at lower prices than have been known here for three years."[44]

Market situations in the East also affected the San Francisco market. If money was temporarily tight in any of the eastern ports that shipped to San Francisco, dealers sometimes sent word to their San Francisco consignees to sell at the prevailing market price and send the money East. In its issue of August 1, 1854, a year the northern economy went into a brief slump, the *Chronicle* noted, "Instructions advising commission merchants to sell and remit by August 1 have caused a depression in our general market."[45]

The traditional way of forcing goods on the market was to present them for auction. A steady stream of auctions in a nineteenth-century commercial city was almost certain proof that the volume of goods had overwhelmed the market and that established merchants were not doing well. When the British dumped huge amounts of goods on New York City after the War of 1812, for example, the city saw a tremendous upsurge in the number of auctions, and a number of established importers were driven out of business. For the surviving New York merchants, though, the cloud had a silver lining, for the English decision to dump at New York, rather than Philadelphia or Boston or Baltimore, was a major factor in that city's becoming the nation's center of commerce. But there were few silver linings by the Golden Gate.[46]

I do not want to leave the reader with the impression that, for the San Francisco merchants, life was unrelieved gloom and doom. Things might be bleak, but there were some bright spots. When Levi Strauss, for instance, instructed his brother to "buy up every yard of canvas and the like that you can get your hands on and keep buying it," he knew what he was talking about. And occasionally the importers would emerge victorious from their skirmishes with the jobbers. In May 1853, for example, the jobbers refrained from buying large amounts of flour, in anticipation of large arrivals, which, they were confident, would break the importers. But by the second week of

June, when the importers' paper, the *Alta*, reported that shipments were "not as large as we anticipated," and the country dealers were pressing them for flour, they finally had to "enter the market" and buy at the prices the importers were asking.[47]

Certainly the jobbers had their own set of problems. As middlemen in the commercial chain, they had payments on two sides. They paid the San Francisco merchants for the goods they bought from them, and they were in turn paid by the country merchants for the goods they sold, but the dependence on credit, typical of the day, could be precarious. The gold rush pattern of credit was succinctly summarized by the *Chronicle* in late November 1854, a low period for everyone: "The country is just now largely in debt to the city, and it is extremely difficult to make collections. Here the jobber owes the importer, the country dealer owes the jobber, and the miner who is looking anxiously for rain, owes the country storekeeper."[48]

Throughout most of the 1850's, a steamship left San Francisco every two weeks for the East. On "steamer days" (the term came from Ohio River shipping a few decades earlier), outstanding debts had to be collected. A hitch anywhere along the credit chain disrupted everything and prevented the full amount of money from being sent East. This happened in the middle of November 1854, when money was tight. One paper explained:

> The trouble is that the country is heavily in debt to the city, for those goods taken in the last thirty days, which the jobbers are now called upon to pay the importers for . . . although the seller on time has good claim on the buyer, yet there is no tangible operation which the former can raise the money upon, if he is necessitated to borrow. We presume however that as the credit system becomes a fixed fact here, in time it will become so systematized as to yield all the conveniences that it is capable of affording to the wants of business.[49]

The jobbers bore the brunt of the inconveniences that resulted from the faulty workings of the system, because they depended on the country dealers for the cash necessary to pay the San Francisco importers. Lacking cash, they could get behind, as happened in the fall of 1853, when the fall trade did not begin until well into October. If they got too far behind, the importers simply stopped extending them credit—even if it meant failure for the jobbers, as in the case of the house of Sherry, Janes, and McRea in the spring of 1855, for example.

The only recourse for the jobber in such a situation was to stop extending credit to the country. This happened in the spring of 1853, but only for a few days. For the most part, the jobbers, along with all the others in the chain of supply, tried to juggle credit and payments.[50]

• IV •

The popular American frontier symbols are the log cabin and the covered wagon. We would be truer to the historical record, I suspect, if we dropped those and substituted the bank. For in those rare instances when the bank did not accompany the settlers west, it preceded them. The westward-moving yeoman of our national myth of expansion may often have been so isolated that he could not hear the barking of his neighbor's dog, but he was rarely so out of touch that he could not reach his banker in a relatively nearby town or city. Frontier areas were chronically short of capital and desperately in need of credit. The bank was a necessary institution if the frontier were to be settled.

So banks came quickly to San Francisco. They came and flew in the face of the California constitution, which reflected what Bayrd Still has called "the normal frontier antipathy to monopolistic associations and creditor institutions." The constitution was pretty straightforward. "The Legislature shall have no power," it declared, "to pass any act granting any charter for banking purposes; but associations may be formed, under general laws, for the deposit of gold and silver, but no such association shall make, issue, or put in circulation any bill, check, ticket, certificate, promissory note, or other paper, or the paper of any bank, to serve as money." Even so, the banks still came. In the early days of the gold rush, anyone with a reasonably strong safe could become a banker, and many of the larger mercantile companies, such as Macondray and Co., stored gold in their vaults. These arrangements soon gave way to the appearance of firms dealing exclusively with banking affairs, while preserving the charming legal fiction that there were no banks around. In 1849, two ex-soldiers, one of whom had come to California as paymaster in the army, opened an Exchange and Deposit Office, and others, including a representative of the Rothschilds of London, were soon on the scene.[51]

These early bankers found a ready business, for, as Ira B. Cross has stated, "Miners were constantly in the market for drafts with which to remit their earnings and wealth to families, friends, and bankers in other cities." The burgeoning California express companies, already in the business of transporting gold and often branches of eastern companies, naturally began to perform this task. Soon one of the largest banks in the state and in San Francisco was Adams and Co., which was connected with the Boston-based express company of the same name. Wells, Fargo, and Co., fast becoming an express power in its own right, also conducted a banking house. In addition to the express companies, eastern banks set up branches in California. In 1850, Willis and Co. of Boston sent out Willis's brother-in-law, Thomas G. Wells, to San Francisco, where he opened the house of Wells and Co. He prospered so handsomely that he bought his brother-in-law's interest in April 1851, only to be burned out himself in the fire of May. By October, his venture had breathed its last, and creditors had to settle for thirty-seven cents on the dollar. (At that, they did considerably better than creditors of other suspended San Francisco banks.) Page, Bacon, and Co., a St. Louis bank, established a San Francisco branch, as did Lucas, Turner, and Co., another St. Louis concern.[52]

As was the case with the importers, the success of a banking house depended in large measure on the connections it was able to establish with someone in the East or upon its ability to devise some gimmick that would enable it to stand out from the herd. James King, for instance, had spent some time in the 1840's working for the powerful house of Corcoran and Riggs in Washington, D.C. In California, he set up his own bank, which prospered in part because it was able to advertise bills of exchange on Corcoran and Riggs. King's bank failed in 1854, when it became involved in financing something called the Tuolumne Hydraulic Association, a shady enterprise that apparently existed more on paper than anywhere else.[53]

The banking house of Palmer, Cook, and Co. set itself up as bondsman for state and local Democratic officials, in exchange for which it had the privilege of being the state and city pet bank as long as it met the interest on state and city bonds, payable twice yearly in New York. After a series of close calls, it finally failed to meet the payments in June 1856, when the vigilantes were destroying the local Democratic party, and it went out of business.

Lucas, Turner, and Co. used family connections. Henry S. Turner had been graduated from West Point in the 1830's and had served in the western campaign under General Kearny. He was also the uncle of Ellen Ewing, who married William Tecumseh Sherman. Turner convinced Sherman that his future lay in banking. He appointed him manager of the San Francisco branch, and was thereby able to have that branch made the depository of War Department funds. Unlike Palmer, Cook, and Co., however, Lucas, Turner, and Co. did not fritter away its funds. Sherman, in fact, was so tight that he refused to act as bondsman for anyone who did not keep on account the full amount of cash expressed in the bond. He was also notoriously stingy in extending credit to the jobbers, whose precarious position in the middle of the credit chain made him uneasy. "I have watched their operations closely," he said, "and I confess they scare me." One jobbing house actually placed a notice in the papers protesting the tight policy of Lucas, Turner, and Co.[54]

Connections with the East, which were so important in starting San Francisco banking, proved eventually to be a curse. At the end of 1854, after Page, Bacon, and Co. of St. Louis found itself overinvolved in midwestern railroad speculation, it secretly sent an agent to San Francisco to bring back some funds from its branch there. No sooner had the agent dispatched the funds to St. Louis, by the first steamer available, than news arrived by incoming mail that the St. Louis bank had failed. When the news got out, there was an immediate run on the San Francisco house, and it was forced to suspend payment "for want of coin." This failure triggered runs on the other San Francisco banks.[55]

The largest bank in the city did not even attempt to weather the storm. Adams and Co. was undoubtedly the single most important financial institution in the state. The express division reached all parts of California and consistently shipped the largest amount of gold dust from the mines to the East. The companion banking house served all portions of San Francisco society. On February 23, 1855, just a day after the close of Page,

Bacon, and Co., Adams and Co. announced that it would not open. Simultaneously, it announced that a suit for dissolution of partnership was being initiated, with Alvin Adams, the Boston head of the entire company, as plaintiff. The two resident managing partners in San Francisco were named as defendants. On application to the District Judge, Alfred A. Cohen, a businessman with the reputation of being a real estate wizard, was appointed receiver of the firm's assets. Considerable resentment surfaced in the press that the bank had not bothered to open on the morning of the twenty-third. Instead, receiver Cohen had spent the night of February 22–23 removing the assets from the premises and depositing them in the vaults of Alsop and Co., commission merchants.

The managers of Adams and Co. admitted that the suit was a ruse, but they maintained that it was the only way they could survive a run on the banks. Since California banks were unchartered, hence unregulated, and it was not legally clear whether a bank could go into insolvency and have an assignee divide the assets fairly, this suit, the managers argued, ensured an equitable distribution of the assets to the creditors. They maintained that had Adams and Co. opened on February 23, a mad scramble would have taken place, with a first-come, first-served allotment of the cash on hand. Some creditors would have received nothing, while others would have been paid in full. They insisted that the suit was intended to give them the chance to spend a few days recalling money from their branches in the interior of the state, after which they meant to drop the suit, reopen the bank, and withstand the run. If they failed to gather sufficient funds to allow a reopening, at least they would have delivered the assets to a receiver for distribution. (Cohen maintained throughout that he had accepted the receivership on the understanding that his services would only be needed for a couple of days.)

The plan had not taken into account the effect of panic on its depositors outside the city. When news of the closing of the San Francisco house was telegraphed to the interior of the state, anxious depositors stormed the Adams and Co. branches there and withdrew all funds on hand. Cohen soon realized that the bank would be unable to satisfy its San Francisco creditors, and he petitioned the court to remove him as receiver. Since the firm was unable to find anyone else who was willing to take the post, it decided to take a chance and go into insolvency. The same judge who had appointed Cohen receiver now ruled that banks could go into insolvency and appointed him temporary assignee. The San Francisco creditors quickly elected three permanent assignees: Cohen, a former state treasurer, and an official of Palmer, Cook, and Co., which had so far withstood the panic. The three then moved the Adams and Co. assets into the vaults at Palmer, Cook, and Co.

But as Adams and Co. had originally feared, another judge ruled that a bank could not become legally insolvent. He voided the order under which Cohen had been removed as receiver, removed the assignees, and removed Cohen as receiver. In his place he appointed Henry Naglee, one of the former military officers who had started the first Exchange and Deposit Office (long since failed) in San Francisco. Naglee had a well-deserved reputation for not waiting on formalities. While serving with the army in 1848, he had been arrested for shooting two Indians. After his release, apparently unable to devise an alternative form of recreation, he had shot another one. Appropriately enough, he had been a collector of the discriminatory foreign miners' tax and a member of the 1851 vigilance committee.[56]

Naglee promptly sued Cohen and the other assignees for recovery of the assets in Palmer, Cook, and Co. He obtained a judgment against Cohen for $269,000, which Cohen refused to pay, claiming that he was entitled to compensation for his term as receiver (not a bad sum for a few days' work). The matter then dragged through the courts for years. But it left in its wake a severely damaged credit system in San Francisco. And for the city's importers, faced with a steamer every two weeks, that was not welcome news.

• V •

It was not an easy thing to be a San Francisco importer in the 1850's. But the importers had no monopoly on hard times. Again and again, the harsh reality of California mocked the expectations of those who had been foolish enough to think that a quick fortune awaited them in the Golden State. As early as 1850, the St. Joseph *Gazette*, back in Missouri, surveying things from its vantage point at the beginning of the Overland Trail, had presciently warned:

> We begin to think with Col. Benton that the discovery of gold in California is a subject for regret rather than congratulations, and that the sooner it is used up, the better. Within the past two years, six persons whom we knew intimately have sought the land of gold, and of these, three are dead. The other three would gladly return, but have expended all the money they took with them, and have not the means to come back. Truly, fortune hunting in California is a poor sport.[57]

The expectations of an eastern lawyer named William Daingerfield were typical, and so was the manner in which the Pacific Coast exacted its toll. In 1853, Daingerfield, recently arrived in San Francisco, received a thousand-dollar fee for successfully arguing one of the endless California land cases in court. That was all he needed to fuel his imagination. "I will make a fortune, and a large one, in the next few years," he boasted to his family back East. "I will have information that I can sell to speculators at a high price, as I will have full knowledge of the character of all the lands put into market, and speculators have already offered me 25 percent to invest for them." It was the classic approach to reality of the hustler: more money can be squeezed out of any situation. Daingerfield estimated that he would make nine thousand dollars in the next year, just for starters. Then, in all probability, the governor would make him a judge. What secrets was he imagining that he could sell as a judge?

One month later Daingerfield had to confess that he had as yet "collected no money from my business here." He tossed this off as "bad luck," but he had also lost an investment in some property in Shasta County that burned down. He had decided to "invest all the rest of my funds in city lots in San Francisco. They can't burn up and must increase in value." But that plan, too, went awry. In December he wrote, "I will make several—(perhaps thousands)—certainly hundreds by our next sale of property." By April, the dream was fading: "Our last sale of property did not command such prices." He had to learn to be content with his more modest fees, and he struggled to put his dreams of being a real estate tycoon or an esteemed and wealthy judge on the back burner.[58]

The dreams were in the air. George Doherty, who published a paper called the *Daily Times*, had to give up the enterprise, and wrote ruefully to his confidant, Rev. John Nobili, president of Santa Clara College, "I am about as far off my 'pile' as I ever was." With the bewilderment typical of those who cannot quite bring themselves to admit that their dreams were unrealistic to begin with, he mused, "I have been very unfortunate ever since I came to this 'blessed' country."[59]

The case of Harvey Lamb offers a more extreme example of the cruel way in which the "Emporium of the Pacific" could treat those who came to it. Lamb arrived in San Francisco in the first month of 1852, full of enthusiasm: "Cleveland can't hold a candle to San Francisco," he declared. True, "Times are very dull here at present," but he was sure that this was only temporary, owing to the fact that the previous winter had been a very dry one. After a month, he was still without steady work, and he began to give serious consideration to going out to the mines. He hung around the waterfront for a few months more, picking up odd jobs here and there, but constant work still eluded him.

In April, he wrote his mother, "I see but little chance of finding anything to do here." So he struck out for the interior of the state, looking for gold or a good paying job. He found neither. By the end of the summer, he was back in the city he had regarded as hopeless only a few months before. After the mines, the city had a different appearance to him. "I wish now I had remained in this city instead of going to the mines," he wrote. "I could have made some money here. [He does not say how.] As it is, I have worked all summer and have made little more than expenses."

By October, still out of work, he hit on a new scheme. "I can find nothing to do here and am going above to Oregon," he announced, "to buy lumber for this market." In true San Francisco fashion, he was becoming a speculator. "What little money I have I intend to invest in that trade, *make or break*." He did not "make." He explained why when he returned: "My speculation in Oregon did not turn out as well as I had anticipated. I could not buy any lumber owing to the late fire in Sacramento which set all the lumber dealers crazy. So I invested what money I had in hogs, and had I succeeded in getting them to market, I should have done very well. But as it is, out of 78 hogs which I purchased in Oregon, only 15 lived to reach this place. I lost about $400 in the operation, my usual luck."

The last we know of Harvey Lamb is his remark at the end of December: "I shall leave again Saturday for the Sandwich Islands." Then he drops out of this history, like so many other nameless and faceless individuals for whom San Francisco was anything but the end of the rainbow.[60]

CHAPTER 3

THE SCAPEGOATS

Then he shall present the live goat, and Aaron shall lay both his hands on the head of the live goat, and confess over him all the iniquities of the people of Israel, and all their transgressions, and all their sins; and he shall put them on the head of the goat, and send him away into the wilderness by the hand of a man who is in readiness. The goat shall bear all the iniquities upon him to a solitary land; and he shall let the goat go into the wilderness. —*Leviticus 16: 20–22*

♦

It is well known that within the last 12 months *54 murders have been committed in San Francisco alone, not one of which has ever been punished, and in some cases the perpetrators have never undergone the least investigation.*

—*Vigilante Robert S. Lammot,*
writing from San Francisco, June 11, 1851

♦

Since the formation of a Vigilance Committee in San Francisco, crime has diminished at a most wonderful rate—scarcely a burglary, murder, or robbery, gunshot, or theft is heard of in the town. —*Vigilante Robert S. Lammot,*
writing from San Francisco, July 9, 1851

♦

Americans of all ages, all conditions, and all dispositions constantly form associations. They have not only commercial and manufacturing companies, but associations of a thousand other kinds, religious, moral, serious, futile, general or restricted, enormous or diminutive. . . . Wherever at the head of some new undertaking you see the government in France, or a man of rank in England, in America you will be sure to find an association. —*Alexis de Tocqueville*

♦ I ♦

As the previous chapter has tried to make clear, the San Francisco importers had many worries, mostly caused by their inability to solve the basic problem of overstocking. However, their adoption of some ancient strategies allowed them to gloss over their own shortcomings. According to legend, whenever bad news—defeat in battle, a famine, an earthquake, a plague—was brought to them, the Persians would kill the messenger who carried the tidings, symbolically blaming him for the disaster. Other peoples mystically deposited their sins on a sacrificial animal and then sent the beast into the desert to die. Americans, too, have always seemed to like externalizing their woes. A people who allow themselves few public doubts about the righteousness of their enterprises, and have virtually no sense of what used to be called original sin, need to blame their troubles on someone else "out there." Sometimes it was the devil, who was unaccountably hell-bent on subverting Plymouth or Salem; other times it was the Pope. The international banking (i.e. Jewish) conspiracy has occasionally sufficed, as have foreign anarchists, socialists, and communists. The San Francisco importers followed the American pattern. The more unable they were to control their own destinies, the more shrill were their cries against others. They spent the years after 1850 casting for scapegoats, and they held a number of auditions.

They tried the federal government first. As the major port of entry into what had become the western part of the United States, San Francisco had a customs house. Besides being the principal source of federal patronage in the area, the House was the federal institution that touched the businessmen most directly, and the businessmen complained about it constantly. One of the standard gripes was that the Collector, a federal appointee, enforced the customs regulations too literally. There was, for example, a regulation that goods imported in foreign vessels had to be unloaded within a certain amount of time, usually fifteen days. When the Collector had the audacity to bring up the rule, he met bitter complaints. One paper summarized them: "This order only benefits a few property owners in town, who offered their stores for bonded warehouses, while it exposes the importer to the risk of fire, and makes him subject to numerous charges, which will consume the value of his merchandise in the course of a few months." This particular complaint came at a time when the market was overstocked, as it normally was. The importer preferred to have goods stay on board ship until he had a reasonable chance of selling them. That way he avoided paying storage cost on goods he might be forced to hold for some time, and he postponed paying lighterage and drayage fees. And also, although the respectable merchants never would have admitted it in the public press, leaving goods on board ship was a neat way of keeping the jobbers in the dark.[1]

The importers had another complaint, which stemmed from the specific application to San Francisco of the old American notion of exceptionalism. Where Americans claimed that they were different from the rest of the world, the western merchants claimed that they were different from the rest of America. Because ships that left the East for San Francisco would often call at one or more South American ports on their way to California, it was possible to argue that all the goods on board had actually been "exported" and then brought back into the country of production. In that case they were subject to an increased duty. For a time the Collector adopted this line of reasoning, much to the discomfort of the San Francisco importers who claimed that the law was never meant for them.[2]

There were other complaints of the Customs House, and running through them all was a single thread. The frustrations and uncertainties the merchants experienced when they dealt with the Collector were magnified out of all proportion and made to symbolize all the frustrations the beleaguered merchants experienced in their own business affairs. One merchant, decrying "the continual vexations of the present Customs House officers," declared: "As long as we have no free trade, we must submit to the payment of duties; but let these be raised on a liberal footing, let the public be acquainted with the new regulations and some time allowed to make the new decisions known. Have we not had plenty of cases where the Collector sustained a point for a month or two, and then changed his opinion? Who can know whether tomorrow will be considered lawful what today is deemed so?" These types of complaints continued throughout the period. In 1856, one correspondent to the *Bulletin* summed up the prevailing attitude: all the collectors, he claimed, had been hopelessly corrupt.[3]

It is rather difficult to work up much sympathy for the merchants on this score. In the first place, the collectors were hardly imposed on them by a remote and unfeeling central government. The importers themselves often had a say in his appointment. Roger Baldwin, who worked at the House, reported in 1852 that the new collector had been "highly recommended by the merchants of this port." Nor were the collectors empire builders who created armies of useless clerks, entirely dependent on themselves. In the summer of 1852, for example, when imports were dropping, the Collector reduced his staff by about half. There was a similar cutback in the fall of 1854.[4]

Nor were the collectors inflexible. In the middle of 1853, Collector Richard Hammond wrote to the president of the San Francisco Chamber of Commerce asking his assistance in evaluating sizes of loads. "When foreign merchandise is entered for warehousing," Hammond wrote, "it becomes the duty of the Collector to convey it to the store, in drays or carts employed on the public accounts, the expense to be defrayed by the person entering the goods. . . . I propose contracting with responsible parties, who will give me ample securities for the faithful performance of their contract, to convey all the merchandise ordered to bonded warehouses at stipulated rates." (The person who obtained this contract would receive a fine patronage plum, but that was understood in San Francisco or anywhere else.) Hammond asked the Chamber and the draymen to meet and decide what amount of goods would constitute a "load," so there would not be constant haggling on the waterfront. Less than a month later, the Chamber sent Hammond a proposed schedule of "loads," and he accepted the proposal in its entirety.[5]

In the same vein, in 1855 the Collector asked the Secretary of the Treasury to exempt San Francisco from the federal regulation requiring importers to produce certified invoices for goods before putting them into a warehouse. Because of the risks of the long ocean voyage, invoices and goods were often sent separately from the East to San Francisco, and the timing was not always right. Mail could sometimes be lost at sea, and the Collector understood the problem of those merchants who "by unavoidable casualty are unable to produce certified invoices upon the arrival of their goods. By being compelled to pay duties immediately, they in a measure lose the advantage of the market, which a warehousing system would procure to them." The following month, he asked the Secretary to exempt San Francisco from a federal regulation that required an entirely new registry when an ocean vessel happened to engage temporarily in the coastal trade. Although this collector was willing to assist the merchants in limited cases like these, he privately informed his superiors in Washington that he thought his predecessors had shown "too much indulgence" to the city's commercial elite. This opinion would have enraged the importers, had they known about it; but it was, I think, accurate. On the whole, the record shows that the collectors were reasonably honest—and certainly they were not blatantly dishonest after the manner of the legendary New York collector Samuel Swartwout, who was known as the uncrowned king of thieves. But the hard-pressed merchants of San Francisco had no historical perspective, even after half a decade. The Customs House was a convenient and often used projection of their own frustrations. As something that was irksome to them and imposed from outside, it was a wonderful scapegoat.[6]

Second, they blamed the East. One eastern practice that increasingly upset the importers of the city—however eastern their origins—was that of dispatching ships to California with "unspecified manifests." Mail and newspapers were sent to California across Panama or Nicaragua, whereas goods and merchandise had to travel around the Cape, and mail often (though not always) reached San Francisco ahead of goods dispatched at the same time. By reading in the newspapers and mail the manifests of the ships that had left the East, an importer could obtain an idea of what items were going to appear in the San Francisco market and could advise his own shippers accordingly. As one importer put it, "We have copies of the manifests of all the different vessels leaving the Atlantic ports for California, so we keep posted as to the goods on the way, and can advise our correspondents more understandingly on what to ship us."[7]

However, with San Francisco overstocked and prices declining from 1853 on, shippers adopted the practice of putting down on the manifest something like "merchandise." In this fashion, they attempted to sneak their goods through the seas and make something of a killing when the goods hit the unsuspecting San Francisco market. The theory was that a shipment might bring higher prices if San Francisco did not know how long it would have to wait for the next shipment. But for the San Francisco merchants, struggling to bring order out of the chaos of the city's commerce, the practice resulted in just another uncertainty.

In June 1855, the *Chronicle* announced that manifests were getting "more and more mystifying," and by August the Chamber of Commerce was trying to do something. Its secretary was authorized to correspond with the Secretary of the Treasury and ask that officer to require that all manifests be fully specified. Apparently that did not work out, for by the beginning of the next year the Chamber was memorializing the legislature: "The trade of California, since its commencement, has always been attended with fluctuations and revulsions of an extraordinary and disastrous character, rendering the pursuits of commerce far more dangerous and uncertain than in any other portion of the Union." As a result, the Chamber continued, there were "the extremes of scarcity and oversupply." Unspecified manifests, the memorial concluded, "defeated the legitimate aims of commerce, in adapting supply to the demand, and entailing losses on the importer, who has been governed by the ordinary statistics of trade." The state senate passed a resolution on the matter, although opponents noted that the system did work to keep prices down for the consumers, no matter what the inconveniences on the San Francisco merchants.[8]

Third, even though it was a bit close to home, the merchants tried to pin the blame on local government. At roughly the same time the manifest controversy was brewing, San Francisco's importers picked up another opportunity to blame their troubles on someone else. The California legislature obliged them. In 1855, as the decline in gold mining was becoming evident, that body reacted to adversity, as it would for decades to come, by attacking Orientals. It passed "An Act to Discourage the Immigration to this State of Persons who cannot become Citizens thereof." It was a simple act, directed at "any vessel arriving in any of the ports in this state." The law stated that, for each person on board the ship who was ineligible for California citizenship, the master, owner, or consignee of the vessel had to pay a tax of fifty dollars. The Commissioner of Emigrants in San Francisco was to enforce the act there. Edward McGowan, a Broderick stalwart, was in office at the time of the passage of the act.[9]

In 1856, the Know-Nothing legislature asked McGowan to report on his enforcement of the act. He replied that he had heard somewhere that ninety-six Chinese had landed in the past five months, but that "in no instance has the tax been collected, as every merchant in this place, and all others who know anything of the laws of the United States, are fully aware of the unconstitutionality of the said law." The Assembly Committee on Mines and Mining Interests, to whom the reply was referred, was furious and demanded that the governor immediately remove McGowan. But the San Francisco merchants, along with their colleagues in the interior of the state, demonstrated a touching affection for the sons and daughters of the Middle Kingdom. For them the Chinese were not competing miners but potential customers. So they sent a memorial to the Mines and Mining Committee "upholding and sustaining" McGowan's policy. Even though the memorial was summarily rejected by the committee and the governor did remove McGowan, the communication itself was significant. It was signed by seventy-six individuals and firms, fully half of whom were commission merchants or importers. Seven other signers were jobbers or wholesale dealers, and ten more were general merchants. Additional signers included one auctioneer, two bankers, and three men affiliated with steamship companies. The memorial was an impressive display of commercial union. And the union was created, not by the common market in which they all struggled, but by a perceived outside adversary.[10]

The immigration act was not the end of the merchants' difficulties with the legislature. Since commerce and mining were the major occupations of the state during the period, and since there were more miners than merchants voting in the state, commerce was a major object of the successive state revenue laws.

In the city, commerce had been from the beginning a principal target of the tax ordinances. As early as 1849, Geary had recommended a series of taxes and licenses upon many commercial activities and persons, such as real estate, auctions, merchants, traders, storekeepers, drays, lighters, and boats.

San Francisco merchants quickly began to claim that they were being made to pay a disproportionate part of the municipal budget. Merchants, cried one paper, were "pounced upon for a most outrageous license . . . while in the meantime the real estate owner goes scot free . . . the whole brunt of carrying on our city government is on the shoulders of the merchants." Some merchants moved to resist the payment of one tax or another, but most efforts never got beyond the talking stage. There were, however, a couple of tax strikes that lasted for a few weeks.[11]

The city's merchants made the same complaint of the state. In 1852, a committee of the Chamber of Commerce wrote the chairman of the Senate Committee on Commerce and Navigation that taxes were too high and that the public expenses ought to rest equally upon "mechanics, merchants, and landholders, and all who participate in its benefits." The Chamber of Commerce was not yet three years old, but it was already beginning to identify commercial interest with the public interest, and it confidently stated, "All classes will concur in providing a remedy for any interest taxed in undue proportion."[12]

It was true, of course, that merchants in San Francisco and in the rest of the state were taxed. Both the city and the state required licenses for virtually every kind of significant commercial activity. "An Act Concerning Licenses," for example, passed by the legislature in 1852, specified that licenses had to be obtained by "every person who shall deal in the selling of any goods, wares, and merchandise, wines, and distilled liquors, drugs, or medicines." Those who did not come under that umbrella, such as express companies, and "each caravan, menagerie, or other collection of animals . . . each circus, rope or wire dancing, or sleight of hand exhibition for reward," received special attention. These overall provisions were retained in the subsequent financial legislation of the state with only minor modifications and were constantly hanging over the head of anyone desiring to engage in business in California.[13]

Special taxes were enacted for certain types of businesses. In 1853, for instance, a tax was imposed on the banks of the state, at the rate of ten cents per one hundred dollars' worth of business transacted. This flat rate was abolished the next year, and a more complicated sliding scale of taxation was introduced. This had the effect of lowering taxes for banks that handled the most amount of money and raising them for the banks that did the least amount of business. Smaller banks, already beginning to feel the pinch of tight credit, were squeezed a bit more by the state.[14]

Consigned goods, a category that embraced a considerable proportion of the goods imported into the Golden State, were also the objects of tax legislation. "An Act to Provide for the Levying, Assessing, and Collecting of Public Revenue," passed in 1852, slapped a tax upon "all and every person or persons selling any consigned goods within this state . . . which tax shall be paid by the person making the sale." The rate was fixed at eighty cents per hundred dollars. In the general revenue statutes of 1853 and 1854 the tax was retained, although it was reduced first to sixty cents, and then to fifty.[15]

Auctioneering, another major element of the San Francisco business system, was also the object of legislation. In 1850, the first legislature imposed a schedule on goods auctioned off. The rate ranged from two dollars per hundred dollars on "wine and ardent spirits, foreign or domestic, and all brewed and malt liquors" to fifty cents per hundred dollars on real estate. The auctioneer was responsible for paying the tax. In 1852 this schedule was abolished, and the tax was set at the flat rate of one dollar fifty cents per hundred dollars, except for real estate, on which the tax remained what it had been. In 1853 the non–real estate tax was reduced to one dollar per hundred, and it was further cut to fifty cents the next year. In 1853 a section was introduced into the law that imposed a higher license fee (as distinct from the tax) upon an auctioneer if he did business in a city containing over ten thousand inhabitants. That proviso was retained in 1854, although the fees themselves were reduced. In other words, it cost more to be an auctioneer in San Francisco than it did in the interior. But San Francisco was where most of the auctions were.[16]

All these taxes were only natural. In a state so much involved with commerce, it was perfectly reasonable that the legislature would turn to commerce to raise the state revenue. However, the tax upon consigned goods and the auction tax contained provisions that tended to draw the different types of businessmen in the city closer to each other, and to allow them all to assume a posture of being commonly aggrieved.

Specifically, the tax upon consigned goods contained a clause that required both the importer and the jobber to pay taxes on the same set of goods: "When any goods, wares, merchandise, or other commercial property shall be sold in one county of this state, for or on account of any person or persons in another county of this state, the same shall be held and deemed to be consigned goods within the meaning of this act." Thus when the importer sold goods to the jobber, the importer had to pay the tax; and when the jobber turned around and sold the same goods to the country merchant, the jobber also had to pay the tax. The Chamber of Commerce, urging repeal of the law, argued, "The tax on consigned goods is peculiarly onerous and compels the payment of a tax upon the same goods several times." The governor took the position that the merchants were generally avoiding the tax, and he tried to get the legislature to make the steamship companies also liable for it. The legislature satisfied neither the Chamber nor the governor in 1853, but in 1854 it voted to drop the offending sentence from the law.[17]

A feature of the auction tax worked in a similar way. The law stipulated that the tax was to be paid if the goods were put on the block, "whether sold or not." As we have seen, it was not unusual for goods to be offered for auction and then withdrawn, if the bids were not up to the seller's idea of a fair price. Also, the auction was often the importer's last resort, his final attempt to establish a public "floor" price for his merchandise. Therefore, it seems reasonable to conclude that this section of the law probably restricted the importer's freedom. It became more costly to use the auction as a testing place, for the auctioneer would require that he not be left holding the tax bill even if the goods were not sold.[18]

State legislation thus had a significant effect. The law, especially the tax on consigned goods, put the importer and the jobber in the same boat, even though their natural business stances were ones of rivalry and opposition. Commerce tended to drive them apart, yet the laws harnessed them together. In gold rush San Francisco, as in virtually every other American city from the days of the Stamp Act until now, there was nothing like the government when it came to uniting competing businessmen!

The gold rush years were years of commercial adversity for the merchants of San Francisco, and the merchants blamed their woes on everything and everyone but themselves—on the weather, market glut, credit uncertainty, especially after the bank failures of 1855, and the government. They were convinced that everyone they came into contact with was conspiring against them. They were never certain how flexible or rigid any particular customs collector would be in interpreting the law. The practice of sending unspecified manifests kept them in the dark in crucial areas. The city and state governments had oppressive taxation policies.

Yet there was a significant difference in the ways in which the unhappy merchants responded to the types of adversity that plagued them. The simplest and most effective way to have dealt with the overstocking about which they complained so bitterly would have been for them all to have agreed to cease ordering entirely and to refuse to accept new merchandise. But since that would have been tantamount to abandoning their individual and collective dreams of instant fortunes, they never did anything like this. They could not stop hustling. In their business letters, they complained about having too many goods on hand, and then they requested more. For example, on July 30, 1853, the firm of Grogan and Lent wrote a supplier in Chile, "Business continues quite brisk . . . flour has advanced more than expected: holders refuse to sell under $18." The letter went on to say that Chilean flour would soon reach $24, and it advised the correspondent to send some "quickly." Two short weeks later, Alexander B. Grogan wrote the same supplier and complained that business was "dull." He placed the blame on "overstocking," which he vigorously denounced![19]

On the other hand, the merchants were capable of common action when the perceived object of their anger was outside the commercial network. The Chamber of Commerce may not have been able to do anything about overstocking, but it was an effective vehicle for dealing with the Collector or for memorializing the legislature. The merchants may have been unsuccessful in most of their attempts to corner the market, but they could act jointly when they thought the legislature was robbing them of their customers. The merchants were unable to police themselves, but they were more than willing to try to police others.

◆ II ◆

Besides these problems special to the nature of their business, the merchants of the young city felt themselves vulnerable—rather more than others—to two other problems: fire and crime. In response to these threats, the merchants became policemen with a vengeance and organized one of the most spectacular examples of mercantile cooperation, the San Francisco Vigilance Committee of 1851.

As a recent student of early San Francisco has remarked, "It would be difficult to overestimate the importance of fire in the total development of San Francisco." In truth, a city filled with crudely constructed wooden houses and shanties and constantly buffeted by brisk winds would have been remarkable had it *not* been ravaged by fire. The section of the city near the waterfront was particularly at risk, because it had so many wharves and storehouses, which in times of commercial oversupply contained a great volume of goods either in storage or awaiting passage to the interior.[20]

Fires occurred regularly in this part of the city. On Christmas Eve, 1849, fire broke out in the exchange building fronting the Plaza (Portsmouth Square) and destroyed nearly two blocks of buildings, at an estimated cost of one million dollars. On May 4, 1850, another fire broke out in a separate exchange building in almost the same location and devastated almost three square blocks of structures, with damage estimated at more than four million dollars. Scarcely two months later, a fire that started in a defective chimney in a bakery on the south side of the Plaza burned an area from the Plaza to the water's edge, causing five million dollars' damage. On September 17, 1850, fire broke out in a hotel fronting the Plaza and burned a four-block area, but damage was held to three hundred thousand dollars. The following year—by coincidence on May 4—an even more devastating fire occurred, started this time in a paint store on the south side of the Plaza. Whipped by shifting winds, it hit eighteen square blocks and several storeships that had been hauled up on the beach. The ships in the harbor itself were saved only by the expedient of razing some of the wharves to cut off the path of the blaze. Damage was variously estimated at between ten million and twelve million dollars. Heinrich Schliemann, the future discoverer of Troy, happened to be visiting the city at the time. He wrote, "The roaring of the storm, the crackling of the gunpowder, the cracking of the fallen stone walls, the cries of the people, and the wonderful spectacle of an immense city burning up in a dark night all joined to make this catastrophe awful in the extreme." A newspaperman reported, "In consequence of the calamitous fire . . . the monetary and commercial relations of almost every person in the city have become deranged and in numerous cases completely shattered." To underline the extent of the destruction, one merchant datelined his next letter, "(What remains of) San Francisco."[21]

Fire compounded the precarious uncertainty of San Francisco life. In December 1850, for instance, one man was writing a letter home. Suddenly he put down his pen. When he returned to his desk, he explained, "I had written so far when I heard the alarm of fire and immediately I dropped my writing materials and ran out. As always on similar occasions the city appeared a perfect bee-hive. The streets are alive with people running in one direction. People have learned by sad experience what a terrible thing fire is in San Francisco, and so, as soon as one is known to exist, everything is dropped at once." Yet, paradoxically, fires performed a useful commercial function. When the market was glutted, fires were one way of seeing inventories reduced. As one man put it, "The only thing that has saved California so far has been the many disastrous fires, at least that has saved the masses of merchants from failing for legitimate causes."[22]

But few people, publicly at least, took that sanguine view. The general mood in the spring of 1851 was better caught by one resident, who penned this somewhat frenzied description: "We live in such a cauldron of excitement in this town that it is impossible to collect our ideas to write a letter: thefts, robberies, murders, and fires follow each other in such rapid succession that we hardly recover from the effects of one horrible tragedy before another piece of unmitigated villainy demands our attention."[23]

There is something pitiable about the hysterical reaction of San Franciscans to the phenomenon of city fires. Cities have always been susceptible to accidental fires—not all great fires in history have been caused by Greeks hiding in horses or mad emperors with fiddles. If there is a constant theme in sixteenth-to-nineteenth-century American urban history, that theme may well be fire. Contemporaries knew it and accepted it, and wherever historians look, they are apt to find it. Take the case of William Penn. He is often praised for his foresight in insisting (vainly, as it turned out) that his city of brotherly love contain a number of spacious parks so that, as he said, "it may be a greene country towne." Penn may well have been a prophet, seeing clearly the dangers of urban congestion. But the rest of his comment is probably more to the point: "a greene country towne that may never be burnt." Besides being pretty and relaxing and healthy, Penn's parks were to function as natural fire barriers. No American city has been spared a serious fire. Mrs. O'Leary's cow could well serve as a symbol of the city in America in the eighteenth and nineteenth centuries. The year 1776 was not just the year of the Declaration of Independence: it was also the year of a devastating fire in New York City in which over a thousand buildings were destroyed. And the city suffered another large fire a scant two years later.[24]

Cities have always been vulnerable to fire in their formative years, and American cities, which exist as arenas for the fulfillment of private greed, were especially vulnerable. All too often, citizens did not want to be diverted from the chase after personal wealth by having to direct some of their wealth into a public fund for an effective fire department, though sometimes necessity left no choice. Boston, for instance, suffered a serious fire in 1676, so great that Samuel Sewall reported "about fifty landlords were despoyled of their housing." Twenty years before even Paris got a fire engine, Boston had the good sense to have one shipped from England. All up and down the "urban frontier," fire was an integral part of the westward movement. In 1807, for example, a Cincinnati newspaper commented, "We seldom pass a week without reading some melancholy account of the disasters occasioned by the most destructive of all elements—fire." Towns like Lexington, Kentucky, and Pittsburgh endured serious blazes, and, as Richard C. Wade says, "Each new outbreak found [each] town somewhat unprepared." Fires roared through St. Louis in 1825, Louisville in 1827, and Cincinnati in 1829. In Chicago in 1834, a fire was started by an accident with live coals that were being carried in a shovel. In 1835, in New York City, a large group of buildings prominently advertised as fireproof were wiped out by a fire nonetheless, and in 1857, twenty-two people perished in yet another Chicago fire.[25]

In San Francisco, though fires were a menace almost from the start, loss of life was actually relatively light, and the city in some ways came off better than other parts of the urban frontier. The merchants took a shorter view; they professed to be outraged by the fires, but the real reason for their feelings may have been one they themselves only vaguely understood—that is, that at some unarticulated level they were realizing that the charred buildings and burned wharves were mute testimony to the fact that San Francisco was not, after all, a glorious place of new beginnings but just another American city. So they reacted in a way that was fast becoming typical. They blamed their problems on someone else. This time it was an organized group of criminals.

Throughout the first months of 1851, the press became increasingly preoccupied with crime in the streets. On New Year's Day the *Alta* cried out, "There are some three hundred thieves in this city, who live by their profession, and prefer to live so rather than work." In the middle of February the same paper, after giving the details of a robbery that had taken place the night before, complained that theft was becoming "far too frequent." Toward the end of that month, it exploded, "No place seems safe from outrage, no person secure, even in his own dwelling." It went on to complain about "the floodgates of crime, which seem opened by the devil's hand and flowing from his infernal abode through our very midst." And in May, the *Herald* warned that "thieves and vagabonds throughout the state" had sworn to ruin San Francisco.[26]

It is difficult to determine accurately the specifics of crime in gold rush San Francisco. The population of the city was shifting, as people left in the summers and returned in the winters. Court records are incomplete. The statistics of the recorder's court, which handled petty crime, exist for only about 35 percent of the period. There are some available fragmentary figures. For instance, the *Alta* published on May 2, 1850, what it called a complete list of arrests from September 4, 1849, to March 26, 1850. The total that the paper gave was 741, mostly for larceny and assault and battery. These statistics led Mary Floyd Williams to assert, "Order was preserved in the city with fair success . . . violence in the city was not of the alarming proportions sometimes attributed to it." If such statistics had been continued throughout the period, there might be a basis for further generalization. But, alas, the figures are not there. However, some contemporary statements regarding crime can be summarily dismissed. One such is the statement in the

Chronicle of December 15, 1853, that there had been twelve hundred murders over the past four years in San Francisco. That would have been almost one murder a day. If they did take place, the newspapers of the preceding four years, including the *Chronicle*, were remarkably loath to report them.[27]

There is no reason to imagine that crime was less of a problem in San Francisco than it was in any other American city, however. Like fires, violence and crime occurred in all large cities in the United States in the nineteenth century. The people did not like these things, but they accepted them. The antebellum view of crime was, like so much else in nineteenth-century America, based on a semisecularized Puritanism. William Bradford had attributed the occurrence of crime in Plymouth to the fact that the colony was such a noble experiment that the devil was working overtime, but nineteenth-century Americans tended to blame crime on devilish persons, sometimes produced by devilish environments, who were bent on illegitimately reaping the fruits of others' honest toil.

Since colonial days, crime had flourished in Boston, Philadelphia, and New York. Bostonians had noted an increase in crime after 1720, and mob violence, for a variety of reasons, was a staple of colonial life. In Philadelphia, the Walnut Street Prison was one of the two largest buildings ever constructed in colonial America. Right after the Revolution, New York City experienced an upsurge in violent crimes. It already had its own criminal area, the burned-out section between Broad and Whitehall streets known as "canvas town." A 1784 grand jury claimed that the section contained "numerous receptacles for the vicious and abandoned," and it sent the sheriff in to knock some of them down. And, as Sidney I. Pomerantz said of post-Revolutionary New York, "Riots were not infrequent." As the cities grew, so did crime. By the 1830's, crime, like the rest of New York, was moving uptown, to the famous Five Points district, a well-known center of vice and crime of all types. In 1842 the Board of Aldermen issued a long complaint:

> The property of the citizen is pilfered almost before his eyes. Dwellings and warehouses are entered with an ease and apparent coolness and carelessness of detection which shows that none are safe. Thronged as our city is men are robbed in the streets. Thousands that are arrested go unpunished, and the defenseless and the beautiful are rav-

ished and murdered in the daytime and no trace of the criminals is found. The man of business, in his lawful calling, at the most public corner of our city, is slaughtered in the sunshine and packed up and sent away.

In 1850, an English traveler wrote of New York, "Probably no city in the civilized world is so fearfully insecure."[28]

Crime, moving west with the development of the country, also took root in cities that were just beginning to grow. St. Louis was hit by a rash of burglaries in 1812 and the police attributed them to "many lightfingered gentlemen." After the War of 1812, the Pittsburgh Moral Society was established out of the feeling that "irregularity and vice" were shaking the very foundations of society. In the 1820's a Cincinnati assemblyman admitted that his city was "famed as a place of iniquity." In the 1830's a wave of domestic violence hit the North. Centered in the cities, most of the mobs were aimed against Catholics and abolitionists and directed by those Leonard Richards called "gentlemen of property and standing." No group had a monopoly on violence. And in 1847 a Chicago paper claimed that it was "getting to be a notorious fact that robbers, pick-pockets, thimble-riggers, etc., are perfectly at home in our city."[29]

But if crime was pretty much a fact of life in antebellum American cities, the legal definitions of crime and the perception of crime as a problem fluctuated extensively. Kai T. Erikson, for instance, has argued that successive "crime waves" in seventeenth-century Massachusetts reflected not so much an increase in crime itself as an increase in the fear of the colonial elite that its authority was declining. The post-Revolutionary increase in crimes against property, Frank Browning and John Gerassi similarly argue, reflected not so much an actual increase in the number of burglaries or thefts as the increased sensitivity to private property that the Revolution inculcated.[30]

It was probably much the same with the crime wave that hit San Francisco in the spring of 1851. It was not so much an actual increase in crime as an increase in the merchants' fear of crime, on which they could blame their uncomfortable feelings of not doing very well in the gold rush city. The anxiety was latent in the majority of merchants, and it only needed an incident to bring it out in the open.

Australian immigrants unwittingly obliged. In the first five months of 1851 alone, 1,648 of them arrived at San Francisco. Almost 80 percent of all the Australians who were going to arrive throughout the entire gold rush period disembarked in that brief period. It must have seemed like an invasion. By February or March of 1851, there was little doubt in the minds of the harried merchants that the fires in the city had all been started by foreign arsonists. Here again, the merchants were adhering to a venerable American tradition. Boston, for example, experienced a severe fire on the night of August 7, 1679, and the public quickly blamed it on outsiders, specifically Baptists and Frenchmen. In San Francisco in 1851, the Australians were made to order.[31]

♦ III ♦

To be an outsider in Anglo-Saxon antebellum America was always to be in a paradoxical position: you were less than fully human, but at times, also you were almost superhuman. You were both more and less than yourself. If you were a native American, you were a savage, but you were also nature's nobleman. If you were a black, you were a gorilla, but you also possessed such remarkable sexual powers that you were the envy of your white masters. And if you were an Australian in San Francisco in 1851, you were an incorrigible criminal, but a criminal capable of organizing your criminality in such a sophisticated fashion that your very success mocked the inability of the Yankee merchants in the city to organize their own affairs profitably. You were, in fact, the most successful arsonist in the history of the world since Alexander the Great gave his virtuoso performance at Persepolis.

The Australian rush for San Francisco had begun in earnest when the ships that had left Australia at the beginning of 1849 returned home in the summer with the news of the discovery of gold. Before that, only a handful of persons had made the journey from Australia to California. Apparently, however, these few included a few unsavory characters, enough to make the Australians as a whole candidates for scapegoat status. Describing the fire of May 4, 1850, Milton S. Latham wrote that it had been started by "Sydney convicts," for the purpose of giving them "a fine opportunity for stealing, which they bravely improved." Undoubtedly some Australians were engaged in criminal activities, although they were hardly the only ones. Furthermore, it was known in California that Australia had been partly settled by convicts, and the popular consciousness generally slurred over the "partly." Even in 1848, however, ex-convicts were a distinct minority of the total number of Australians embarking for California. According to one calculation, 13 percent of those who came from Sydney in that year were ex-convicts. But fully one-third were free immigrants who had originally been transported to New South Wales at the expense of the British government. The greatest concentration of ex-convicts apparently came from Tasmania, and even from there they were only 20 percent of the total number of people who made the journey.[32]

The numbers were never very large, in any event. According to the state census of 1852, there were 2,228 Australians resident in the city. Far from being a collection of hardened criminals, they seem to have been a collection of families trying for the second time to improve their lot. Many had left Ireland for Australia in the early 1840's and had moved from there to California at the end of the decade. The sex ratio of those who listed Sydney as their last place of residence, for instance, was 151.69 males per 100 females, whereas the figure for California as a whole was 1,213.91 per 100. Almost two-thirds of the former Sydney-ites lived in family groups. As two demographers have put it, "It is clear that the males from Sydney differed from the other males in California: they had brought their wives and their children with them." In their family structure, the Australians living in San Francisco were more "American" than most of the Americans living there. That may have been part of the rub.[*33]

The public perception, as mirrored in the press, was angry: "The state of California has been made the grand rendezvous for the transported felons of Great Britain, who have either managed to escape or have been assisted in their embarkation from the penal colonies." By 1851, "Australian" was virtually synonymous with "criminal." "Much as we desire the extension

*Numbered notes marked with an asterisk contain material that may be of particular interest to the reader.

of liberal principles and their enjoyment by the oppressed of all nations," the *Alta* said, "we do not wish to stand side by side at the ballot box with the escaped felons of England."[34]

It may be, as has been suggested, that "any group which had made two major migrations must have included a large number of very aggressive and competitive persons." But that does not explain the antipathy to them in San Francisco. The Americans who came to California were not noted for their passive behavior, as the Mexicans, Chilenos, and Chinese discovered. One of the slang phrases then current in San Francisco was "to see the elephant." The term had originated in the East, after the first exhibition of a live elephant in 1796. It generally meant that you had gone to the edge, that you had experienced the ultimate possibility of a particular situation. J. S. Holliday sums up the meaning of the phrase this way: "suffering a severe ordeal, facing one's worst expectations, overcoming the meanest realities; in a word, knowing the Truth." Or, as Lawrence Ferlinghetti and Nancy Peters explain, "The sardonic application of the term in the gold rush to mining life meant to have seen it all and come away with no illusions." In non-literary San Francisco, the phrase seems to have had a rather more aggressive meaning. As one man helpfully defined it, to see the elephant meant "to shoot three Indians, hang two greasers (Mexicans), kill a grisly bear, and dig a seven pound lump of gold." What a marvelous mix of the infantile hope and depraved racism that was so much of the westward movement! Certainly those Australians who were Irish were eligible for the contempt with which the East welcomed the Irish in the 1840's, and with which the Americans in San Francisco were familiar. As foreigners in California, the Australians were regarded as poachers in the Garden of Eden.[35]

On the other hand, the Australians were also consumers, and we have seen that businessmen who needed consumers tended to oppose anti-foreigner legislation and activities. However, two things combined to minimize the Australians' importance in this regard. First, the crimes attributed to them were crimes against merchants. Fire increased the amount of money necessary for the conduct of business. Every time there was a fire, additional construction costs had to be borne, and the fact that there were so many fires contributed to the high rate of interest. Second, the market was so overstocked that two thousand or so Australians could hardly make an appreciable dent in the supplies. In the developing commercial equation in San Francisco in 1851, fire plus crime plus overstocking equaled Australian scapegoats.[36]

◆ IV ◆

The immediate series of events that culminated in the eventual formation of a vigilance committee began with the robbing of Jansen's store on February 19, 1851—the event that begins this book. The Jansen crime was brazen and spectacular, but the significant outcome involved what did *not* happen. The city was excited for a weekend, but by Monday morning the two Australian prisoners were back in jail, and the merchants were back in their offices, gearing up for what they hoped would be a profitable spring trade. As long as the trading season lasted, the business of San Francisco was business.[37]

A few hotheads like Coleman tried to keep the robbery before the public over the next few months. On March 9, for instance, there was a public meeting to protest the jailing of a local editor by a judge. Coleman attempted to incite the meeting to do something about the two thieves. Even though he was not a lawyer, he did not like losing cases. But, as the press reported, "As the people had assembled for a different object, Mr. Coleman did not succeed in arousing his audience to a very high pitch of excitement."[38]

The disastrous fire of May 4 stirred things up once again. Loss in life and property was high. With fire raging through the business district of San Francisco, merchants were faced with a choice: should they help the community fight the fire, or should they look out for themselves? For some merchants, private concerns overtook public ones, and they unwisely chose to stay in their offices guarding their money. Unaware of what had happened in New York in 1835, they assumed that the buildings could withstand the blaze—so merchants were burned along with their precious wealth, thereby contradicting the old adage that fools and their money are soon parted.

It quickly became an unchallengeable point of public dogma that the fire had been started by a group of Australian arsonists. As the *Herald* complained a few weeks later, after another fire, the city contained "an organized band of incendiaries . . .

whose fixed determination seems to be to desolate our city and ruin it beyond redemption." In an attempt to forestall further blazes, a loose group of young merchants like Robert S. Lammot organized a volunteer fire patrol. It was modeled on one that had been set up a few months earlier on the outskirts of the city and was under the overall direction of importer Frederick W. Macondray. The formation of the patrol was coupled with a denunciation of the police for letting criminals run amok through the city. The *Alta*, though it must have known that the police had been prompt enough in the matter of the Jansen robbery, declared: "A large portion of their body offer protection to, rather than a check upon, the disorderly and the vicious. Men get appointed sometimes as policemen who are no better than the unhung who prowl about our streets at night for theft and robbery."[39]

More plausible, perhaps, than that makeshift explanation is another, that the merchants were groping toward a scapegoat. The spring trade had come early that year, and by May it was almost spent. Yet the importers still found themselves, by their own reckonings, loaded down with supplies. They had time on their hands and no remedy in their heads. Trying to stop fires was at least something. They could only blindly hope, as the *Herald* put it, that "property being secure, business would once again flourish."[40]

Thus the city's merchants entered the summer doldrums with a lot of inventory and a lot of time. The inventory would have to wait until the fall, but the time could be used to think. The results of their thinking began to be reflected in the press. On June 4, the *Alta* ran a piece praising "The Spirit of Lynch Law," and it complained the next day that fire alarms were getting to be too frequent. On June 8 it editorialized, "If there are fifty men in this city which deserve hanging, they ought to be hung, and we hope they will be hung. They never will be, of course, with the consent of the lawyers." And on the same day, a correspondent who signed himself "Justice" urged the formation of a vigilance committee.

So, for no immediate reason, a vigilance committee was formed. There was no spectacular crime, as there would be in 1856, to precipitate the formation of a committee. Rather, it just happened that two merchants met on the street and began rehashing the regular topic of conversation—how bad things were. They decided that things were not merely bad, they were terrible, and so they went off to see Sam Brannan. He had been, in February, one of the vociferous proponents of the idea of hanging the two Australians first and asking questions later. These three men, plus Brannan's clerk, decided to call a meeting of the merchants. At the third such meeting, a draft document was approved and signed. It is worth quoting extensively:

> Whereas it has become apparent to the citizens of San Francisco that there is no security for life and property, either under the regulations of society as it at present exists, or under the laws as now administered—therefore the citizens whose names are hereunto attached do unite themselves into an association for the maintenance of the peace and good order of society and the preservation of the lives and property of the citizens of San Francisco and do bind themselves each unto the other to do and perform every lawful act for the maintenance of law and order and to sustain the laws when faithfully and properly administered, but we are determined that no thief, burglar, incendiary, or assassin shall escape punishment either by the quibbles of the law, the insecurity of prisons, the carelessness or corruption of the police, or the laxity of those who pretend to administer justice.

The document went on to say that the body was going to deal with crime in an unspecified way, "as a majority of the committee when assembled shall determine upon." What all this might mean was anyone's guess, and probably even those who signed were not sure themselves. At any rate, the "constitution" was not meant to be distributed to the press, and the committee kept its existence a secret.[41]

A decision on what a vigilance committee would do, however, was soon forced on the putative vigilantes when Jenkins was brought to their rooms. After he had been executed, a coroner's jury was set up. It took testimony from the police who had been on the scene, trying to save Jenkins, and from anyone else it could. It concluded that Jenkins had been killed "by strangulation, by being suspended by the neck with a rope . . . at the hands of and in pursuance to a preconcerted action on the part of an association of citizens styling themselves a committee of vigilance." More provocatively, the jury named nine men, all members of the committee, as directly involved in the murder.[42]

Brannan, who had favored summary execution in February, and who had supposedly screamed out, just before Jenkins was hanged, "Every lover of liberty and order lay hold of this rope!" was one of those implicated by the testimony before the jury. He published an indignant card in the papers, categorically denying that he had had anything to do with the affair. Brannan's card drew an angry retort from Broderick, who had been on the scene trying to stop the hanging and who had implicated Brannan before the coroner's jury. Broderick's reply, published in the press, stated that Brannan's remarks were absurd, since everyone who had been there knew that Brannan was one of the leaders in the execution, and anyone who knew anything knew what kind of man Brannan was: "Of that gentleman it is unnecessary for me to say anything further, notorious as he is for his violence and contempt of law. He is widely known as a turbulent man, ready to trample upon all laws that oppose his private opinions or private ends." Although this was not quite up to C. H. Webb's later quip that Brannan was "a thing of booty and a bore forever," for 1851 San Francisco, it was not bad!*[43]

The vigilance committee then decided that there was safety in numbers. So it published a communication in the papers of June 14: "We, the Committee of Vigilance, remark with surprise the invidious verdict rendered by the coroner's jury. . . . We desire that the public will understand that [the nine men named] have been unnecessarily picked from our number, as the coroner's jury had full evidence of the fact that all the undersigned were equally implicated with their above-named associates." Attached to the statement were 180 names. (Ultimately, no legal action was ever taken against them for their part in the Jenkins hanging.) At the same time, the committee published its bylaws. They indicated that the committee had settled on deporting criminals as its main task. "The Committee of Vigilance," the laws read, "will ever be ready to receive information as to the whereabouts of any disorderly or suspicious person." When such characters were found, the committee promised that they would be "notified to leave this port within five days."

Through the summer, the vigilance committee functioned openly and called a total of 91 persons before it. The overwhelming number were laborers from Australia. Of the 91 called, 41 were discharged, 15 were handed over to the authorities, 14 were deported from California, 14 were strongly advised to leave, 4 (including Jenkins) were hanged, and one man, a Mexican, was publicly flogged. The outcome of two cases was unstated in the committee papers. The charges on which persons were brought before the committee ranged from murder and larceny to being "a desperate character." One man was deported for being the "keeper of a suspicious house," another for being "a suspected immigrant," and a third for being "a bad man." The committee was rather narrow in its approach. It generally attacked Australian immigrants and attempted to disrupt their normal activities by closing their boardinghouses, killing and deporting a handful, and throwing the fear of the committee into the rest.*[44]

The committee divided itself into an executive committee, which ran things and did the paper work, and a general committee, which assented to the proceedings of the executive committee and did the footwork. It was the overwhelming opinion of contemporaries, and it is the overwhelming judgment of subsequent students, that the executive committee was composed of some of the leading merchants in the city. One of the vigilantes put it succinctly, "The vigilance committee was composed of the most intelligent, best educated, and property owning classes of the city." Another vigilante called the committee "the salt of San Francisco," another "the best men in the city," and still another "first class men." They were, of course, talking about themselves, but contemporaries agreed. One resident, for instance, wrote that the committee was composed of "the first and best men in the community." There is little reason to question that appraisal. Since a virtually complete roster of members of the committee has survived, it is possible to be reasonably precise. Of the more than 700 names assembled by Porter Garnett and Mary Floyd Williams, almost half (49.9 percent) can be identified. The commercial makeup of the committee is striking: 89 men (at least 12.5 percent of the signers) came from the importing sector (importers, commission merchants, and auctioneers), and another 116 (16.3 percent) were merchants of one sort or another. Importers and merchants thus accounted for almost one-third of the members. There were also 22 bankers (3.1 percent). As might be expected in an organization that denounced "the quibbles of the law," lawyers formed a very small part of the committee. I have been able to identify only nine, or slightly more than one percent.[45]

When one looks at only the executive committee, which actually ran things, the commercial orientation of the organization is even more evident. No formal list of the executive committee has survived, so I consider as members all those who are recorded as having cast more than one vote in that body from June 26 to August 20, 1851, the time of the committee's greatest activity. Of these 23 men, 20 are identifiable, and 14 of them were engaged in one type of commerce or another. Nine (39.1 percent) were engaged in importing, and another five (21.7 percent) were merchants. Without a doubt, the 1851 vigilance committee was a businessmen's club.[46]

Opposition to the committee arose during the hanging of Jenkins and was never absent during the time of the committee's activity. Public officials, at least formally, tended to oppose the committee, which had had the arrogance to claim that it had been forced into existence because public officials were not doing their jobs. The governor of the state, Democrat John McDougal, issued a proclamation in which he argued, "No security of life and property can be guaranteed, except the constitution and law are observed." Aware that the vigilance committee was directing its energies against immigrants, the governor went on, "We owe it to ourselves to impress upon the strangers who have settled among us, unacquainted with and perhaps entertaining prejudices unfavorable to the practical operations of our peculiar institutions, that our government is a government of laws." He demanded that the committee immediately disband. The committee refused, and that was that.[47]

The mayor of San Francisco, Whig Charles J. Brenham, who had been elected a few months earlier on a vague retrenchment-and-reform platform, also issued a proclamation urging the committee to disband. Brenham was particularly upset by a resolution that the committee passed in early July: "Resolved that we, the Vigilance Committee, have the right to enter into any person's or persons' premises where we have good reason to believe that we shall find evidence to substantiate and carry out the object of this body." The mayor solemnly denounced the no-knock search policy: "They claim and exercise the right of domiciliary visits, without any accountability and with a character not known under any but Inquisitorial governments. The great and sacred right of *habeas corpus* has been rendered by them ineffectual. . . . Any combination of citizens whose proceedings are not controlled by law can have only an insurrectionary tendency." But like the governor, the mayor was not inclined to carry his opposition any further.[48]

Practical opposition in the city appears to have been directed by Broderick, who was already a power to be reckoned with in state and city politics. He organized a series of meetings of the "law-and-order" group, as those who opposed the committee called themselves. On at least one occasion, he disrupted a vigilance rally. Law-and-order handbills were circulated throughout the city until the mayor ordered the practice stopped for fear that it would only serve to exacerbate tensions. One such flyer asked, "Shall we tolerate in this enlightened age a Danton, a Robespierre, or a Fouché, and the paraphernalia of a secret inquisition for the suppression of our laws and courts?" However, the opposition was unable to hinder significantly the operations of the committee, though it was able upon occasion to disrupt it.[49]

By the middle of August the committee seemed to be winding down. Besides Jenkins, it had hanged one other man, James Stuart, on July 11. (The unfortunate Berdue, accused of being Stuart and having robbed Jansen back in February, was awaiting trial in Marysville for another of Stuart's crimes. The vigilantes, when they discovered that a man captured in a sweep of Australian boardinghouses was actually the real Stuart, sent word to the sheriff in Marysville and obtained Berdue's release.) On August 14, the committee sentenced two of its last prisoners, Robert McKenzie and Samuel Whittaker, captured on July 24 and August 11, respectively, to death.

When Governor McDougal learned in Sacramento that the two executions were imminent, he rushed down to the city. He obtained a writ of habeas corpus from a local judge, and the governor and the mayor personally delivered the writ to the sheriff, former Texas Ranger Colonel Jack Hays, at 3:00 A.M. on August 20. Hays executed the writ by breaking into vigilante headquarters that very night and spiriting away the two prisoners. He deposited them in the county jail, where they remained while the committee pondered this insult and how to respond to it. The next Sunday, August 24, two contingents of vigilantes stormed the jail during church services and grabbed the two men. They pushed them into a wagon, which raced through the city at breakneck speed. Upon arrival at the committee rooms, the two were immediately lynched. In the twisted logic of vigilantism, the two were described in the press the next day as having been "rescued" from the authorities!

In response to the opposition, the committee argued that it really did not like what it was doing, but that "the general insufficiency of the laws and their present maladministration" left it little choice. As one citizen put it, "Extreme cases require extreme remedies." The *Herald*, which supported the committee, observed, "But the Sabbath was made for man, not man for the Sabbath, and the citizen is not made for the law, but the law for the citizen." The paper charged that the opponents of the committee were "wanting in that common sense for the exigencies of society which in every free country should mold and fashion the actions of the judiciary." As to the domiciliary visits, the *Herald* sniffed, "It is a power no honest man need dread." The secretary of the committee put its case in a nutshell: "He [Broderick] did not think that the people should take the law into their own hands, that was the substance of his position. . . . I had nothing to say against Broderick in his position, because his theory was good enough, but there is a time when men should take the law into their own hands." Or, as another resident claimed, there was a "higher law," which had to come into play when "honest and well-disposed citizens have suffered till patience cannot be a virtue." The substance of the committee's justification was therefore conservative. It claimed that it was only trying to restore effectiveness to the law. Perhaps nothing better illustrates the essential fragility of American society in the 1850's than this: conservative businessmen along the Pacific were using the same arguments as radical abolitionists along the Atlantic. Both groups were ready to destroy a government to advance their aims.[50]

How effective the vigilance committee's efforts really were is impossible to say. Probably there was some decrease in crime, but not a drastic decrease, as pro-vigilance papers claimed. The committee was not very successful in stopping fires, however, for on June 22 another blaze broke out. The committee quickly spread the story—though it had no evidence—that it had been arson, started by Australians for the purpose of embarrassing the committee. It failed to find the incendiary, but a street mob had the pleasure of stomping to death two alleged arsonists and whipping "a Mexican with a long and unpronounceable name."[51]

The "rescue" and murder of the two prisoners on August 24 were the high point of the activities of the vigilance committee. Toward the end of August, with the fall trade season starting soon, the committee began to lose momentum. Being a vigilante was hard work and practically a full-time job. One merchant member of the committee wrote in July that he generally rose at dawn and worked until around six in the evening. Then he had to go to the rooms of the committee and take part in the proceedings there for a few hours. Once a week, when he was on vigilante duty, he had to stay up most of the night, and still be ready for work at six in the morning. A schedule of that sort was tolerable during the summer doldrums, but hardly possible during the periods of heavy trading that were fondly expected in the fall.[52]

Toward the end of August, a group of committee members began meeting in an effort to put together a slate of independent candidates for the fall elections. On August 27 they published their ticket, along with an address that urged the populace to "trace the troubled waters back to their source, and the explorer will find his journey terminate at the ballot box." "Sweep clean the Augean stables of legislation," it declared; "purify the ermine, and show by your votes that honesty and virtue are at a premium in the public estimation." The ticket turned out to be a mixture of the most popular and strongest Whigs and Democrats already nominated by their respective parties, plus some independents. The election results were mixed. Every independent candidate who was also on a Whig or Democratic ticket was victorious, indicating that in close races the independents possessed enough strength to make the difference. On the other hand, every independent candidate who was not on one of the major tickets was roundly defeated. The independent ticket could not muster anything near the political muscle of the established parties. The vigilance committee itself took no formal stand in the election, and the fourteen members who presented the ticket were careful not to claim that they were acting for the committee. But it was entirely understood that the ticket was, in fact, a vigilante ticket. After the election, the president of the executive committee announced that the committee's work was over and it adjourned, although it did not formally disband.[53]

More importantly, its memory survived. It was a truly spectacular example of harried merchants acting together in something of a common interest. If another "extreme case" were to arise, the precedent of an "extreme remedy" would be at hand.

A view toward the bay, filled with ships at anchor, from Kearny Street in 1850

Early morning on the Vallejo Street Wharf in 1852

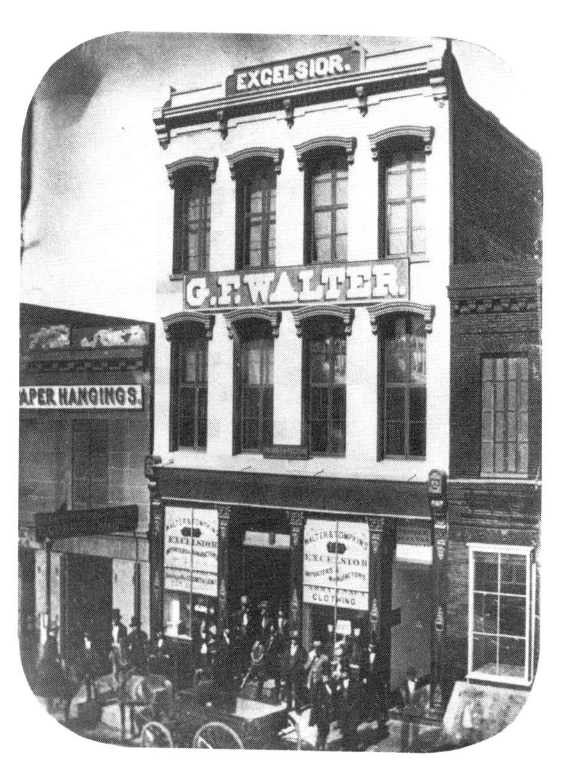

The Excelsior Building, 1856

The Wells Fargo Building, 1852

Montgomery Street, 1850

Contemporary sketch of the hanging of John Jenkins at the hands of the 1851 vigilance committee

Broderick Engine Co. No. 1, with St. Mary's Catholic Church in the background

Three nineteenth-century San Francisco firemen. David Scannell, who had been sheriff in 1856, is seated.

David Broderick

David Terry

Milton Latham

William Coleman

James King

Sam Brannan

First Methodist Episcopal Church, 1854

First Baptist Church, the original site of John Pelton's school, as it appeared the day before it was torn down in 1853

Fort Gunnybags, 1856

Vigilantes surrounding the California Exchange and capturing a law-and-order armory inside on June 21, 1856. A few hours earlier Judge Terry had stabbed the vigilante officer Hopkins.

CHAPTER 4

THE POLITICIANS

And they told Moses, "We came to the land to which you sent us; it flows with milk and honey. . . . Yet the people who dwell in the land are very strong, and their cities are fortified and very large. . . . We are not able to go up against these people; for they are stronger than we." —*Numbers 13: 27–28, 32*

♦

They have done me the honor of electing me a member of the Whig Central Committee, which I am not sorry of, as it will give me an acquaintance with a great many merchants of this town (of whom it is principally composed).

—*Businessman Robert S. Lammot,*
writing from San Francisco, March 25, 1851

♦

Sol has been elected City Attorney with a salary of $4,000 per annum. He will be able to throw a good many fees in my way, by employing me on behalf of the city to aid him in important suits in which the city is concerned. My friend Capt. Garrison, the agent of the Vanderbilt line, has been elected mayor and from that source I shall get some good fat fees.

—*Lawyer Joseph B. Crockett,*
writing from San Francisco, September 15, 1853

♦

The political activity which pervades the United States must be seen in order to be understood. No sooner do you set foot on American ground than you are stunned by a kind of tumult; a confused clamor is heard on every side, and a thousand simultaneous voices demand the satisfaction of their social wants. Everything is in motion around you.

—*Alexis de Tocqueville*

♦ I ♦

With the possible exception of the federal government's failure to have completed a transcontinental railroad on the day before yesterday, probably nothing was so frequently and regularly denounced in the press of gold rush San Francisco as was politics. Public officials, the standard line went, were nothing more than thieves, who sought office for the sole purpose of fleecing the public and enriching themselves and their friends. One newspaper referred to the city council as "those who have preyed like hyenas upon the people," and characterized the political system as one of "official jobbing" and "official corruption," which had turned San Francisco into a "bankrupt city."[1]

Such a set of scoundrels was able to perpetuate itself for two reasons. The first was the general apathy of the respectable citizens, who were too absorbed in their own pursuits to assume any measure of civic responsibility. "Our property holders," the *Alta* complained, "have held themselves by far too much aloof from municipal concerns." Second, political violence and fraud were widely practiced, making it virtually impossible, even if the spirit were willing, to topple the rotten system. Gangs of hired bullies, or "shoulder strikers," controlled the polls and prevented honest citizens from casting their ballots. Professional ballot box stuffers were constantly at work to make sure that those honest men who fought their way to the polls would be on the losing side when all the ballots were counted.[2]

These charges about political violence and fraud were adopted by the vigilance committee of 1856 and used as a justification for its own extralegal activities. At a mass meeting on June 14, 1856, called to rally support for the committee, a ballot box with a false bottom was displayed as evidence that voting fraud was widespread in San Francisco. A month later the committee issued a long document, entitled "Official Corruption," in which it explicitly adopted the entire series of accusations on this topic that had been floating through the press for the preceding five years.[3]

The vigilantes' version of the nature of the San Francisco political system won quick and general acceptance. Less than a decade later, William H. Brewer, an assistant to the state geologist, wrote: "Previous to 1856 it was terrible—its fame for murder and robbery and violence spread over the world. It was even vastly worse governed than New York, and by the vilest politicians. They held elections, and by election frauds, double ballot boxes, etc., legally kept their power. Robbers were policemen and murderers were judges."

For a century after the Civil War, the notion that San Francisco politics in the gold rush era was a corrupt mess was a staple of the imitative phase of scholarship. In the analytical phase, qualifications began to appear, and quite correctly, for it is clear that the politicians, though certainly not blameless, were perhaps no better than the public deserved.[4]

Two distinguishable issues are involved in evaluating the city's politics. One is the deeds of the city's politicians, and the other is the process by which the politicians were chosen. I am going to talk a bit about city expenses and the like somewhat later, in the context of a discussion of the movement for a nonpartisan form of political organization. For now, I should like to discuss the process by which public officials were chosen. Briefly, I want to argue that, although some violence and fraud did exist in the political arena, they have been greatly exaggerated. I believe that a close examination of the canvasses reveals that a stable and coherent political system existed in San Francisco. The major "crime" that was connected with politics was that otherwise well-connected men, the type who were to become vigilantes, were on the losing side more often than they wished to be. To put it another way, when the business hustlers, who were not doing well, looked out over the city, they thought that they saw that the political hustlers, mostly Democrats, were doing quite well. And that galled them no end.[5]

• II •

In a way, gold rush politics in San Francisco began in the spring of 1851, when incumbent mayor John Geary, whose accession to the office of alcalde in 1849 had put an end to the factional bickering that had followed the American occupation of Yerba Buena, announced that he would not stand for reelection. Geary shortly thereafter left San Francisco, and San Francisco's loss was others' gain. Geary subsequently served as a successful territorial governor of Kansas in quite difficult times, and after the Civil War he became governor of Pennsylvania. His withdrawal from city politics in 1851 opened the way for citywide organizing efforts by groups that claimed a loose allegiance to one of the national parties.

A brief survey of the results of the succeeding elections might be helpful at this point. Even though I tend to agree with Barbara J. Fields that in the historical profession "pure pedants are increasing in numbers and influence," I ask the reader's indulgence for a few rather pedantic paragraphs.[6] Here is what happened.

In the 1851 elections, the Whigs swept all the citywide offices, six of the eight seats on the Board of Aldermen, and four of the eight seats on the Board of Assistant Aldermen. At the 1851 county elections, the Whigs and the Democrats split the two seats in the State Senate, and the Democrats carried the Assembly delegation four seats to three. Of the remaining county offices, the Whigs carried six and the Democrats five, giving each party a total of ten county offices. At the 1851 county election, the Democrats also "elected" an unopposed slate of city candidates. This resulted from an ambiguity in the new city charter granted by the legislature earlier in that year. The charter provided that city elections should be held in April 1851 and "thereafter annually at the general election for state officers." The Democrats, who had lost in the spring elections, contended that the charter mandated another city election in the fall. The victorious Whigs argued that "thereafter annually" meant starting in 1852 and did not bother to put together a ticket. The courts eventually decided that a city election in December had been proper, unseated the Whig government, and installed the Democrats.

In 1852 the Whigs carried the city offices eight to four, the Board of Aldermen seven to one, and the Board of Assistant Aldermen six to two. In the county elections the Whigs and the Democrats once again split the two Senate seats, with the Whigs carrying the Assembly delegation four to three. The Whigs also carried the two other county offices that were contested—all in all, a very Whiggish year.

The situation changed abruptly in 1853, as the Democrats

carried all the city offices, four of the eight seats on the Board of Aldermen, and five of the eight seats on the Board of Assistant Aldermen. The Democrats also won three of the four Senate seats and all nine Assembly seats, in addition to all the other county offices. The election was a stunning Democratic triumph.

There was yet another change in 1854. The Know-Nothings carried all the citywide offices, either with candidates of their own or with candidates from the other parties whom they endorsed. The Democrats were able to retain only two seats on the Board of Aldermen and one seat on the Board of Assistant Aldermen. On the county level, both Know-Nothing candidates (one Whig and one Democrat) were elected to the Senate, and all the Know-Nothing candidates (five Whigs, two Democrats, and two independents) were elected to the Assembly. The Democrats did manage to retain the three county supervisorial posts that were outside the city limits, but their defeat in 1854 was nearly as complete as their victory had been the year before.

In the 1855 city elections, the Democrats staged a comeback. They captured six of the nine citywide offices that were contested and eight of the sixteen seats on the common council (four on each board). In the county elections that fall, the Democrats gained further ground. They swept all county offices, both Senate seats, and all nine Assembly seats. By the end of the year, they were in a strong political position.

This survey was necessary to establish a simple point. For all the talk of corruption and fraud that we have encountered in the historical literature, and shall encounter in contemporary appraisals of city politics, the San Francisco political system was a competitive one. The Whigs won in 1851 and 1852, the Democrats in 1853, the Know-Nothings in 1854, and the Democrats in 1855. Opponents of the Democrats were victorious in three of the five years in which contested elections were held. If the San Francisco democracy was a corrupt political machine, it was a remarkably inefficient one.

♦ III ♦

As the municipal elections of 1851 approached, one paper remarked, "An election canvass always turns everything topsy-turvy, upsets the ordinary business of life, sets a large number of people crazy, and produces a general disorganization throughout all the ramifications of society." Business, the paper went on, almost came to a standstill: "The transaction of ordinary affairs is deferred, creditors postpone payment, expeditions are put off until 'after the election.'"[7] The paper was undoubtedly reflecting on the sporadic canvasses in San Francisco over the preceding few years, but it could also have been reflecting on the entire national antebellum experience. For this was, as Michael Feldberg has said, a "turbulent era." In a book of that title, Professor Feldberg has attempted to construct a classification system for the various riots and disorders that punctuated the life of early nineteenth-century America.

One of the Feldberg categories is useful here. He argues that there was a distinguishable phenomenon called the "election riot." According to Feldberg, "the election riot occupied a twilight zone between political and recreational violence." Its object was "not to destroy the opposition party as a political organization. Election rioting usually did not have ideological content; the rioters did not fight to advance or defend political principles. Rather, they fought because it was entertaining, and because it was a way of preventing the other side from getting votes."[8]

This classification seems very persuasive. It would serve to explain a scene like this one in 1855 San Francisco:

> About half past one o'clock, a Democrat accused a Know-Nothing of circulating spurious Democratic tickets. . . . The accusation brought on high words and then blows. The Democrat drew a revolver and then beat his opponent over the head, but the belligerents were finally separated. The affair occurred in the midst of a dense crowd and several policemen tried to get at the combatants, but the Democrats managed to carry off their man, and after they supposed him to be beyond danger of arrest, they gave three cheers for the Democratic party.[9]

Every society seems to need a place in which adults can legitimately hit one another. We do the hitting somewhat vicariously today, but in gold rush San Francisco, people could not gather before a screen and watch twenty-two sometimes grown men stomp on each other for a few hours on the Sabbath. Pushing, shoving, punching, screaming, and yelling around the polls had to do.

The election riot was not an isolated occurrence. Feldberg points to an 1834 riot in Philadelphia as "typical of the political violence of the era." A Whig mob stormed a Democratic gathering, tore up their banners, and worst of all, tore down their hickory pole! The Democrats retaliated by breaking into Whig headquarters and tearing up the whole place. That same year, in New York, the militia had to be called out to put down a disturbance that grew out of an election in which the mayor was to be chosen directly for the first time.[10]

Riots moved west when the country did. An 1820 Indiana newspaper complained that a recent election "exhibited such a degraded state of society as outrages all the usual principles of civilization, or rules of social order and morality." Speaking of the entire trans-Appalachian frontier, Malcolm J. Rohrbough observes, "The whole election process loosed elements of rowdyism and boisterousness, not infrequently lubricated with corn whiskey." So we should not be surprised to find the election riot residing in San Francisco. It is undeniably true that elections, marked by almost nightly torchlight processions, mass meetings, parades, and rallies, quickened the pace of life in the town. But it is surprising that a close examination of contemporary accounts reveals that San Francisco elections were generally conducted in a peaceful and orderly manner. Let's look at those accounts.[11]

In late March 1851, both parties held primaries before the municipal elections. The *Herald* reported that the Democratic primary "passed off very quietly and without any unpleasant disturbance. Notwithstanding the rain which fell for most of the day, there was a pretty good turnout of the voters interested in the election." The Whigs held their primary soon after, and the same paper remarked, "Every ticket had its rivals, and the friends of each were anxious in pushing their favorite. As far as we observed, notwithstanding the press around the ballot box, the utmost order and decorum prevailed—all went on smoothly." The press did not mention how the general election on April 28 went, but we can assume, given the general willingness of the major dailies to denounce politics for the slightest reason, that their silence on the question of violence indicates that the general election was as peaceful as the primaries had been. A glimpse into the situation can be gained from a letter William Weston wrote his father on the day after the election. Weston described the elaborate torchlight parades that took place on the night before the contest and said, "It was the most exciting election I ever witnessed—many rows and fights—but no lives were lost, although pistols were fired two or three times during the day." There was, in other words, much "excitement," but not much violence.[12]

In September of that same year, in the county election, the voters had three tickets to choose from—the regular Democratic and Whig tickets, and also an independent ticket put up by the 1851 vigilance committee. The primaries of the major parties were held about a month before the election. They were apparently hotly contested, yet there was little mention of fighting at the polls. A newspaper column on the Democratic primary reported that there was "great spirit" displayed, and that "none of the delegations was elected without a sharp struggle—except in the eighth ward." Concerning the Whigs, the same paper told its readers, "Great activity prevails among the friends of the various candidates and a multitude of tickets are in the field." The primary itself it termed a "sharp contest." But neither primary was apparently stained with any violence worth recording.[13]

As for the general election, one daily summed it up as "a very quiet and orderly election." Another paper was more enthusiastic: "Yesterday was one of the quietest elections ever seen anywhere, and by far the most quiet ever witnessed in San Francisco since the American occupation . . . the day was rightfully dull in incident. With the exception of one or two very small fights in the sixth ward, which were easily stopped, nothing occurred to mar the harmony and good feeling with which all parties appeared to work." In 1851, then, there were two elections and two primaries connected with each. Six times during the year, San Franciscans voted without appreciable violence.[14]

It might be possible to argue that such peacefulness, especially in the fall elections, was a direct result of the activities of the vigilance committee. But at the next election, in 1852, when there was no vigilance committee, things were still peaceful. The *Herald* remarked after the general canvass: "The election passed off yesterday in this city with the utmost quiet and decorum, no single breach of the peace having come to our knowledge. Our citizens have good reason to felicitate themselves on this most gratifying result . . . no commendation is too high for such remarkable self-restraint." In another column, the paper continued in the same vein: "One thing was the subject of universal remark—that although disorders and disturbances were expected to prevail on all sides, very few scenes of violence occurred throughout the day. There were, of course, disputes and wordy warfare, and occasionally jostling, but, take it altogether, we have never witnessed a more quiet election." The *Alta* concurred in this judgment:

> Contrary to the expectations and anticipations of all, the election yesterday was conducted in a quiet and orderly manner. In fact, it could favorably compare with any of the oldest and best regulated communities in the Atlantic states. . . . It is a great cause of congratulation on all sides that the long-expected day has come and gone, the people have expressed their will, and there are no terrific scenes or disgraceful proceedings to record the event. . . . There were perhaps one or two knockdowns and disagreeable disputes in different portions of the city, but they resulted in nothing. It was a peaceful election, as all who made themselves conspicuous around the polls appeared to be busy and had no time to spend in idle arguments.[15]

At the next set of elections, in 1853, many tickets were presented to the voters. In addition to the regular slates, candidates ran on an "Anti-Extension Reform Ticket," a "True Independent Ticket," a "Mechanics' Lien Ticket," a "Regular Mechanics Ticket," a ticket organized by "a large and respectable meeting of mechanics," and, finally, an "Independent Reform Club Ticket." Yet the large number of tickets in the field did not affect the nonviolent pattern of voting that had characterized the preceding two years. The *Alta* did say that, during the Democratic primary in August, "The order preserved at some of the polls was not the best." But the only disturbances it reported were in the first ward, where a brief scuffle between rival factions resulted in one of them withdrawing from the polls and holding a rump primary elsewhere. As for the Whigs, the paper reported that their primary "passed off in a very orderly manner. There was a great deal of interest in the result, and a number of carriages was provided for the convenience of the voters. The vote polled was a comparatively large one for a Whig primary election."[16]

The general election itself was quite orderly. "Our own citizens deserve praise at least for the good-natured manner in which the toilsome business was conducted," the *Alta* concluded. "Few rows of any kind, as far as we can learn, occurred at any of the polls. From 8 o'clock in the morning to the setting of the sun, our streets wore a holiday appearance."[17]

The 1854 elections broke the pattern. As in 1853, many tickets were presented to the electorate. Both the northern (Tammany) and southern (Chivalry) Democrats offered slates, as did the Whigs. The Know-Nothings offered a ticket composed mainly of Chivalry Democrats and Whigs. More candidates appeared under such labels as "Independent Citizens Ticket," "Floating Ticket," and "Cuidado Ticket."[18]

Both the Tammany and Chivalry Democrats held primaries, which were apparently quite orderly. The Chivalry-leaning *Herald* noted of the Tammany primary, "As might be expected everything passed off with remarkable quietness, there being, of course, no opposition." The Whig primary, however, was marked by instances of disorder. In one ward, an attempt was made to storm the polls and carry off the ballot box, and this forced the election inspectors to flee for a time. In another ward, "All was progressing quietly until some evil-disposed person suddenly jerked the ballot box from the table and dashed it on the floor, scattering it in every direction; at the same instant he drew from his pocket a handful of tickets and cast them among those from the box." A Democratic paper, doubtless with great exaggeration, commented, "The scenes of rowdyism and violence which were enacted exceeded any of the kind ever before witnessed in this city . . . the polls in nearly all of the wards, where there was any opposition, were beset with shoulder strikers and bullies, and to suppose that any respectable man would allow himself to be hustled about by such a crowd is preposterous in the extreme."[19]

The general election was wild. The *Herald*, which had supported many of the winning candidates, reported, "It is generally conceded that the election yesterday was more peaceable and orderly than any election ever held in this city." But it had to concede that there had been some rowdyism: "We are not yet progressed far enough in the arts of civilization and peace to expect that the entire day would pass off without some disturbance. Toward evening, when the closing of the polls occurred, considerable excitement prevailed in some of the wards."[20]

That was an understatement, to put it mildly. Things actually had begun to get wild in the second ward early in the afternoon, after Ned McGowan and Paddy Martin, Broderick allies, arrived at the polls with Tammany tickets that were the same size and color as their own tickets. The Know-Nothings learned that the two were trying to pass themselves off as

Know-Nothing workers and persuade unsuspecting Know-Nothing voters to cast what were actually Tammany ballots. The Know-Nothings also heard rumors that Martin was offering an inspector of elections $2,000 to stuff 300 Tammany votes into one of the boxes. A gambler friend of Martin's had supposedly wagered $20,000 on the reelection of Mayor Garrison, a Democrat, and Paddy was apparently trying to help the cause along.

The Democrats also had reason to be concerned about the second ward. They had intelligence that some of the special policemen hired by the city to keep order at the polls were using the authority of their badges to push the Know-Nothing ticket into the hands of intimidated Irish voters. So both sides sent in reinforcements. Roving bands of Democratic and Know-Nothing workers spent the rest of the day ambushing each other and scuffling around the polling place.

The election was only a bit more peaceful in the fifth ward, which spread out from the foot of Market Street. There, Jacob Ritchie, the Tammany candidate for ward assistant alderman, tried to steal some tickets from a Know-Nothing worker named Isaac Hillman. He did not succeed and had to content himself with yelling, "No man shall electioneer that damned Know-Nothing ticket in this ward! You belong in the third ward, and by God, you won't stay here!" (The third ward was a merchant stronghold, and it was staunchly Know-Nothing.) When a fellow worker came up to protect Hillman, Ritchie turned on him and shouted, "What have you got to say, you Know-Nothing son of a bitch?" News of the fracas quickly circulated, and Know-Nothing contingents arrived to keep Ritchie at bay. After the polls had closed, Ritchie and Bill Matthews, the Tammany candidate for tax collector, tried to storm the ballot box. Ritchie drew a pistol, but thought better of it when someone from the crowd shouted, "If you fire that pistol, your body will be riddled with balls!" Outnumbered, the two withdrew.

Ritchie and Matthews had not received any help because Democratic activists were gathering at the sixth ward, west of the lower waterfront. Garrison had heard that there, as in the second ward, Know-Nothing policemen were electioneering their ticket. So he descended on the polls with a contingent of party loyalists. He tore the badge off one of the offending policemen and then mounted a box to give a fiery harangue. News that the mayor himself had arrived drew a large and angry Know-Nothing crowd to the place, and a free-for-all ensued.

The outnumbered Democrats were about to retreat when runners reported the news of the incident to the second ward. Two hundred Irishmen, led by the volatile Tammany worker and political brawler Billy Mulligan, immediately headed down Kearny Street to the rescue. Broderick intercepted them and tried to stop them, but Mulligan, shouting "Let's get even!" drowned him out. Mulligan's rangers reached the sixth ward in a matter of minutes. As a newspaper drolly remarked the next day, "The arrival of the troop did not contribute to pacify matters."

While all this was going on, some Democratic workers in another ward were passing the time in Barry's saloon as they waited for the polls to close. Tony Durkin, a waterfront laborer, was very grateful that the proprietor kept his glass quite full. But the reason became clear when Barry asked Tony to do the boys a favor. As Durkin later recalled, "I went with him across the street to the polls where a bottle containing drink was passed." But he needed a trifle more courage. As he put it, "I objected to it [the bottle] as being watered and said I wanted prime liquor, which they sent for and handed to me. I drank and became pretty well lit." He was ready. "Barry urged me to go in and seize the ballot box," he recalled. "I got into the room where the ballots were being counted and got hold of the box and threw it over my head among the crowd." Durkin then passed out. As the bystanders gathered up the box, Tammany workers were undoubtedly adding a nice number of never-cast Tammany ballots to the pile.

In 1855, stability returned to the electoral process, in both the municipal and county elections. The two Democratic factions came together, partly because a number of the Chivalry Democrats threw their lot in with the Know-Nothings. The Democratic candidate was James Van Ness, a city councilman who had survived the Know-Nothing sweep the previous year. The Whigs did not offer a slate, so the opposition to the united Democracy was itself united under the Know-Nothing banner. The Know-Nothings, as was their practice, did not hold a primary, and it appears that the Democratic primary, with the exception of a minor election riot to which I alluded earlier, was peaceful. The *Chronicle* did not even consider it worth mentioning. "The whole affair was as flat as dishwater," it complained, "there not having been an eye blackened, a coat torn, a hat stove in, or a watch stolen."[21]

At the municipal election at the end of May, according to the *Herald*, "An almost incredible degree of quiet and order characterized the entire proceedings of the day; there were but few disturbances worthy of note and but few attempts to vote illegally." The *Chronicle* concurred: "It was eminently peaceful. . . . Never in the city has there been such quietness about the polls. There was more sobriety than we ever witnessed at a municipal election before." At the county elections in the fall, the peacefulness evident in the spring still held. The Democrats and the Know-Nothings presented candidates, and even the Whigs, though nearly moribund, managed to put together a pretty full slate a few days before the election. The Know-Nothings broke with their custom and held a primary, which apparently was quiet, even though there were competing tickets in some of the wards. The Democratic primary, too, was fairly quiet, except for a spectacular gunfight between John Bagley and Robert Cushing, on the one side, and James P. Casey, on the other. This dispute was a continuation of a fight that had occurred in June, when, at the Democratic primary to elect delegates to the state convention, Bagley and Cushing had attempted to remove Casey from his position as sixth ward inspector of elections. The gunfight was an isolated incident, however, and voting proceeded routinely throughout the rest of the city.[22]

The 1855 fall elections marked a return to the pattern that had existed before the 1854 melees. The *Alta* wrote a glowing report:

> Yesterday was the proudest day for San Francisco she has ever seen. We speak not of the results, but the manner in which the election was conducted was honorable, and would reflect credit on any city in the world. All through the day the city was quiet as the sabbath. Business was in the main suspended, and men gave their attention to the election. Quietly they went and deposited their votes, and lingered around the polls for a while, happy to witness how great a change has come over San Francisco in the last two years. Some three or four trifling affrays occurred, but they were quickly quelled, Whigs, Democrats, and Know-Nothings all joining in to hustle the disturber out of the way, and establish a good name for the city.

The *Chronicle* took the same line: "So far as the conduct of the people was concerned, it may be said that we have never had an election so orderly and quiet."[23]

To sum up, although the city press complained throughout the early 1850's about election-day violence, in only one series of elections, that of 1854, were there reports of specific incidents of serious violence connected with the voting. In all the other elections—two in 1851, one in 1852, one in 1853, and two in 1855—the unanimous testimony of the papers was that the voting was conducted in an orderly and peaceful manner.

◆ IV ◆

The question of fraud is more difficult to examine, since, obviously, the essence of a successful election fraud is that it remain undetected. It is only when fraud is done up in grand style, on a truly spectacular scale, that it can easily and confidently be detected. Such was the case, for instance, in Kansas City in 1859. These kinds of obvious frauds were extremely rare in San Francisco.[24]

Sometimes the accusation of fraud could serve as a convenient face-saving device for an editor anxious to explain the defeat of a candidate or party he had supported. In 1854, for instance, the *Chronicle*, a paper with Whiggish and Know-Nothing leanings, reported that the vote of the Democratic first ward showed a decrease of 247 from the past election. The paper sniffed, "The natural inference must be that there was some kind of rascality in the voting or counting last year." But at the same election, the vote in the second ward showed an increase of 251 over the preceding year, and, perhaps not coincidentally, the ward went from being straight Democratic in 1853 to being straight Know-Nothing in 1854. The *Chronicle* refrained from suggesting that fraud might be involved there.[25]

Some fraud did occur, and in a few isolated instances it was truly spectacular. The most celebrated instance involved James P. Casey, whom we have already met in a political shootout and whom we shall encounter later on a vigilante scaffold. During the 1855 county elections, Casey was serving, as he had before, as sixth ward inspector of elections. Outside the city, in the first district of the county, a supervisor's race was taking place. Using a part of the election law that allowed the citizens at the polls to choose from among their number inspectors and judges of the elections if the officials who had been elected to these positions were absent at the time of the voting, three of Casey's friends showed up early at an isolated polling place. Finding no one else there (not unusual), they assumed the positions themselves. At the end of the day, they reported that their precinct had cast 150 votes for none other than James P. Casey—who was not even known to be a candidate. A Democratic judge sitting on the Court of Sessions declined any responsibility over the matter, and Casey was declared legally elected as supervisor of the first district.[26]

Though this case is extreme, most accusations of fraud that were made in the 1850's do not hold water, or if they do, the fraud seems too minor to have swayed a particular election. Many of the allegations collected by the 1856 vigilance committee were general and vague. Various Irishmen were denounced for reasons such as "his only support comes from corrupt politicians," or "he is one of the tools used to excite the Irish population to rows and fights around the ballot box on the days of election," or "he is a violent man," or "he has derived his principal support by holding some public office," or "he was a general bully at the election time." Most of these unspecified accusations were akin to that which a certain E. W. Crowell directed against one Daniel Sweeney: "I can only speak generally and not refer to any particular act."[27]

Other allegations were more specific. One man, for instance, claimed that there was fraud in the first ward—a waterfront ward with many laborers—in the election of 1854. The Democrats did carry the ward in 1854, but they had also carried it in 1853 and they were to carry it again in 1855. Most tellingly, they were also to carry it in 1856, when the vigilantes controlled the election machinery and a number of Broderick's first ward operatives had been driven from the city. That they carried it in 1854, then, must be attributed to their good organization in the ward and to the voluntary affinity of Irish laborers for the party of Jackson. It was similarly alleged that there was fraud in the sixth ward in 1854. But in this election the Know-Nothings carried the ward, even though the inspector and judge of elections were Democrats.

It is worth noting that most of the allegations that floated through the city in the early 1850's concerned primary elections, and most of those concerned the Democratic primary. In most of these instances, the loser of the primary, either the northern or southern wing of the party, accused the winner, either the southern or northern wing, of fraud. Most of the accusations were long on passion and short on specifics. And most of the allegations concerning the general elections were of the same character. For instance, after the defeat of many of the candidates it favored in 1853, the *Alta* fumed, "There was more money spent in this city on Wednesday to influence votes, legal and illegal, than was ever expended for a similar purpose in any city or state in the world." Of course, mountains of evidence would have been needed to sustain such a charge, but the *Alta* did not concern itself with pursuing that sort of investigation.[28]

Other allegations that ran through the gold rush years were more pointed, and similarly lacking in evidence. After the 1852 elections, for instance, one paper noted, "There are loud complaints of foul play manifest in the enormous vote of the eighth ward." The vote of that ward was in fact up about 15 percent over the total in 1851, but since the vote of the entire city was up almost 30 percent, the increase in the eighth ward does not seem extraordinary. Again, after the 1855 elections, one paper said, "After the polls were closed last night, someone observed, 'The election is just begun.'" The specifics were that "a rumor that about 300 votes had been stuffed into the eighth ward ballot box had obtained general circulation." That rumor may or may not have been true, but it is noteworthy that the election results would not have changed had those votes not been counted.[29]

Finally, the false-bottom ballot box that allegedly was used to perpetrate the 1854 frauds (exactly which one was never made clear) was said to have been found just occupying space in someone's cellar by the vigilantes in 1856. It was a marvelously convenient discovery, and one that Bancroft accepted at face value. But not all contemporaries of the vigilantes were so unskeptical. Sherman, not an unbiased observer, called the discovery "humbug." Though he admitted that the box could have been used at some primaries, he thought it was "never used at the public polls."[30]

There were, however, two specific and rather interesting claims of fraud concerning the 1855 elections. Depositions given to the vigilantes asserted that many second and seventh ward votes were fraudulently cast for the Democrats in that election. Both these wards had been predominantly Democratic in 1853, however, so it appears that in 1855, after flirting with the Know-Nothings, they were simply returning to the Democratic fold.

The voting behavior of these wards points to an important fact: the Know-Nothings, as opposed to the Whigs, could at times beat the Democrats on their turf. Why could they do what their predecessors the Whigs could not? I shall return to this point when I analyze the Know-Nothings a bit later.

My final judgment on fraud corresponds closely to that of the *Herald*, as it took stock after the 1856 elections. In the months preceding that canvass, the vigilance committee had made a great effort to drive from the city alleged ballot box stuffers and to destroy the local Democratic organization. Yet, as the anti-vigilance *Herald* could not resist observing, the total number of votes at the 1856 election was not appreciably different from the total cast at the previous election. This meant either that the charges of ballot box stuffing had been greatly exaggerated over the previous years, or that the People's Party, the political arm of the vigilance committee and the victor in the 1856 election, had stuffed in precisely the same quantities as had the Democrats before them. The *Herald* obviously preferred the first explanation. "After this test," it said, "all that has been trumpeted to the world of ballot box stuffing at the last election falls to the earth." I agree. It is impossible to argue that the San Francisco political system before 1856 was built on systematic violence and fraud. If you want a reason why the Democrats were able to win elections in gold rush San Francisco (and remember, they did not win even a majority of them), and why they were able to recover from the drubbing the Know-Nothings gave them in 1854, you could do better than cry fraud. You could listen to what the anti-Democrats said only in private: "California ought to be Whig and I believe is, but here as almost everywhere, the Democrats are under better organization."*[31]

• V •

There is one further question that has to be considered before we leave the political arena: From whom did each of the parties derive its strength? We can approach that question by combining the voting results with the researches of Roger Lotchin, probably the best modern historian of gold rush San Francisco. Lotchin has made a thorough study of land use differentiation in the gold rush port as revealed by United States Coast Survey maps of 1853 and 1858 and city directories.[32]

Lotchin describes the situation in 1850 as follows: "The retailing, wholesaling, manufacturing, and middle-class residential section was a half-moon shaped area fronting the old cove in the north part of town. The outstanding characteristic of these locations was proximity to the waterfront and to each other. Lower class residents tended to be on the periphery of this indiscriminate grouping, although they too were close to the water." Between 1850 and 1857, change occurred, comparable to changes in other nineteenth-century cities, which involved "the sorting out and separating of the various activities that had been in 1850 located contiguously." By 1857 the city had a new shape:

> The wholesaling part of the business community had migrated eastward toward the water. The middle classes had erupted over the hills to the west, and, to a lesser extent, into the Rincon Hill area south of Market. The retailing section tended to stay where it had been, or to spread out to the west and south, following its retreating customers. The resettling gave the retailers a position between the wholesalers and the middle class residences. Unlike retailing, petty manufacturing, such as blacksmithing and coopering, did not follow the middle class ascent of Russian and Nob hills. Indeed the migration of these artisans was north and south, away from the central position they had formerly held.

If we combine these findings with the voting behavior, we can draw a rough outline of voting groups and party affiliations.

The first ward, north of Jackson Street and east of Montgomery Street, embraced a large waterfront area that included two frequently used wharves on Broadway and Pacific streets and a large section of the northeastern part of the city, bordering on the Telegraph Hill area. According to Lotchin, as the period under study advanced, this area became more and more working class, as the middle class residents continued the westward migration to Stockton and Dupont streets. By 1856 it was reported that "many hard characters, notorious for their turbulence . . . lounge about the wharves." This movement of people appears to have correlated closely with a change in the political complexion of the ward. In 1851–52 it tended to be anti-Democratic, especially in choosing state and county officers. In the county election of 1851, for instance, the only Democrats to carry the ward were those who had been endorsed by the independent, vigilance-related ticket. In 1852, the ward was almost straight Whig. But in 1853, the only Whig who carried the ward was the candidate for state comptroller. The ward remained heavily Democratic from 1853 through 1855.[33]

The second ward embraced most of the northwest part of the city, including North Beach and Russian Hill. This area of the city appears to have been a mixed one throughout the first half of the 1850's. It apparently contained, in uncertain mixtures, the fringes of the laboring groups, who moved north from the original area of settlement, and the middle classes, who moved west from the same starting point. Perhaps because of this mixture, the ward tended to vote erratically throughout the period. It was, for instance, heavily Whig in the 1851 city elections, but rather evenly split in the 1851 county elections. It was heavily Democratic in 1852 and 1853, heavily Whig and Know-Nothing in 1854, and Democratic in 1855.

The third ward, like the first, was on the waterfront. Montgomery Street, the western boundary of the ward, is regarded by Lotchin as a kind of dividing line between laborers and managers. Even east of Montgomery, less than half the population was labor, and the proportion quickly lessened the farther you went west. The ward itself contained Clay Street, where most of the larger produce merchants in the city conducted business. In 1851 and 1852 this merchant-dominated ward went Whig, with only four exceptions: at the county elections of 1851 it voted for four Democrats who had been endorsed by the vigilance committee ticket. In 1853 it remained Whig on the state level but split its city and county vote between Democrats and Whigs. In 1854 it went heavily Whig/Know-Nothing and in the 1855 city elections voted straight Know-Nothing. In the fall of 1855, it remained predominantly Know-Nothing, although the Democrats did pick up some strength.

Of all the areas of the city, the fourth ward was the one most affected by the westward trek of the middle classes. Lying directly west of the old downtown section, it was intersected by Dupont, Stockton, Mason, and Taylor streets, where Lotchin estimates the middle class proportions as, respectively, 60, 75, 60, and 75 percent. Up to 1855 the ward returned rather consistent anti-Democratic pluralities. At the 1855 county elections, the same trend that was evident in the third ward was noticeable here as well: from being straight Know-Nothing in the spring, the ward allowed the Democrats to gain ground in the fall.

The fifth ward was the lower waterfront, and it contained the important Market Street wharf. Also within its boundaries was the corner of California and Front streets, around which were clustered the leading commission houses in the city. At the edge of the ward was Sacramento Street, on which the majority of large dry goods dealers were situated. This was the most consistent anti-Democratic ward in the city. Through 1852 it voted for only three Democrats. As we have seen in other wards, these were men who had been endorsed by the vigilance ticket of September 1851. It split in 1853, but returned to its normal posture the next year, when it voted for only one Democrat. And in 1855, at both elections, the Know-Nothings carried the entire ward.

The sixth ward included a large area west of the lower waterfront. Its population was probably much the same as that of the second ward—workers and middle class people both, migrating south and west, respectively. Its behavior was, like that of the second ward, erratic. It went heavily Democratic in the spring of 1851, but then heavily anti-Democratic in the fall of 1851 and in 1852. In 1853 it split, and in 1854 it went moderately Know-Nothing. It remained moderately anti-Democratic in the spring of 1855, but by the fall the Democrats had picked up strength there and were able to win a majority of the offices. At the end of 1855, then, the voting behavior of this ward closely resembled that of its neighbor to the north, the fourth.

The seventh ward embraced a large area of land south of Market Street along the coast. Its population was undoubtedly the most disparate of any ward in the city. Within its boundaries were Happy Valley, Pleasant Valley, and Rincon Hill, which were from an early date almost exclusively middle and upper class areas. Yet another part of the ward, the area bounded by Market, Mission, Stewart, and Second streets, was an area in which laborers outnumbered everyone else 89 percent to 11 percent. Its voting reflected this heterogeneity. In the early years, it tended to divide pretty evenly between the Democrats and the Whigs, but in 1853 it went heavily Democratic. The next year it reversed itself and went heavily Know-Nothing. In the city election of 1855 it was heavily Know-Nothing, but in the fall, as we have seen in other wards, the Democrats gained ground, although the anti-Democrats still carried the ward.[34]

Ward eight, the extreme southwestern part of the city, and the three districts in the county, outside the city, were substantially Democratic strongholds during the period. Unfortunately, little can be surmised about their populations.

It seems safe to conclude, after all this, that Democratic strength tended to be greatest in the areas of the city that were populated by immigrants and laborers; conversely, anti-Democratic strength tended to be greatest in areas of upper and middle class residences and/or large mercantile establishments. This was certainly the case with the first and fifth wards. The voting behavior of the second, third, fourth, sixth, and seventh wards was also consistent with a vague businessman-laborer political division.

This does not mean that every Irish laborer was a Democrat, or that every Yankee businessman was a Whig or Know-Nothing. What Robert Kelley says about New England in the 1850's is appropriate for San Francisco as well: "What cultural historians usually discover is that specific groups of people lean but marginally in a particular direction. Yankees . . . leaned . . . Republican in sufficient numbers to give that party a specific character, although many Yankees were strong Democrats."[35]

The political situation in San Francisco was thus quite similar to that in other northern and midwestern cities. In New York, Boston, Pittsburgh, Detroit, and virtually everywhere else, Irish Catholic laborers were Democrats.[36] But for San Francisco, it is important to note that in 1855 the Democrats appeared to be picking up strength in areas of the city that formerly had been hostile to them. The fifth ward remained solidly anti-Democratic, but the second, third, fourth, and sixth wards, all of which contained significant numbers of nonlaboring people, turned out to vote for the Democrats in greater numbers than they had in former years. For the staunch anti-Democrats, the decline of the Know-Nothings in 1855 seemed ominous: where, now, could the anti-Democrats go?

CHAPTER 5

THE ADVERSARIES

When the Lord your God brings you into the land which you are entering to take possession of it, and clears away many nations before you . . . you shall make no covenant with them and show no mercy to them. You shall not make marriages with them. . . . For they would turn away your sons from following me to serve other gods. . . . Thus shall you deal with them: you shall break down their altars, and dash in pieces their pillars . . . and burn their graven images with fire.

—Deuteronomy 7: 1–5

♦

The Know-Nothings have done the job
Wide-awake boys acted accordin'
If you want to get a lick
Just say you're a mick
And they'll kick you on the other side of the Jordan.

—Jingle in San Francisco, fall of 1854

♦

Are you willing that a company of ignorant, bigoted, priest-directed, Bible-hating foreigners should come to our shores and, by political influence, withhold from our schools the fountain of everlasting life, the fountain from which our Republic came?

—"The Schools Demanded by the Present Age," sermon delivered by Rev. Edgar Lacy, May 11, 1856, San Francisco

♦

Religious zeal is perpetually warmed in the United States by the fires of patriotism. These men do not act exclusively from a consideration of future life; eternity is only one motive to the devotion of their cause. If you converse with these missionaries of Christian civilization, you will be surprised to hear them speak so often of the goods of this world, and to meet a politician where you expected to find a priest.

—Alexis de Tocqueville

◆ I ◆

The political disappointments of the Democracy's opponents were part of a larger set of disappointments that pervaded the entire city. For beneath the façade of glittering expectations and the reports of progress that informed a work like the 1855 *Annals of San Francisco*, there was always an undertone of darkness and gloom in the gold rush port.

When the hustlers' anticipated riches did not materialize instantly, they first tended to lower their sights a bit. Milton Hall received a rude shock when he arrived. "I have been here fifteen working days and have only worked five out of that time," he sighed. "A man has to be pretty well acquainted before he can get any jobs." It was a dreadful thing not to be able to find work in the place you yourself had trumpeted as the end of the rainbow. One unemployed laborer reported, "There are 42 men boarding with me, and they are swearing from morning to night."[1]

During the prosperity of 1852, Roger Baldwin wistfully described how his fellows were making out. "I see or hear of every day some acquaintance who has made his pile," he wrote, but he tried to keep up his own hopes: "I don't despair yet of being somebody." Then came the lament, "I wish I could get rich a little faster, but I don't see my way out of the woods for a long time to come." In the same vein, Andrew Davis tried to put the best possible face on his own failure to strike it rich quickly. "I regard the time passed to make large fortunes in a few days without capital," he wrote, apparently believing that such a time had actually ever existed in San Francisco. But he was unwilling to give up the dream. "The time for a straight-forward legitimate business is as good as ever," he insisted. Similarly, one would-be magnate had his eyes warily on the calendar: "One year in California, and I can't say that my pile has grown as rapidly as I would have wished." But his hope, if not eternal, was at least biennial. "The end," he claimed, "is not yet." Robert S. Lammot had drawn up a five-year plan for himself, and it was proving to be as unsuccessful as later Soviet versions would be. His results were all too common in the city: "Two years passed out of the five, and no money made yet."[2]

Some tried to be philosophical about the whole experience. "Californians are properly divided into two great classes," Daniell opined, "lucky and unlucky. I place myself toward the foot of the latter." His hope did not die easily either, for he went on, "But never mind. It is always darkest just before the day, and my time will come yet." Perhaps, though, his most genuine thought was the one that he saved for the end of the letter: "Oh, how I should like to be in Roxbury this winter!"[3]

For some the gloom was more severe. One person wrote of the gold rush sardonically and said, "The grand finale . . . will be what is vulgarly called the *bust up* and a scattering among the sons of California, the lucky ones perhaps having enough money to pay their passage home to their mamas and papas while the other portion will serve for subjects for newspaper paragraphs referring to 'Great Spread of the Anglo-Saxon Race,' 'Enterprising Expedition of our Countrymen,' or 'Wonderful Adventures of a Party of Americans.'" A two-year resident confessed, "Mother, it is mighty hard to make money here. I have worked night and day for two years and am $3000 worse off than when I commenced." Summing up the prevailing frustrations, one merchant grumbled, "There is a great deal of moonshine about the large fortunes made here." A laborer reflected, "How sadly disappointed people are when they arrive here. They all form a very wrong idea of the place, about making fortunes in a hurry." He urged his father to get the word to two of his friends that they ought not come to California, "for they will be very sorry if they set their feet on this place, or they will be different from all that come here now."[4]

Through all these reflections ran the nagging realization that San Francisco was not really all that different, that people who had failed in the East would fail in the West, that there was no pot of gold at the end of the American rainbow. One merchant, seemingly resigned to the situation, commented: "I cannot think that the good time of last summer will ever come to San Francisco or to California again. The whole country is fast settling down to the confirmed order of the older states, ruining thousands." Another resident wrote in similar tones, "California has become almost an old state. It is not new enough for the spirit of the age."[5]

But if California was not new enough, was anything? In 1855, one merchant noticed a "general desire to leave this country." John Banfield wrote, unconvincingly, "I do not yet regret that I came out here." And another laborer, who was temporarily (and unsuccessfully) at the diggings, put the matter more graphically. Speaking of a steamer that had recently sunk with a large loss of life, he confided to his father, "To express my honest opinion it is about as well for one third to two thirds to get wrecked or drowned before ever reaching California, as to get here and be as awfully deceived as they will be."[6]

For countless immigrants, life in San Francisco meant terrible loneliness in the midst of the frenzied activity that was necessary just to keep one's head above water. One lawyer wrote, "California is only a sort of theater." A merchant complained of "this land of strangers where nothing but the merciless grasp of the money getter greets you on every side." Another merchant added, "Friends are of but little service here. Everybody is intent on making money and have but little time to talk without they are well paid for it." Reflecting on "disinterested friends," one woman told her sister that "this climate seems peculiarly unpropitious to the growth of such specimens." A Land Commissioner complained, "There is not a soul with whom I can converse as with a friend in this whole Babel of California. Intense selfishness locks up every bosom and nobody has the time or inclination to do anything but make money." And another resident sadly concluded, "It is difficult to find friends in this part of the globe."[7]

In a society that tended to equate personal worth with personal wealth, any confession of failure had to be kept as private as possible. "I am well, but not making money very fast," a laborer told his wife. Then he added, "But I don't want you to tell anyone so." Later this same man cautioned his wife, "Write me if you ever hear any remarks about my driving a team. I never thought much of this business myself and only took it to make some money. It is honest anyway, and that is as much as any of them can say."[8]

Even though associational life flourished in the gold rush city, the lack of a more personal group to which one could belong only reinforced the sense of having nowhere to turn. One laborer told his wife, "This is not much of a place for pleasure, unless it is to be found in one's own family." For the young unmarried men who formed such a large part of San Francisco's population, the loneliness was particularly hard. One resident noted, "If only I had someone to live for, who was dependent on me . . . some kind of restraining influence—in fact, a home." Another complained, "We are almost exclusively a nation of men. Money is the god of our idolatry—our minds are sufficiently active—our hearts as barren as the sun-burned hills." As he described not the 1980's but the 1850's, he was depressed: "It's nothing but men, men, men, all day long and all looking just alike—between 25 and 30, with shiny hats, mustaches, and great boots pulled over their pants as they go stamping through the mud." Another man summed up his constant loneliness this way: "I have made one discovery, that my only true friends are a very small circle—*at home*."[9]

For women, the frustration could be intense. Lura Smith, writing to her sister, exclaimed, "How anyone can live, write, or do anything else with two children to take care of, I can't see!" And the loneliness could be devastating. "I want you to write as soon as you get this," Mary Banfield pleaded as she closed a letter to her mother. "And don't send a half sheet, write a full one about all the folks." Finally, Lura Smith's sad remark on December 26, 1854, might stand as a summary of gold rush society. "I am quite glad there was no one to wish me a Merry Christmas," she wrote. "It would have been such a mockery."[10]

It is against the background of this sense of frustration and failure that we ought to take a look at two groups that I have so far mentioned only as part of the general framework of the San Francisco population in the 1850's. The two groups were adversaries, and their interaction did more than anything else to change the face of the city by calling forth the vigilance committee in 1856. They were the Know-Nothings and the Catholics, and both must be understood in context.

♦ II ♦

Let us return to the spring of 1851, when Geary's decision not to run for reelection as mayor opened the way for competitive politics in the city. After the Whigs and Democrats had held their primaries and conventions, a new element entered the political arena. Shortly before the election, a group of prominent individuals, including Geary, large landowners such as Samuel Brannan, Joseph L. Folsom, and William D. Howard, and a number of merchants, tried to put together an independent ticket headed by Alexander Sibley, a commission merchant. Sixty-three individuals and business firms, claiming the support of "four hundred others," signed a public appeal in which they stated their belief in an independent ticket, which could remain disengaged from state and national politics and could concentrate exclusively on the interests of the city. Of the sixty-three signers, thirty-one can be identified from the contemporary city directories, enough to make it apparent that this was an upper-crust effort. More than half of those identified belonged to the major business occupations of the city—the importing sector, retail merchants, and bankers. Lawyers formed the largest group (eight), and there were five importers, five merchants, and four bankers or brokers. However, the backers of this independent effort were unable to test the electoral prowess of their candidates because the ticket withdrew a few days before the election.[11]

The independent ticket that grew out of the 1851 vigilance committee owed something to this spring precedent. But whereas only sixty-three names had publicly stood behind the independent effort in the spring, an impressive 373 endorsements were mustered by the organizers of the fall ticket. More than half the signers and firms can be identified from the directories, indicating that this, too, was an upper-level movement. Importers and merchants predominated among the sponsors, with, respectively, seventy-two and seventy-six of their numbers represented. Together, these two groups accounted for at least 40 percent of the total signers, and 70 percent of those who could be identified.[12]

Another political petition appeared just before the 1852 election. This time the cause was a "Union ticket," which consisted mainly of men who had been nominated by their respective parties, and four who were not. The presentation of the ticket followed the pattern that had emerged in the two 1851 elections. A few days before the election, an appeal signed by prominent citizens appeared in the press. It urged the voters to discard the tired distinctions of party and vote for the best men, that is, the men endorsed by the signers. A total of 119 people signed the appeal. Nearly 69 percent are identifiable and, as in the fall of 1851, merchants and importers led the way, with 30 percent and 17 percent, respectively, of the total number of signers belonging to these two groups (68 percent of the identified signers).[13]

There was another effort in 1853. This time the banner was "Anti-Extension Reform," the main stimulus for the effort being opposition to the bill to extend the shoreline farther into the bay. Although the bill had failed in the legislature that year, the forces of Democratic Governor John Bigler were expected to introduce it again at the next session. A total of ninety-eight persons, of whom fifty-eight can be identified, signed a public appeal that stressed the baneful effects of party politics. Once again, importers and merchants led the list, accounting together for 44 percent of the signers.[14]

In sum, nonpartisan politics had become an established part of the political life of San Francisco by 1853. The issues might change, but the form remained the same. The obvious question follows: how effective was this form of politics at the polls? Since the nonpartisan tickets tended to be a conglomeration of Whigs, Democrats, and self-proclaimed independents, no precise answer is really possible; but it appears that, with the exception of the ticket growing out of the vigilance committee, the nonpartisan efforts did not fare well. By my calculations, that ticket controlled roughly 890 votes, or about 15 percent of the total cast. The 1852 Union ticket was even less successful. It was able to control 482 votes, about 6 percent of the total. In 1853, because of the large number of tickets, the situation was a bit more complicated. But it does not appear that Anti-Extension Reform, by itself, counted for much in the minds of the voters. The Whigs who were also on the independent ticket ran, on the average, about 13 percent ahead of Whigs who did not receive the independent endorsement. On the face of it, this indicates strength reminiscent of the 15 percent the vigilance ticket had gathered. But there is another aspect to consider: Anti-Extension Reform candidates who were not on the Whig ticket ran, on the average, 26 percent behind Whigs who had the independent endorsement. On balance, then, being a Whig counted for about twice as much as being an independent. Receiving the independent endorsement helped a Whig, but not possessing the Whig endorsement hurt an independent twice as much. So it appears that, although political nonpartisanship developed quickly in San Francisco, it was not the road to electoral success. Through 1853, the business-oriented sponsors did not have much to show for their efforts.[15]

The willingness of a core of the city's upper crust to raise repeated challenges to the city's standing political order probably reflected the fact that San Francisco, as we have seen, had not been good to them. It is a time-honored American tradition that troubled businessmen turn to politics for help. But there was another source, I think, of their willingness to approach politics outside the traditional categories. That source was more national in scope. During the early 1850's, in state after state, the differences between the two established parties were becoming increasingly indistinct. This had a profound implication for the political system of the nation as a whole.

Politics in general, as David Potter has pointed out, is less concerned with the attainment of one value than with the reconciliation of a number of them. But if the process of reconciliation goes too far, then the existing political parties lose their distinctiveness, their meaning, and their value. In that case, political expression has to find other channels. This was precisely the national political situation in the early 1850's. Michael Holt, a perceptive student of pre–Civil War American politics, describes the situation:

> The two party system collapsed because Whig and Democratic voters lost faith in their old parties as adequate vehicles for effective political action, and they lost faith because social, economic, and political developments between 1848 and 1853 blurred the line that divided Whigs from Democrats on a host of issues. Voter loyalty had always depended on the popular perception that the parties were different from each other, that they offered real alternatives to hostile voters in elections, and that because of that choice, men had a real chance to control government. Once agreement, or seeming consensus, on issues had replaced conflict between the parties at the national, state, and local levels, therefore, the ties that bound voters to their old parties frayed and often completely snapped.

In a nutshell, "What destroyed the second party system was consensus, not conflict."[16]

The disintegration of the older parties, which would have occurred some time or other in San Francisco in any event as part of the national process, began there sooner because the city had been settled when it was. For in antebellum America, as one of its historians has written, "local and state politics touched the lives of people more often and more directly than national politics": in nineteenth-century cities, there was always a strong undercurrent of feeling that local politics ought to reflect exclusively local concerns and that national issues ought not to have a place in city elections. This was the mood in San Francisco. As one paper noted before the 1852 election, "On the Presidential question the community is fairly divided, but on no other single issue will there be a strict party vote."[17]

The interest in local issues naturally tended to be strongest in a city's formative years, when there was a host of problems that were obvious to everyone. Streets had to be paved, sewers constructed, wharves built; public health and safety had to be at least marginally ensured. As Gunther Barth has put it, the residents of instant cities wanted "instant government." A consensus emerged in which there was fundamental agreement on two key propositions: first, the government ought to do these things as quickly as possible; second, the government ought to do these things as cheaply as possible.[18]

In many frontier cities in the nineteenth century, a kind of bipartisan boosterism based on these two somewhat inconsistent propositions emerged. Antebellum political parties could rarely be accused of consistency. As one student of antebellum politics has written, "The major parties in both party systems put forth and supported at different levels of government a bewildering array of policies that were at times inconsistent, contradictory, and at odds with their heralded principles." So, even though a basic tenet of the national Democratic party was that the state ought not do too much in the way of internal improvements, on the local scene that doctrine was pure heresy. In Pittsburgh, for example, as Holt explains, the major political battles concerned "the extent and location of public improvements in the city." That there should be improvements financed by the public was taken for granted. In Chicago, the local Democrats pushed internal improvements with a fervor that would have gladdened the heart of Henry Clay. Mass bipartisan meetings to demand harbor improvements and canal construction were a staple of life in the early years of the city.[19]

By the same token, with an inconsistency that was only rarely acknowledged, city residents constantly complained about the costs of the improvements they were demanding. Irritation with the cost of government issued in periodic attempts to pinch pennies whenever possible. Kansas City at the end of the 1850's reduced the salary of the important city engineer to the princely sum of $200 a year. Milwaukee officials, like their counterparts in San Francisco, were constantly accused of being spenders without reason. So, as a result of what Michael Frisch calls this "low-tax ideology," cities constantly had to go into debt to make ends meet. In the early 1840's, a relatively small city like Richmond, Virginia, was spending almost half its entire budget to pay the interest on its debt, and in the 1850's, a larger place like Chicago had a floating debt of over a quarter of a million dollars. But in city after city, the fact of municipal indebtedness, which had been spawned by a broad consensus on the duties of government, was regarded as an indication of pervasive corruption, and it increased the desire of the men of commerce to attempt alternate political arrangements. The fact of political consensus paradoxically led to political splintering.[20]

City politics are thus apt to be consensual for a period after the city's founding. San Francisco's formative years happened to occur at a time when national politics itself was becoming more consensual, and thus the consensual tendency was reinforced in the gold rush port. But the national consensus presaged a breakdown of politics as usual, and the appearance of independent tickets in San Francisco from 1851 on indicated that the breakdown was well under way there within three years after the discovery of gold.

♦ III ♦

The Know-Nothings in San Francisco must be understood, I think, in the context of this type of independent, nonpartisan politics. The party was much more than an anti-Catholic phenomenon. It was that, of course, but, more fundamentally, it was the continuation, by another name, of the nonpartisan efforts of 1851–53. The strong affinity between the 1851–53 efforts and the Know-Nothings was evident in the name assumed by the new party. Although it was called "Americans" or "Know-Nothings" in the press, it called itself the "Citizens' Reform Ticket." This designation located it squarely in the nonpartisan tradition. The affinity was also evident in the manner in which the "Citizens' Reform Ticket" was presented to the public, for the Know-Nothings simply imitated the practices of the earlier independents.

Those tickets had been put together by a group of men consulting privately and had been published in the press only a few days before the election. The Know-Nothings adopted the same procedure in 1854. Both the Democrats and the Whigs held primaries and nominating conventions during August and published the lists of their candidates before the end of that month. During the time that such normal pre-election activity was taking place, there was some speculation in the press that "the admixture which has stirred up the political cauldron in the Atlantic states" was secretly organizing in San Francisco. However, there was no definite information available on the progress or scope of this organization.[21]

The election was scheduled for September 6. On September 1, the newspapers carried announcements of a "Citizens' Reform Ticket," headed by a merchant named Lucien Hermann. Hermann happened to be a Roman Catholic, however, and this precipitated something of a crisis within the ranks of the new independent movement. On September 5, the eve of the election, Hermann was dropped from the ticket and replaced by Samuel P. Webb, a man who was living in San Francisco after a stint as mayor of Salem, Massachusetts. Hermann's disgruntled supporters hastily patched together a "Cuidado" ticket, with Hermann the mayoral nominee, but this ticket proved to be a negligible factor in the actual voting. The fact that a Catholic such as Hermann could have been nominated at all by the Know-Nothings for the highest city office indicates that anti-foreigner or anti-Catholic attitudes were not the overriding reasons for the organization of the new party.[22]

This is not to say that those attitudes were absent from San Francisco during the period. Historians have long recognized that gold rush California spawned a number of antiforeigner activities, which were directed mainly against Mexicans and Chinese. As we have seen, an anti-Australian impulse was an integral part of the 1851 vigilance committee. Privately, anti-foreigner sentiments had been circulating in San Francisco almost from the beginning of the American occupation. As early as 1850, San Francisco merchant Charles Hosmer wrote to a relative about a foreign miners' tax recently imposed by the legislature: "The tax upon foreigners in the mines is likely to produce some trouble (*but the tax is right*), and they will be *obliged* to submit. The universal Yankee nation is here, and their rights there are none to dispute."[23]

The phrase "universal Yankee nation" points to an aspect of early San Francisco, and the West in general, that is relevant here. The westward movement, with its centrifugal and frankly acquisitive tendencies, never sat that well with what was left of the New England mind. To the true New England mentality, which believed in order, stability, and regularity, the movement west could have only one real purpose—the re-creation of New England. The president of Harvard, Edward Everett, though he could not stem the move to California, counseled those bound for the Pacific to "take the Bible in one hand and your New England civilization in the other." His advice was heeded by many. One of the leading Protestant divines in the new city of San Francisco, Timothy Dwight Hunt, made no secret of his goal to "make California the Massachusetts of the Pacific." Stephen Webb, another Massachusetts native, who became the Know-Nothing mayor, had the same chauvinistic attitude: "Everywhere over our surface, in New England fashion, arise the spires of churches and schoolhouses. All the influences which have followed it [San Francisco] and crowned it with glory are New England influences."[24]

Within this tidy transplanted New England version, there was certainly very little room for foreigners (one cannot very well call them immigrants in this context, since all who came to San Francisco—New Englanders included—were immigrants). But they could hardly be ignored. The gold rush period was also the period of the heaviest immigration, in proportion to the existing population, that America has ever experienced. In the decade after 1845, 1.2 million of these immigrants were Irish. In the letters of the transplanted New Englanders and others, immigrants—that is, foreign-born immigrants—were often mentioned in the context of politics and associated (rightly, as we have seen) with the "low class" Democratic party. Writing of the 1851 elections, William K. Weston said, "All the artifacts that the 'bartenders' and 'subtreasurers' of New York, Baltimore, Philadelphia, New Orleans, and New South Wales, aided by the convicts of Van Dieman's land, could work and devise, could not secure the Locofocos victory." Similarly, at the end of 1851, an outgoing Whig alderman wrote that the new

Democratic officials were "a set of Locos, among whom was *an Irish drayman who can scarcely write his own name*!"[25]

The Irish in San Francisco, like their counterparts in most other antebellum American cities, tended to be manual laborers, often on the wharves and docks. In Boston in the 1840's, almost half of the city's Irish-born were unskilled day laborers. In New York during the 1850's, almost three-quarters of the immigrant ferrymen in the harbor were Irish. In Kingston, New York, three-quarters of the Irish population were unskilled. In Chicago, the Irish lived in the second ward by the river, near the wharves and a canal construction project, and more than half of them labored as unskilled workers. In Milwaukee, the Irish were, as sociologists like to say, overrepresented at the bottom of the occupational hierarchy, and they quickly formed their own ethnic enclaves, parishes, and militia and fire companies. In San Francisco, they generally clustered together around the waterfront, where most of the unskilled jobs were to be had.[26]

The reason for the Irish concentration at the bottom of the San Francisco economic pyramid was twofold. First and most obviously, the Irish, being an agricultural peasantry, did not have the skills that would have allowed them to rise quickly in an urban and commercial society. As a sympathetic historian has written, "Irish immigrants were probably the least sophisticated Europeans entering the United States in the first half of the nineteenth century." And they did not have any connections. This is a less appreciated but just as important reason. Whereas most Americans set themselves up as San Francisco merchants, using contacts—sometimes very flimsy but still a thread—that they had developed in the East, the Irish were entirely on their own.[27]

In all American cities, "respectable" people looked upon the Irish with distaste. They were regularly lampooned on the New York stage, where the "drunken Irish buffoon" could always break up the audience. The Irish (and the Germans who arrived at these shores during the same period) were, of course, no strangers to liquor, and they had the extreme misfortune to land in the post-alcoholic republic. By the 1840's, drinking was no longer a patriotic duty. Spirits had become demon rum, and temperance was an integral part of the pietistic Yankee morality that shaped so much of antebellum high culture. By 1851, the American Tract Society had flooded the land with over five million temperance pamphlets. In such an atmosphere, denunciations of "KING ROTGUT" easily spilled over into condemnations of "IRISH GROG SHOPS." There was more to it, of course, than their lack of skills and their drinking habits. As Lawrence J. McCaffrey has quipped, "If the Irish had stepped off the boat wearing linen suits and patent leather shoes, waving the American flag in one hand and a university degree in the other, they might have been considered more respectable. But they still would have been labeled enemy aliens." For most of them were Catholics, and I shall have something to say about that a bit later.[28]

As was the case in the rest of the nation, the "respectable" people of San Francisco did not roll out the welcome mat for the Irish. For instance, speaking of her next-door neighbor, one woman, the wife of a drayman, wrote, "They are low Irish, so we keep just as clear from them as we possibly can." Two years later, living in a different house, this same woman complained, "We have nothing to say to our neighbors on either side. . . . They are Irish, and to say that they are intemperate, liars, and thieves, etc., would not be exaggerating." In April 1856, she reported "a grand flare in the street" between two Irish women. "Mrs. E. invited Mrs. H. to settle it by fighting, but she backed out, knowing she would get beaten—so they only brandished case knives and used tall language in so loud a voice that we could not help hearing a part." Fortunately, this appalled native of Long Island concluded, "All we have to do is let them alone and they will leave us to ourselves—for they see that we are not of them." She was able to say this despite the fact that "Mrs. E." was a Mrs. Edwards, "the same one that assisted me when I was sick."[29]

The Know-Nothing party in San Francisco fed upon these anti-Irish notions and served to sharpen them. As one paper drily remarked, "The Know-Nothings appear to have no particular affinity for the Broderick Democrats, and there will be no love lost there." After the 1854 election, laborer Thomas T. Seward gleefully wrote his wife, "There is one thing certain—foreigners won't have much show here the next twelve months. Webb, the mayor-elect, says that if there is any vacancy, and he cannot get *Americans* to fill them, he will leave them go vacated." Another laborer, Milton Hall, was somewhat annoyed that the Know-Nothing victory had not been more complete:

> The Know-Nothings swept all before them, and I am glad of it. The old fogey parties of Whigs and Democrats was nothing, only in name, and it was time they was broken up and turn their attention to something for the good and preservation of the country, for if they do not stir the premises, priestcraft will get a hold, and once got the D——l could not move them . . . by fraud and deception they got one Irishman in the common council and he has a right to appoint policemen, which he did, and both *rank pats* . . . my vote was challenged by a rank Irishman, and I had to swear it in.[30]

By the beginning of 1855, the following jingle was making the rounds of the city:

> The Know-Nothings have done the job
> Wide-awake boys acted accordin'
> If you want to get a lick
> Just say you're a mick,
> And they'll kick you on the other side of the Jordan.

The fact that the above letters were written by laborers says a great deal about the dual character of San Francisco Know-Nothingism. On the one hand, the Know-Nothings were "non-partisan," but political, businessmen-reformers. On the other hand, anti-Catholicism gave the political efforts of the city's businessmen an appeal beyond the business sector. For, as R. A. Burchell put it in his book on the nineteenth-century San Francisco Irish, "The Reformation was still a live event for the nineteenth century mind, which regarded the event with either disgust or adulation." The Know-Nothing victory in 1854 demonstrated that the combination of these two elements could be politically potent.[31]

♦ IV ♦

We have now arrived at the central issue separating the Irish from their hosts. A walk close to the city's waterfront, where a good number of the Irish resided in the 1850's, would have made the difference quite clear: on Vallejo Street stood St. Francis of Assisi Church; on Market Street there was St. Patrick's; and on the corner of California and Dupont, the cornerstone of St. Mary's Cathedral was laid in 1853. Where the Protestants had ministers, the Irish had priests.[32]

The history of the religious tensions between Protestants and Catholics in nineteenth-century America has been written, and it has been written well. Most students of American history know that when Samuel F. B. Morse was not inventing the telegraph, he was writing anti-Catholic polemics, that the fraudulent *Awful Disclosures of Maria Monk* was gospel truth for fearful Protestants, and that mobs stormed and burned convents and churches in the 1830's and 1840's. And thanks to John F. Kennedy, most people now know that there was a time in Boston when employment notices carried the sentence, "No Irish need apply." The writings of Richard Hofstadter and David Brion Davis, among others, have helped us understand that the hostile reception accorded Irish Catholics exposed deep and fundamental tensions and fears in American society. In that vein, I should simply like to offer one set of observations that I think might help clarify what happened in San Francisco.[33]

To be a native American in the antebellum nineteenth century meant that, rhetorically at least, you had no doubts you were the new Adam riding the mighty westward course of empire. What is less appreciated, I think, is that to be a Catholic in the same period in America meant that you had, if possible, even fewer doubts about yourself than the native Americans had about themselves. You were a member of an institution that had existed for almost two millennia. That institution had seen empires rise and fall, potentates come and go. America, far from being the last best hope of mankind (the church, after all, was the only hope), was simply one more land to be conquered. To be an American Catholic meant that you had a pretty fundamental confidence that, when the dust had settled, America would have been converted. As early as 1843, citing the founding of Holy Cross College in Worcester, Massachusetts, the Catholic Boston *Pilot* predicted that "Catholicism will obtain an ascendancy over all the minds in the land." Marcus Lee Hansen caught this conviction perfectly in his quip, "The oldest institution in the western world was not going to revise its program because a few Yankees looked on it with disfavor."[34]

In significant ways the church's program *was* at variance with the standard American vision. Nativists were not whistling in the dark when they raised the question of whether one could be both a Catholic and an American, as those terms were understood before the Civil War. American religion and politics, for instance, were both based on a loose congregationalism, whereas nineteenth-century Catholicism was rigidly hierarchical in its own structure and generally reactionary and monarchist in its political leanings. The American bishops had fought incipient congregationalism, disguised as lay control of parishes (trusteeism) in the 1820's; when the principle reared its head once more in the late 1840's and early 1850's, they were ready again. There were ugly scenes in Chicago, for example, when the local bishop tried to wrest control of some church property from a group of nuns. In another Chicago quarrel, this one over a church deed, the bishop allegedly attempted to have the church raised four feet off the ground to prevent the laity from getting into it. Also, where the standard American creed preached self-reliance and the worth of the individual, nineteenth-century Catholicism rested upon an extraordinarily negative view of human nature. As one devotional manual put it, "The corruption of our nature, the perpetual rebellion of human passions, the constant lusting of the flesh against the spirit, puts us in the necessity of offering a continual violence against ourselves."[35]

These surface incompatibilities became more apparent in the early 1850's, at precisely the time San Francisco was being settled by both native Yankees and Irish Catholics. It was not entirely unreasonable for nativists to suspect that the Catholics were preparing to launch their long-expected American offensive. The Irish were becoming naturalized, and in those places where they waited until naturalization to vote, they were beginning to vote in large numbers. Given the rather exalted position of the bishop in Catholic theology, and also the attempts of Bishop Hughes in New York to start a Catholic party in politics in the 1840's, who could say with certainty that the bishops were not secretly instructing the ignorant peasants how to vote? After all, Hughes was the kind of man who could tell Orestes Brownson, "I will suffer no man in my diocese that I cannot control. I will either put him down, or he shall put me down." Hughes and the bishops like him were, in fact, in the process of becoming bosses in their own right. One could say that the ecclesiastical machine was perfected long before the political machine was, and the machine was getting its own wigwams (as Tammany's original New York headquarters had been called). Large buildings, churches and schools, mute testimony to the Catholic determination not to go back to where they had come from, seemed to be going up almost everywhere. There was a notable pickup in Catholic construction during the early 1850's.[36]

Education was a particular source of controversy. All sorts of attempts to come to an accommodation on the issue of Bible reading in the public schools foundered—often simply because most Protestants did not see that a problem existed. They were content in their illusion that, so long as the schools did not teach Methodism and Presbyterianism, they were nonsectarian. They did not realize, or preferred not to realize, that the schools taught a kind of generalized Protestantism.[37]

Those few Protestants who acknowledged the true state of affairs also ran into trouble. They tried to adopt the policy of having the Bible read in the schools without comment. But for two very specific reasons, this was unacceptable to Catholics. First, Catholic theology reserved exclusively to the *magisterium* of the church the right authoritatively to interpret Scripture. As a priest put it: "The Catholic church tells her children that they must be taught their religion by AUTHORITY. . . . The Protestant sects say, read the Bible, judge for yourselves. The Bible is read in the public schools, the children allowed to judge for themselves. The Protestant principle is therefore acted upon, slyly inculcated, and the schools are sectarian."[38] Within the framework of then-current Catholic theology, he was entirely correct.

Second, in 1844, Pope Gregory XVI, in a letter to Italian bishops, had prohibited Catholics from using vernacular Bibles that had not been approved by the bishops and did not have explanatory notes. (Explanatory notes in Catholic Bibles proved that Protestantism was heretical, and explanatory notes in Protestant Bibles proved that the Pope was the Antichrist!) In America, the authorized version was the Douay Bible, which contained a host of explanatory notes. Therefore Catholic children, even if they were permitted to read their own Bible, had to read notes and comment, since both were right there on the very pages of the text.[39]

The upshot was that in the early 1850's, the Catholic bishops of America deliberately and consciously adopted a ghetto strategy. They determined to build a set of parallel institutions. The 1852 Council of Baltimore told all bishops to "see that schools are established in connection with the churches." And in private, Hughes fumed that the public schools were hotbeds of "Socialism, Red Republicanism, Universalism, Infidelity, Deism, Atheism, and Pantheism." Three thousand miles distant, Bishop Alemany chimed in with a complaint that "the great emigration brings Protestantism and immorality." For him, they were two sides of the same coin. So San Francisco Catholics adopted their own ghetto strategy. As soon as a Protestant orphan asylum began to be organized, they initiated their own. As the bishop said, "If we have not a Catholic institution to maintain our orphans, many of our Catholic children . . . will receive a Protestant education."[40]

I should like, in concluding this section, to speculate that Americans and Catholics inevitably came into conflict with each other for two reasons. First, they were both, on the surface, totally sure of themselves. There was no room for compromise. In the 1850's neither the American Adam nor the bark of Peter really wanted to accommodate the other. A Protestant newspaper in San Francisco was not entirely off the mark when it complained that a Catholic school would teach every pupil that "every child outside of that church, every playmate it should meet in the open school, was a little heretic, to be shunned like the devil himself." Second, the leaders of both groups were afraid of the seductive power of the other group. As Tocqueville had noticed, at a deeper level than rhetoric, the Americans were afraid of the individualism they so grandly celebrated. They were willing, even eager, to give themselves over to a larger mass that promised security. The Catholics had a Mass that did just that, and promised security in spades. The celebrated conversions of Orestes Brownson and Isaac Hecker and (later in California) former governor Peter Burnett, might have been straws in the wind. Catholicism might indeed expose the fundamental futility of the endless chase after wealth that was American society. In places where Americans were unsure of themselves, they had to resist Catholicism with a vengeance. And San Francisco, where the dream of wealth had drifted away in the billowing fog, was a place where Americans were very unsure of themselves. On the Catholic side, the antebellum bishops were afraid, to put it bluntly, that the laity would become Americanized. They were afraid that the laity would be seduced by the seemingly limitless opportunities beckoning to those whose only other alternative had been to stay at home and watch the potatoes turn black. The ogre of trusteeism, which surfaced again in the 1850's, showed the bishops what a fragile hold they really had on their flock. A ghetto strategy and a fortress mentality would prove useful tools to keep the faithful faithful. If nativists had not existed, John Hughes and his fellow bishops would have been forced to invent them.[41]

♦ V ♦

In San Francisco, as elsewhere in the north, the specific *locus* of religious controversy was the school system. Northern common school reformers before the Civil War always regarded themselves, as Mary McDougall Gordon has written, as being "Patriots and Christians," and in San Francisco the first schools had a distinctly religious emphasis.

Even as early as 1847, when only a few children played on the muddy streets of San Francisco among the arriving pioneers, the second issue of the *Star*, the city's first newspaper, called for "some immediate action on the part of the citizens . . . in reference to the establishment of a school." The editor said that he had "counted the other day about forty children from the ages of five to thirteen, in the different streets at play, who ought, instead of wasting their time in idleness, to be at school." The paper proposed that private subscriptions be used to finance a school and that a board of trustees be elected to run it. This appeal was more or less ignored, but a few months later a private school was opened by a recently arrived Mormon named William Marston. This school functioned for about a year with an enrollment of about twenty-five students.[42]

In the fall of 1847, the town council appointed a committee to build a schoolhouse. The school was completed by December, but since the committee had neglected to provide some of the necessaries, notably books, students, and a teacher, the schoolhouse was not immediately of any use. In February, however, the council ordered a general election to choose school trustees, on whom would fall the responsibility of putting the schoolhouse to use. The election was held, the trustees were chosen, and a teacher was hired. (William Marston's application was rejected when one of the trustees discovered that it was studded with misspellings and grammatical errors.) The school was formally opened in April. Tuition was charged, but only for those who could pay; for the rest, the school was free.

This school lasted only one month—after which the remaining handful of students, the teacher, and the single remaining trustee joined the other trustees and virtually the rest of the city in the rush for the gold fields. When the furor of the gold rush died down, San Francisco followed the lead of most of the eastern commercial cities in two respects. First, it continued to place emphasis on formal schooling. Second, it initially tried to satisfy the demands of formal schooling by elaborating a network of charity and entrepreneurial schools. The first educational institutions to appear were private schools, which paralleled the one previously run by Marston. The most successful of these was a school housed in the basement of a Baptist church, which was conducted by a former schoolteacher from Massachusetts, John C. Pelton. Other schools were soon opened, including two connected with Episcopal churches and one connected with a Catholic church. In addition, there was at least one school, and probably more, not connected with any particular church. In 1850, Colonel Thomas J. Nevins, who had come to San Francisco as an agent for the American Tract Society, opened a daily school and a Sunday school.[43]

As had happened before the gold rush, the council took action on education only after these private schools were functioning. Pelton's school did not charge tuition, and by 1850 he was finding it very difficult to keep the school going. He petitioned the council to assume the expenses and make it a free public school. The council was willing to take over the school, but it favored the earlier scheme of charging tuition for those who were able to pay. Eventually the council reversed itself and struck out in the direction of Horace Mann and New England. In April 1850, it adopted "An Ordinance for the Regulation of the Common Schools." This was an ambitious-sounding plan, but the schools were a long time coming. When John Swett became the principal of the Rincon School two years later, he described the school as containing "neither blackboard nor map." It had only "a small table for the teacher and one rickety chair." The school board was not overly generous to the pupils either, for "the children furnished their own ink bottles, their pens, and their papers." School officials like Pelton had to appear periodically before various city agencies to plead for funding to keep the schools going.[44]

In 1851 the legislature passed a bill organizing public schools throughout the state. As had been the case in the city, the legislature decided to use the existing private schools as the nucleus of the public school system. The act stated: "If a school district be formed by the enterprise of a religious society, in which all the branches of education in the District schools shall be taught . . . such schools shall be allowed to receive a compensation from the Public School Fund, in proportion to the number of its pupils." Although the State Fund apparently existed more on paper and in the fond wishes of the State Superintendent of Public Schools than anywhere else and this section of the act therefore could not have any real effect on the Catholic schools operating in San Francisco, some evangelists in the city objected. Referring to the immigrant sisters who made up most of the staff of Catholic primary schools in those days, one paper said, "It is plainly impossible for teachers from Belgium or France, or any other foreign country, to educate our daughters as they ought to be educated." At the next session of the legislature, the earlier act was replaced by one decreeing that any school receiving state money must be "free from all denominational and sectarian influence whatsoever." This made the question of funding the Catholic schools in the city moot.[45]

Unfortunately, the legislative records are too meager to sustain an investigation of what interests were responsible for the change in 1852, but in 1853 the legislature again changed its mind—this time under clear pressure—and reverted to the funding arrangements it had decreed in 1851. The Catholic bishop, Joseph Sadoc Alemany, had written to the Superintendent of Public Instruction, Democrat John Marvin, and requested the change: "I would respectfully ask you the kindness of using your influence toward a pro-rate appropriation of the collected funds for the number of children taught in these Catholic schools." Marvin obliged the bishop, and in his report to the legislature he stated his reasons:

> A considerable number of students are taught in churches for the want of school houses. They are for the most part in charge of the pastors of the same, from the choice of the parents of the children. This is more particularly the case with regard to the Catholic population of

the state. It appears that in these schools all the ordinary branches of a common school education are taught, and in order that this class of school may receive their portion of the school money, some change in the school law is required.

The legislature obliged Marvin and agreed to fund the Catholic schools.[46]

Not surprisingly, San Francisco's Catholics were strongly in favor of the funding, mainly because they objected to the Protestant flavor of the city's public school system. They particularly objected to the reading of the King James Bible, which was required at the close of each school day and for a more extended period every Monday morning. One Catholic parent asserted that a public school teacher had whipped his son for refusing to participate in these exercises. The Catholics also objected to some of the textbooks that were used in the public schools—including a reading text that contained the phrase "marshalled monks." These complaints were fairly typical of Catholic objections to American public schools in general. Catholics in New York used to complain that some of the public school textbooks "abounded in false and contemptuous passages regarding the Catholic Church." In Philadelphia in 1834, the bishop had successfully lobbied the school board to have a life of Luther removed from the public school reading list. Catholic charges that their children were whipped for refusing to read out of the King James Bible also cropped up in the city of brotherly love. (Protestants, for their part, professed to be appalled at the influence "the dictation of Jesuit bachelors" had on the education in Catholic schools!)[47]

Soon after the passage of the 1853 law in California, there were three Catholic schools, called "ward" schools, as opposed to the regular public or "district" schools, operating in the city and serving roughly one-third of the total number of school children in San Francisco. These schools received state funds, channeled through the offices of the County Assessor, Democrat James W. Stillman. The Catholics also claimed that their schools were entitled to a share of the city school funds. By threatening to withhold from the city its share of the state funds, which were also channeled through his office, Stillman secured for the Catholic schools some of this city revenue as well. In 1854 and 1855, then, San Francisco witnessed the strange situation of a Know-Nothing city government funding Catholic schools.[48]

Just how Catholic the ward schools were, or how Protestant the district schools were, is not easy to determine, despite the complaints of abuses on record. On the whole, the judgment of a recent historian, that "the San Francisco school system was less aggressively Protestant than some eastern ones," is probably correct. It does seem clear, for instance, that the teachers in the district schools voluntarily began to drop the Bible-reading exercises. John Swett later wrote that the teachers "thought that under the conditions of a cosmopolitan city, in which there were large numbers of children of Catholics and Jews, it was an unwise policy to continue the reading of the Bible as a school exercise." Lee S. Dolson suggests that the teachers might have had less ideological reasons for this concession, since "a possible shrinkage of enrollment, among those offended by religious exercises, could result in a consolidation of classes and losses of teaching positions." Whatever the precise reason, reading of the Bible in the city schools was quietly dropped at approximately the time the ward schools began receiving state assistance. On the other hand, at least some Catholic teachers were dismissed from the district schools at this same time by the City Board of Education.[49]

It is also difficult to ascertain what proportion of Catholic children in the city attended the Catholic schools. Jay Dolan has estimated that in antebellum New York, about 20 percent of the Catholic children were in Catholic schools; the figure was probably about the same in San Francisco. In the ward schools, Catholic children were required to be at school at 8:00 A.M. From that hour until 9:00 A.M., they received religious instruction. At 9:00 A.M. all non-Catholic students (there were approximately 100 attending the Catholic schools) were required to arrive, and normal instruction would begin. I have not been able to discover conclusively to what degree religious training was carried out during the rest of the day. One correspondent of the *Herald* insisted, "The Sisters [the nuns who taught in some of the ward schools] do not make proselytizing any part of their business, nor do they try to crush a Catholic translation of the Bible on children of other creeds. But they try to counteract any predisposition to evil that they may find in a child." In the same vein, a correspondent of the *Bulletin* stated that a ward school for girls was well attended because the parents, "Catholics or Protestants," simply wanted their girls in such a school. This writer maintained that there was "no religious instruction given during the time the Board of Education has prescribed for secular education."[50]

Others in the city were quick to see ill consequences. One person wrote to the *Bulletin* and argued with Know-Nothing flavor that the Sisters could not help being biased:

> Those "Sisters"—who are put forth by the priests and other dignitaries in this city, as qualified to teach our American youth—are mostly of *Irish, French, Italian*, or *Mexican* birth and education. What education they have has been imparted in monasteries and nunneries, in circumstances exceedingly unfavorable to the enlargement and liberal development of the mind, and even a correct understanding of our *free American system of education.*

The *Pacific*, an evangelical Protestant weekly, argued that the issue was not merely whether the ward schools specifically taught religion:

> It needs not that any extraordinary effort be made by teachers, or fellow pupils, to make a few children thus situated in a school, feel a sense of degradation most keenly. The effect would be the same in the minds of a few Catholic children in a large Protestant school, where there were exercises in which they could not freely join. To be singular is disagreeable even to grown people, but to children it is intolerable.

This was very close to what the Catholics had argued in 1853![51]

In 1855, the legislature, spurred by the Know-Nothing city government, repealed the 1853 statute. The new school law forbade any further division of the school fund. The same legislature also passed a law granting the city of San Francisco a new charter, and in May 1855 a new set of major city officials was duly elected. Minor officials, including a newly organized and ward-based Board of Education, were not chosen until the regular county elections in the fall. Since the ward schools were under the jurisdiction of the county, and since the old City Board of Education remained in something of a limbo throughout the summer, the ward schools continued to operate from May until after the fall elections. Thus they functioned for four months after they supposedly had been legislated into oblivion. The Board of Education elected in the fall was equally divided between Democrats and Know-Nothings. In case of a tie, the mayor, a Democrat, was entitled to cast the deciding vote.[52]

The Board invited the functioning ward schools to come under its jurisdiction and thus to form one common school system in the city. This invitation was extended by unanimous vote. The Board also appointed a committee of three Democrats and one Know-Nothing to examine applications for teaching positions in the common school system. Common school teachers were generally appointed for a term of one year. They had to demonstrate that they were "of good moral character and of sufficient learning and ability," and that they possessed "a competent aptness and fitness for teaching." The teachers from the ward schools (all of them men) appeared at the examination, but the nuns who taught in them did not. After the completion of the formal examination, two of the Democrats moved that the committee go to the convent and examine the nuns. They stated that they were also applicants for positions in the schools. On a straight party vote, the entire Board approved the suggestion. "My God, has it come to this!" exclaimed one Know-Nothing sympathizer, "that in San Francisco we are compelled to be at the beck of 'Lady Superiors'?" (Perhaps the visibility in Catholic institutions like schools and hospitals of women who were busy with other things besides bearing children was especially distasteful to some of the rabid Know-Nothings.)[53]

The examination was held at the convent. During the course of the questioning, it became clear that the nuns would consent to teach only classes composed exclusively of girls. When the Board learned this, it quickly persuaded them to withdraw their applications. At the same time, the Board decided to hire a good number (variously reported at from nine to seventeen) of the ward school teachers. In order to absorb these men, some of the old district teachers were "reassigned"—which meant in fact that they were often discharged, because they were reassigned to schools that did not yet exist.[54]

The Know-Nothings on the Board of Education were upset at being forced to accept some of the Catholic teachers at the expense of some of the Protestant teachers. At the time that it had originally invited the ward schools to come under its jurisdiction, the Board had also been inclined to pay off the ward teachers for their summer work, even though the ward schools had ceased to exist legally in May. The Know-Nothings had been willing to go along with this peace offering. But after some of the ward teachers were hired for the common schools, the Know-Nothings changed their minds and began to agitate the question of paying the ward teachers for their summer work.[55]

This controversy tied up the Board for about a month, but at last they agreed to throw the whole matter to the courts by setting up a test case. One ward teacher, William Hammill, and one district teacher, John Swett, were ordered paid. The Board then appointed one Democrat and one Know-Nothing from its membership to argue the case for and against paying Hammill before a judge. This arrangement fell through when Hammill demanded his money immediately, and surreptitiously received it, rather than waiting for the case to be decided. After two more months of haggling, the Know-Nothings on the Board fell back to their original position and consented to the paying of the ward school teachers for the summer.[56]

But then the Common Council, which had to approve the appropriation, became entangled in the same arguments that had tied up the Board of Education. Suits and countersuits were threatened by the Democrats and Know-Nothings. The Know-Nothings argued again that the existence of the ward schools after May was illegal, and the Democrats countered that the ward schools had remained public schools until the fall. This controversy dragged on in the Common Council for more than a month and was extensively reported in the press. Finally, at the end of April, all of the suits were dropped, and the ward teachers were paid, as the Board of Education had originally resolved.[57]

The ward school affair heightened the discussion of religious matters in San Francisco, and, reflecting the trend of the times, it did much to create the climate by which the independent and nonpartisan efforts of the merchants could succeed under the Know-Nothing banner. The 1840's and 1850's were a volatile period in American religious history. Two events centering on a Catholic university in St. Louis illustrate how quickly religious tensions could become violent. The first one took place in 1844. Because of carelessness on the part of a custodian in the dissecting laboratory, a group of boys stumbled on a heap of cadavers in the yard outside St. Louis University. Word quickly spread throughout the city that the Jesuits, who directed the university, were torturing Protestants and bringing back the Inquisition. In short order, a mob invaded the laboratory and smashed a good amount of equipment. Ten years later, during an election, some Whig and Know-Nothing inspectors refused to let a few Irishmen vote. When a scuffle ensued, one of the Irishmen stabbed a boy. Shortly thereafter, a nativist mob stormed through the Irish neighborhood and smashed houses at random. The violence ended only when the mayor persuaded a group of prominent Protestants to inspect the buildings of the university and verify that the Jesuits had not stashed an arsenal there.[58]

With this as the national backdrop, it is hardly surprising that, as the ward school affair was dying down, another religious controversy erupted in San Francisco. Enter, for an encore, the Holy Bible! Although the Bible had been quietly dropped from the public schools around 1853, during the time that the ward school system was being funded, the question of the reading of the Bible in the schools was reopened. At the end of November 1855, one person wrote to the *Bulletin*:

> The State knows no Protestant, no Romanist, no Jew, no Mahomedan. All that she knows, and all that she should know under the circumstances, is that the Bible—*and it alone*—teaches fully our duty to our fellow citizens: and this being the case, this book should not be excluded from our schools, but should be the first placed in the hands of the youth committed to her charge . . . none will be so silly to assert that an obedience to the precepts inculcated in the Bible can make other than honest and worthy inhabitants.[59]

This sort of evangelical sentiment was challenged, in both moderate and full-blown fashion, and gradually a middle-of-the-road position emerged. This consisted of admitting that the Bible could be sectarian and divisive, yet arguing that there was still enough common ground for it to be read without offense at school: "Let every teacher be perfectly free to open his school by reading a portion of the Scriptures and by prayer, or not, just as he chooses: neither required nor prevented. Let every teacher take whatever version he likes best. If he is a Catholic, then read a chapter from his own version of the word of God. If he be a Jew, then the same from the Old Scriptures." Or, as the matter was put by another correspondent, "We need the Bible in the schools because we are indebted to it for our civil and religious institutions and also because of its literary value . . . but I am opposed to any sectarian interpretation of its teachings—let all read and interpret for themselves."[60]

Full-fledged attacks on reading the Bible in the common schools came from James King, editor of the *Bulletin* and highly evangelical in other respects, and from John S. Hittell, who was a reporter for the *Chronicle*—two men who despised each other but were as one on this question. (King had bitterly assailed Hittell's impudence in writing a book entitled *The Evidence Against Christianity.*) Hittell staked out his position early in 1855 in a long letter to the *Chronicle* that attacked the major assumption of the Bible proponents. "I deny that the Bible is the sole foundation of morality," the letter declared. It then went on to connect the Bible and funding controversies:

> The use of the Bible in the schools aids the Catholics in securing a division of the public school money. They claim that it is contrary to the doctrines of their church, and the complaint is so reasonable that the skeptics and the indifferentists, who form a large portion of all American legislatures, very frequently take sides with the Catholics, and secure the latter their share of the school money. . . . If we exclude the Bible from the state schools, we deprive the Catholics of their chief pretext for a division of the public money, and increase our chances of maintaining the unity of the system.[61]

King argued that the Bible was sectarian: "It does teach *a* system of theology." He also, with his usual flair, agreed with Hittell: "If the Protestants insist on having their Bible read in the common schools, then we are in favor of Catholics, Jews, Mormons, Mahommedans, and Infidels each having their portion of the school fund allotted to them, or, in other words, *break up entirely the whole school system!*" In sum:

> So long as one solitary citizen—Catholic or Jew, or of any other faith—is desirous of using the common schools for the purposes of educating his children, and is deterred from doing so because of the introduction of the Bible as a class book therein, the rights of such a tax payer should be regarded, and the Bible not forced into the hands of his children. . . . The Common Schools, we take it, are not designed to teach religion at all, but simply to impart to the children the rudiments of learning as applied to the secular affairs of everyday life.[62]

Such attacks on the reading of the Bible in the schools did not go unanswered. In May 1856, a prominent Congregationalist minister, in a sermon that attracted considerable attention in San Francisco, strongly defended Bible-reading in public schools. In the homily, entitled "The Schools Demanded by the

Present Age," the Reverend Edgar Lacy complained that he had recently attended some of the school examinations, but "I did not hear the Great Cause of all causes and the Maker of all mind so much as once alluded to. The Father and Author of all, who is present in all his works, seemed to be ignored entirely." Lacy went on to connect the ward school affairs to the Bible controversy:

> It is a fact, my hearers, that the Bible has not a place in the schools of your children. . . . How must children feel toward a book that is not considered proper to be read by them at school? . . . how easily it makes them think that the sacred book is of an ambiguous character. . . . Are you willing that a company of ignorant, bigoted, priest-directed, Bible-hating foreigners should come to our shores, and, by political influence, withhold from our schools the fountain of everlasting life, the fountain from which our Republic came?[63]

Reviewing the ward school affairs and the Bible controversies at the beginning of 1856, the *Pacific* warned, "The Church which draws the life blood out of Catholic countries to support itself and educate the people to superstition and bigotry is just as content to draw what it can from the veins of this country." The paper admonished all to beware "this politico-religious church." With that phrase, the *Pacific* got to the heart of the matter, for the terms of the controversy were not nearly so important as its political meaning. As 1854 had demonstrated, in San Francisco religious controversy was the one and only key to successful nonpartisan politics.[64]

CHAPTER 6

THE VIGILANTES

Then Joshua said, "Open the mouth of the cave and bring those five kings to me from the cave." . . . And when they brought those kings to Joshua, he summoned all the men of Israel and said to the chiefs of the men who had gone to war with him, "Come near and put your feet upon the necks of these kings." . . . And afterwards Joshua smote them and put them to death, and he hung them on five trees.

—*Joshua 10: 22, 24–26*

♦

The commerce of this port is very uncertain.

—*Customs Collector Milton Latham, writing from San Francisco, February 16, 1856*

♦

A certain daily evening newspaper in this city. . . . Its solid columns of folly, filth, falsehood, malignancy, hypocrisy, and ridiculous self-conceit long ago forced us, for the sake of our own peace of mind and self-respect, and respect for the editorial profession, to form a resolution never to look at it again.

—*Frank Soulé, writing in the* Chronicle *about the* Daily Evening Bulletin, *edited by James King of William, January 27, 1856*

♦

James King of William is no more! . . . One martyr more for liberty has paid the penalty for speaking what he thought . . . the bold denouncer of wrong, the fearless antagonist of crime, the brave citizen, who risked life and reputation, happiness and home, in the Herculean task of tearing the mask from vice and laying villainy open to view, lies in his bloody shroud, because he felt it his duty to expose evil and possessed the daring to do it.

—*Frank Soulé, writing in the* Chronicle, *May 21, 1856, after the death of James King of William*

♦

In America I saw the freest and most enlightened men placed in the happiest circumstances the world affords; but it seemed to me as if a cloud habitually hung upon their brow, and I thought them serious and almost sad, even in their pleasures.

—*Alexis de Tocqueville*

♦ I ♦

James King was the kind of person who could always be relied upon to produce controversies to order. He was born in Georgetown, Maryland, in 1822, and he quickly demonstrated the qualities that were to bring him renown and an early death in gold rush San Francisco: restlessness and an insatiable desire for notoriety. While still a young man, he took to calling himself James King of William (his father was named William), because he could not bear being confused with the other James Kings who lived near Georgetown. He spent his early manhood in a number of places, clerking for businesses in Pittsburgh and elsewhere in Pennsylvania, and then in Michigan. After that he worked for a time for *Kendall's Expositor*, a Democratic campaign sheet published in Washington, D.C. Later he was employed by the *Washington Globe*, and then by the banking house of Corcoran and Riggs in the nation's capital. Ill health forced him to leave the humid climate of the Potomac, and he headed for California on the advice of a brother who had been there with John C. Frémont.[1]

On his way to California, he heard about the discovery of gold, and when he arrived at San Francisco, he immediately struck out for the mines. He did a brief stint there, not striking it rich, but spending enough time to acquire standing as a genuine '49er. After leaving the gold fields, he dabbled in banking in Sacramento for a brief period, but left in the middle of 1849 and went back to Washington. There he established lines of credit between Washington and San Francisco and made arrangements for dealing in exchange. He had decided to become a San Francisco banker. On December 5, 1849, he opened the banking house of James King of William in San Francisco.

King used his former connections well, advertising bills of exchange on Corcoran and Riggs. At least part of his early business consisted in joining with that Washington house in dealing with claims on the federal government for supplies and property used during the Mexican War. In addition, he became an extensive dealer in the bonds that were issued as California merrily went about violating the provision in its constitution limiting the public debt to $300,000. By his own account, he was more heavily involved in this sort of activity than anyone else in San Francisco. When the legislature passed the law funding the debt of San Francisco, King, as a leading banker in the city, was named to the body supervising the operation, the Commission of the Funded Debt. An 1851 source estimated his wealth at $125,000, and by 1853 that figure may have been as high as a quarter of a million dollars. Together with many other young businessmen, he was a member of the 1851 vigilance committee, and for a time, his bank was used as a depository for the funds of the committee. He was also one of the fourteen members of the vigilance committee who were prime movers in the presentation of the independent ticket at the fall elections in 1851.[2]

King had a penchant for the dramatic and was given to the grand gesture. For instance, in September 1851, with considerable attendant publicity, he offered to lend the city $5,000, interest free, to tide things over in the treasury. The offer was politely declined. In late 1853 he served as foreman of the Grand Jury and caused quite a stir when that body returned indictments against the city treasurer and two former city officials for the improper handling of city warrants. When the Grand Jury report was attacked in the press, King was quick to take to the papers himself and deliver vigorous counterattacks, in which he claimed that his life had been threatened. (The indictments were quashed on the technicality that two members of the Grand Jury were not American citizens.)[3]

In 1854, when his bank failed, King managed to persuade the banking house of Adams and Co. to take over his assets, and he went to work for them as a cashier. In the opinion of William T. Sherman, King was in such a terrible financial position at this time that the arrangements with him greatly weakened Adams and Co. and may have contributed to the spectacular failure of that bank in February 1855.

Adams and Co. was the second bank King was associated with that failed within the space of a single year, and he hastened to put some distance between himself and Adams and Co. He spent the months after the failure writing to the papers and telling anyone who would listen that he had realized that Adams and Co. was in a precarious financial position in January and February 1855. According to him, the reason for the failure was the bank's unwillingness to heed his advice. He claimed that Cohen, the receiver, was a crook, and that Palmer, Cook, and Co., which received some of the funds, was desperately short of specie. Things became so bitter that Cohen finally challenged King to a duel, which King declined on moral grounds. Out of work for the summer, King finally hit upon an occupation that would support him and allow him to keep his name before the public, to continue his accusations against Cohen, and to protest his own innocence in the Adams and Co. failure. He started a newspaper.[4]

On October 8, 1855, the first issue of the *San Francisco Daily Evening Bulletin* appeared, with James King of William announced on the masthead as editor. It was a small sheet, of only four pages, four columns each—nothing in size compared with the city's major papers, the *Alta*, the *Herald*, and the *Chronicle*, which had seven columns per page. Phenomenal increases in advertising and circulation soon allowed King to enlarge the size of the paper, however, and by March 1, 1856, less than six months after it had first appeared, the *Bulletin* was equal in size to San Francisco's major dailies. The paper took the city by storm, and by the time the final size was attained, King was editing the liveliest and most controversial paper in California.

King's extraordinary success did not stem from the adoption of any themes strikingly new to California journalism. On the contrary, most of his material was quite stock. He denounced municipal corruption, often with more heat than light, but so did virtually every other newspaper in the city. He professed himself appalled at the amount of city, county, and state expenditures, notwithstanding that in his more solvent days he had speculated in those very expenditures. Other San Francisco editors also attacked the city and county budgets, but they tended to support the consolidation bill pending before the legislature. This bill was designed to merge the city and county governments into one and to put something of a lid upon public expenses. Following the lead of the other dailies in San Francisco, King deplored crime, called for more and better schools, and published the news from the Atlantic Coast and Europe whenever a steamer arrived from the East.

King's unique contribution was undoubtedly his style. His paper was a reflection of himself: it was reckless, extravagant, often wrong, but never dull. Thus, he would not merely denounce political corruption, he would attack specific persons. In one of his first editorials, he wrote: "Of all the names that grace the roll of the political wire-working in this city, the most conspicuous of all . . . as high over his compeers as was Satan over the fallen angels, and as unblushing and determined as the dark fiend, stands the name of David C. Broderick." King admitted that "David Cataline Broderick" was "not directly chargeable with all the acts of violence and bloodshed at the polls," but "*his* mind is the Pandora's box whence spring all these evils." He also used information he had acquired as a member of the Grand Jury, to the effect that Palmer, Cook, and Co. was acting as bondsman for state and local officials. Soon after he started his paper, he took out after them, calling them "the Uriah Heeps of San Francisco bankers."[5]

King was a vain and ungracious man, quick to assert his own superiority in trivial encounters as well as major ones. On the day after the first issue of the *Bulletin* appeared, the morning papers published notices of its existence, tendering King the usual compliments (an old citizen of California, honest man, etc.) and paying the usual compliments to the paper (well-edited, neat in appearance, etc.). King responded in the evening edition of the *Bulletin*, "Some of you we thank, and some of you we don't." He went on to say that he had heard that some people were about "pitching into us," but that if they knew what was good for them, they would reconsider.[6]

It would require an overly long list at this point to detail all the persons and institutions King attacked in the course of his editorship. Besides Broderick and Palmer, Cook, and Co., and the other newspapers in the city, he attacked James Van Ness, the Democratic mayor of the city. One of the mayor's duties under the charter of 1855 was to preside over the recorder's court, the agency that handled petty crimes. Van Ness was too lenient in this duty to suit King's views. He called the mayor "The tool of Mr. Broderick, and the aider and abettor of thieves and ruffians." He scolded Van Ness in no uncertain terms: "You have not punished as their crimes deserve. You have been afraid to do so, either because you wished their services in bullying or stuffing ballots at the next election, or else feared the exercise of those arts against yourself." This was King at his most typical: Van Ness was either in league with alleged ballot box stuffers, and thus damned, or he was not in league with them, but was equally damned. King's barrage finally became too much for Van Ness, and one morning he opened the recorder's court with a passionate denunciation of King, calling him a "malignant misanthrope," to which the editor retorted that the mayor was a "stupid old ass." The point of all this is not in the mutual recriminations. Rather, it is that by the spring of 1856, King was a figure of major importance in San Francisco, so much so that the chief official of the city did not consider it prudent to ignore him.[7]

There were many other objects of King's ire. When the Italian gambler, Charles Cora, shot and killed a United States marshal, King editorialized that if the alleged murderer should escape from jail (he did not), then the keeper of the jail, our old friend Billy Mulligan, should be hanged. He went on to suggest that perhaps the sheriff should be strung up as well, just for good measure. When Cora's lawyers managed to secure a hung jury (the facts presented in court did tend to show that the marshal was the aggressor in the affair), King urged a revival of the vigilance committee. King also attacked gambling, dueling, houses of ill repute, nonobservance of the Sabbath (especially by Germans), a dinner honoring Tom Paine, a book attacking Christianity, the harbor master ("The fact that he is a friend of Broderick," he wrote, "is *prima facie* evidence against him"), and, once his journalistic success was assured, the business partner of the man from whom he had borrowed the money to start the *Bulletin*.[*8]

Sometimes King deliberately tried to stimulate a revival of popular justice. Just before Christmas of 1855, for example, Charles Collins, who owned a hat store on Commercial Street, was attacked by an irate customer to whom he had refused to sell a hat on credit. Collins told the customer, George Lane, that he still owed him for two hats he had bought on credit the year before. Lane swore that he had already paid for those hats and demanded to see Collins's books. When Collins refused and told Lane to come back the next day, Lane became enraged and, Collins reported, "commenced pushing me and upsetting a desk and the goods upon it . . . at the same time using very violent language." A crowd gathered and Lane left. Collins then told the crowd that he had a gun in the back of the shop and Lane had better not return if he knew what was good for him.

When Lane heard about the threat, he returned and dared Collins to try it. Collins retreated to the upstairs of the shop, and Lane departed. The police arrived soon after. Collins described the attack, but the police officer told him not to worry about it, that Lane got that way when he imbibed too much. The officer guessed that Lane would be back in the morning to apologize. Sure enough, he was. But King fumed. "Matters have come to a pretty pass, indeed, when an honest tradesman dare not exercise his own discretion," he wrote. His remedy was simple: "Call on the people! In five minutes a hundred men can be collected."[9]

The foregoing is enough to demonstrate that very little in the gold rush port escaped King's attention; but King did not write in a helter-skelter fashion. His successful pursuit of the martyr's crown made him a local legend, but his subsequent halo has obscured the main thrust of the editorials that he penned. Beneath the seemingly endless flailing at corruption, and under the fury that marked his more extreme suggestions, such as lynching the sheriff, lay a consistent purpose—King's deliberate attempt to agitate religion, and in that way prepare the ground for successful nonpartisan politics. Reminiscing in the 1880's, the merchant and vigilante leader William T. Coleman stated that King "had aroused a Roman Catholic influence hostile to himself by ill-advised strictures on one of their clergy." Time had perhaps dimmed Coleman's memory, or perhaps the apotheosis he was getting from Bancroft was mellowing him. In any event, in the 1850's King's "strictures" were hardly "ill-advised" in a political sense.[10]

In March 1856, the *Bulletin* picked up a charge that had originally been made by a Know-Nothing member of the Board of Supervisors, that the county hospital was costing too much. The management of the hospital had been farmed out by the county to the Sisters of Mercy. This order of Catholic nuns had a well-deserved reputation in San Francisco for selfless charity in ministering to the sick. In the fall of 1855, for instance, the Customs Collector reported to the Secretary of the Treasury that a steamer had recently arrived "with many cholera patients on board." He went on to say that "the chief care of the sick was bestowed in a most self-sacrificing manner by the 'Sisters of Mercy,' who nursed the sick passengers day and night so long as their attentions were needed." The county may also have been willing to place the hospital under the experienced direction of the Sisters of Mercy because of the condition of the Marine Hospital, which the Collector described as "disgraceful." Pigs, chickens, and goats wandered through its open verandas. It had virtually no grounds, which had the effect of making it "literally a prison house even to the convalescent." Patients on the third floor had to use the facilities on the second, even though many of them were "scarcely able to crawl up and down the stairs." Besides its regular duties, the Marine Hospital also had to examine patients who had contracted diseases "in San Francisco . . . after their discharge from vessels." In a port like San Francisco, where cholera might always be ready to jump from the next ship into the city, the need for a well-run county hospital was rather urgent.[11]

King complained that the bills that the Sisters presented to the Board of Supervisors were not being properly audited. He argued that the Sisters ought to be reimbursed on the basis of an itemized list of expenses, rather than simply receiving the $4,000 a month that the county gave them: "This 'going it blind' does not strike us as being the best way of managing this business." King moved from this suggestion to the argument that the Sisters were guilty of religious bias in the way they ran the hospital. The Sisters had, he said, moved some of the patients into "rooms not so eligible, and taken the rooms thus vacated for the purposes of fitting up a chapel for the benefit of the Catholic patients, whilst a Protestant clergyman is compelled to hold his services in the room to which the patients have been removed, and which is not so suitable." Then he introduced a political element: "If these charges should prove to be true—and we have them on good authority—we incline to think it will turn out to be the wire-working of political tricksters, who, making a little capital on the score of being friendly to the 'Sisters,' expect thus to ride into office by bartering their votes and consciences along with the people's money for purposes wholly foreign to the object for which our taxes are levied."[12]

Since King was a major figure in the city by this time, these charges were quickly investigated by the Grand Jury, which reported that the Sisters were using all the money they had received from the county for the purposes of running the hospital and that the room that was being used for a chapel had previously been condemned by the hospital's medical staff and had been turned into a chapel at the Sisters' own expense. Undeterred, King's attack took on a whining tone: "It will be seen that the Jury endorse the County hospital. The Chapel business is all right. *We don't*, and what little faith we had in the management of that business is about all gone today, because, on application by our reporter this morning at the hospital to be admitted, the answer he received was that they did not care about admitting anyone at that moment, '*but that anyone from Mr. King would certainly not be admitted!*'" King declared that he suspected that that order had been the work of one Father Gallagher, an adviser to the Sisters, and that if that turned out to be the case, "the reverend gentleman will regret it."[13]

In King's next attack the following day, the question of how much the hospital actually cost became a side issue:

> Does that gentleman [Father Gallagher] believe that the contemptible fear of losing a few subscribers from among our Catholic friends will deter us from pitching into him if we have any cause. . . . We beg to suggest to his reverence that if he thinks American Catholics are to be led by the nose like a parcel of Chilean peons, and made to come and go at the beck of the priest, we incline to think he will find ere long, he has made a great mistake. The Catholics of this city have not been treated well, anyhow, in the matter of pastors. They have not had the best men, as the size of their congregation fully entitles them to, but a parcel of old fogies, among whom we have heard one of the Frs. Gallagher mentioned, have been saddled on them against their wishes.[14]

In succeeding issues for the week following, King stated that since Gallagher was a Jesuit he was not worthy of any confidence, and he asked whether the priest had taken out his naturalization papers. Informed that neither Gallagher nor Archbishop Alemany was a Jesuit, King replied, "We are glad to hear it." He assured his readers that he personally had not the slightest desire to meet the "sleek and well fed" clergyman, only the "suffering humanity in all their wretchedness, who have the misfortune to be placed under his merciless protection." He did admit that he would like to hear Gallagher preach, just to see for himself what sort of sermons such a man could possibly deliver. When twenty-five Catholics published a card defending the hospital and stating that Gallagher had nothing to do with its operations, King retorted by accusing the priest of "low cunning and church Brodericksim." After a week, King finally managed to get one of his reporters into the county hospital. He headlined the resulting story as follows: "INHUMAN TREATMENT OF AN IDIOT—BAD QUARTERS—STARVING—FILTH—GRAND JURY VISIT—UNWHOLESOME FOOD—PATIENTS BORN IN THE UNITED STATES FIGHTING FOR SOMETHING TO EAT—PARTIALITY TO CATHOLICS—ROBBING THE PATIENTS OF THE LITTLE MONEY THEY HAVE LEFT."[15]

Even granting the nineteenth-century proclivity for journalistic overstatement, these were strong words. But King was no fool. He always denied that he was a Know-Nothing—the party was, he said, "too harsh against citizens of foreign birth"—but he clearly attempted to keep alive the issues on which the party had thrived, however briefly, in San Francisco. And, he said, "We are content to take the Know-Nothings rather than no party at all"; he wanted a party that was not a party in the traditional sense, a nonpartisan party like the one he had helped to organize after the 1851 vigilance committee. Mostly, he offered the frustrated, harried, failing businessmen in the city a scapegoat for their ills. The commercial climate was poor, he claimed, because a corrupt alliance symbolized by Broderick, Father Gallagher, and Palmer, Cook, and Co. was milking the city dry.[*16]

King's explanation was aided by commercial conditions, for the city's merchants were again in bad straits. In the spring of 1856, a number of larger merchants, in a last-ditch attempt to bring order into the marketplace and profits into their pockets, formed a significant cartel. In February, the *Chronicle* noted what it called a "frenzy" in flour. Throughout March, it kept referring to this movement, but contended all the while that another speculation in this product would net those involved nothing: "There seems to be a strong movement in flour of a speculative character, but upon what ground the parties interested base their expectations of any material advance now, we are entirely at a loss to conceive." The price of flour rose as the available stocks were brought under more disciplined control, but meanwhile the speculators spread the story that the existing stocks of flour were dangerously low and that there was not enough flour on hand to feed the state until harvest time.[17]

By the beginning of April, speculation in flour was in full swing. The *Chronicle*, though it remained skeptical, reported on April 3 that heavy sales were being made daily. A few days later, when the transactions were "both numerous and significant," according to the *Herald*, the *Chronicle* debunked the entire movement. It warned those taking part that there was not a scarcity of flour, but more than enough to satisfy the wants of the entire state. The paper did not think that the country dealers would be fooled by the speculators. Alexander B. Grogan privately advised Faxon D. Atherton in the same vein: "Strong efforts are being made to sustain the flour market, but I have no faith in the speculation."[18]

Grogan and the *Chronicle* were correct, and the bubble began to burst around the end of April, with disaster for the speculators. By the beginning of May, Grogan could report, "Flour and wheat are arriving quite freely from Oregon, and the price is going down, notwithstanding all the efforts of the speculators to sustain it." In the middle of the month, he wrote that some of the speculators were privately making arrangements to ship some of the flour to Australia, and that all that was happening in the San Francisco flour market was a series of "sham sales, made and reported to bolster the price." As evidence that the speculation was actually faltering, he stated that some of the smaller dry goods firms in San Francisco had recently failed. By July, the whole fiasco was over. Grogan penned an obituary for the movement: "The bankers are afraid of anyone who had meddled in flour, and are very tight with them."[19]

But by July other things had happened. In April, in the middle of the Gallagher controversy, the Catholics confidently purchased a Baptist church that had fallen into disuse and began to prepare it for Catholic services. And early in May, a group of dissident Democrats, in a bit of maneuvering before the state convention that was to be held later in the year, published in the *Bulletin* an attack upon the Collector of the port, Milton S. Latham, for corruption and unfair patronage policies. The Purifiers, as the dissidents called themselves, accused Latham of being too partial to the Tammany wing of the party in the distribution of jobs.[20]

The background to the controversy was that in California's Democratic party in the 1850's, state patronage had usually gone to the Tammany wing and federal patronage to the Chivalry. After the Democrats lost control of the state in the 1855 elections, Latham, who wanted to do more in politics than count bags of flour for the rest of his life, decided to use the defeat of the state party to try and broaden his own political base.

In the beginning of 1856, he began to hire Irish political operatives like John McDougal and Edward Gallagher as draymen, Martin Gallagher and William Bagley as watchmen, and Peter Burns as a laborer. These were all hard-and-fast Broderick men. Latham was simply trying to buy some credit with Tammany, which was not a bad strategy for a political climber. The "Purifier" letter, which was written by anti-Tammany Democrat R. Shoyer, fumed that Latham was spreading patronage around too widely. The Chivalry would have preferred that Tammany stay out in the cold for a season or two.[21]

In view of King's past performances, the Purifiers had every reason to believe that King would go out after Latham. But King, quite uncharacteristically, came to the Collector's defense. He wrote, "As Collector of this port, as far as our information goes, Mr. Latham has discharged his duties faithfully." James King defending a public official was enough to suggest that something unusual was going on, and a few days later the mystery began to unfold.[22]

A letter to the *Bulletin* from "A Purifier" said, "It has been more than hinted that there are other causes besides those suggested in your editorial [for defending Latham]. . . . We entertain too favorable an opinion of you to believe that you would be swayed by any personal considerations." It was clear that the Purifiers had something on King, and that unless he changed his tune, they would reveal it. King took the hint, and in the next issue of the *Bulletin* on May 10 he sided with the Purifiers. Latham had, he said, appointed "some of the most notorious scoundrels that infest our city" to official positions, and he urged the Collector to sack them at once. King undoubtedly hoped that that would be the end of the affair, but one of his many enemies could not resist the temptation to see him squirm a bit more.[23]

Supervisor Casey had recently purchased the *Sunday Times*, in order to have an organ to express his anger against the credit policies of some of the city's banks. The paper was so vitriolic that at one point banker William T. Sherman, with all the subtlety for which he would become famous during the Civil War, told Casey that he would "pitch him and his press out of the third story window." The Sunday, May 11, issue of the *Times* ran a letter from "Caliban." The author, who said that he was composing the letter on Friday May 9 (before King's concession on May 10), argued that the reason King was defending Latham was that his brother Thomas King had a position at the Customs House. (In fact, Thomas King was a register clerk there, at $3,000 a year.) Further, "Caliban" went on, the reason that King had been attacking the new marshal was that this brother had been a disappointed aspirant for that position.

James King's initial reaction was to hope that the Caliban letter would not attract much attention in the light of his May 10 editorial. So most of the Monday, May 12, issue of the *Bulletin* was given over to reprinting Reverend Lacy's May 11 evangelical sermon, "The Schools Demanded by the Present Age," accompanied by King's favorable commentary on it. But the Caliban letter was the talk of the town. So Thomas King had to spend most of Monday trying to track down Casey to discover, if he could, the true identity of "Caliban." On Tuesday, May 13, Thomas King published a card in the morning papers in which he stated, "I never applied, nor thought of applying, for the position of U.S. Marshal." Rumors abounded that Thomas King had given Casey until 10:00 A.M. Wednesday to tell him who "Caliban" was or to "face the consequences." Casey refused.[24]

By Wednesday, the King brothers evidently calculated that it would be better for them to try to shift the focus of the controversy away from themselves and onto Casey. For what was at stake was James King's self-appointed position as nonpartisan moral leader of the city. In the *Bulletin* on Wednesday May 14, in a devastating personal mudslinging editorial, he lumped together all the dirt he could gather on Casey, whose paper had trapped him. All the material he collected was already public knowledge: that Casey had once been an inmate of Sing Sing prison in New York, that he was a political brawler, and that he had been fraudulently elected to the Board of Supervisors. All in all, King concluded, Casey deserved "to have his neck stretched."

The paper was hardly on the streets with this blasting editorial when Casey stormed into King's office and screamed that he did not like to have his past raked up. King, seemingly unperturbed, asked Casey if the facts in the editorial were true and then ordered him to leave. Later that same afternoon, as King was walking home from the *Bulletin*'s offices, Casey shot him.[25]

King staggered across the street to the offices of the Pacific

Express Co. (an agency that, ironically, had been started by former employees of Adams and Co. and that King had occasionally criticized in the *Bulletin*). Soon he was being attended by a score of doctors—enough, Bancroft remarked, to kill anyone. Until he died, notices of his medical condition were posted every half-hour outside the offices of his paper. Casey was immediately whisked off by a crowd of police and his friends (two overlapping groups) to the jail.[26]

Events then moved on two levels. Publicly, an angry crowd soon gathered in front of the jail. Thomas King, whose job at the Customs House had more or less started the whole affair, mounted the steps of the jail and began shouting that Casey was "a Sing Sing bird and a tool of Broderick." He demanded Casey's head. Mayor Van Ness arrived and tried to get the mob to disperse, but his appeal was ignored. Fearing for Casey's safety, the Mayor then asked the federal authorities to let him be stowed for the night on the revenue cutter *Marcy*, at anchor in the bay. The authorities, having no desire to become involved in the affair, refused. The arrival at the jail of some volunteer military companies helped calm things down a bit there, and the county officials also allowed a delegation headed by respected commission merchant Frederick Macondray to inspect the jail and satisfy themselves that Casey was securely locked up. This done, the crowd slowly drifted away.[27]

In the meantime, on a more private level, a group of merchants who had been members of the vigilance committee in 1851 began to move. They held a secret meeting at the Society of California Pioneers. Within a few hours, a call to the members of the old committee was composed and placed in the papers. Significantly, they were ordered to assemble at the Know-Nothing hall. Advice was also given to the city's editors concerning the kind of press coverage that would be expected. The next morning, with the city in a complete turmoil, the streets around the Know-Nothing hall were jammed with people, all anxious to get in on the expected vigilance activities. The nucleus of merchants arranged to keep the crowd outside, or, as one of the merchants put it more delicately, "The men who were entitled to lead stepped forward." Absolute secrecy and absolute obedience were quickly decided upon as the procedural foundations of a new vigilance committee, and the executive committee, to whom the absolute obedience would be due, was selected. The men inside also determined that the organization would be modeled upon military lines, that Casey and Cora (who was in jail for the shooting of the United States marshal, Richardson) would be executed, and that the committee would then proceed to the deportation of undesirable characters. It was also decided that immediate steps would be taken against the *Herald*, which had the temerity that morning to editorialize against the formation of a vigilance committee. Only then were the doors opened, and the members of the impatient crowd allowed to sign their names to the roster. Each man was assigned a number by which he was to be known, a military company in which he was to serve, and a password that would admit him to vigilante headquarters. The new vigilante was then sent to a predetermined location to begin drilling.[28]

The commercial orientation of the new committee was, if anything, more pronounced and more public than had been that of its predecessor. Sherman, who was in a position to know, wrote to a friend that "all the large merchants" were "active controlling members" and that "most of the rich men are contributing means and countenance *sub rosa*." One of the vigilantes (James Dows) later recalled these contributions:

> The expenses of the committee were very heavy, but we had no difficulty in meeting them. Our collections amounted to several hundreds of thousands of dollars. Men who did not belong to the committee at all, wealthy houses, merchants, bankers, and others, responded liberally to the demands made on them for contributions. When we came round to make collections, they would inquire how much was their share, and whatever we said, they would draw out a check to that amount.

The British consul in the city reported to London that the committee "consisted of the leading merchants, tradespeople, and mechanics—all business is at a standstill." One participant later recalled, "I have seen at one time, not less than five men, members of the Vigilance Committee, with muskets in their hands taking their turns at guard, not one of whom was worth less than half a million dollars." An opponent characterized them as "commission agents, grocers, liquor dealers, auctioneers, clerks, ship captains, speculators in real estate, and dealers in dry goods and hardware." And the editor of the *Herald*, the only major paper in the city that opposed the committee, remarked with some wit: "We are told that in the center of their seal there is a large eye and the words VIGILANCE COMMITTEE, SAN FRANCISCO. It cannot be said of this committee of vigilance eye, as of Banquo's, that there is no *speculation* in it!"[29]

Unfortunately, a complete roster of the membership has not survived, and thus an analysis of the complete committee is impossible. However, the membership of the executive committee, which was in 1856, as it had been in 1851, the guiding spirit of the entire committee, has been preserved. Thirty-three of the thirty-seven members can be identified. Almost 60 percent of the executive committee was composed of importers and merchants. The importing sector contributed fourteen men (37.8 percent), and another eight (21.6 percent) were merchants. In addition, four (10.8 percent) were bankers. There was not one lawyer on the executive committee. When the editor of the *Herald* called the 1856 committee a "mercantile junta," he was entirely correct.[30]

The swiftness of the organization of the vigilance committee, within a day after the shooting of King, indicates, at the very least, that the merchants of the city were much more organized than they had been in 1851, when a vigilance committee was started without a clear structure or program. Five years of general commercial adversity, petition writing, occasional political activity, and the taxation policies of the state and city governments had brought them together. In addition to its much more sophisticated organization, the new vigilance committee was different from its 1851 predecessor in another important respect. This difference was reflected in its constitution, which, though essentially following the 1851 document, added a few new twists, all relating to politics:

> Whereas it has become apparent to the citizens of San Francisco that there is no security for life and property either under the regulations of society as it at present exists, or under the laws as now administered, and that by the association together of bad characters, our ballot boxes have been stolen and others substituted, or stuffed with votes that were never polled, and thereby our elections nullified, our dearest rights violated, and no other method left by which the will of the people can be manifested: therefore the citizens whose names are hereunto attached do unite themselves into an association for the maintenance of the peace and the good order of society, the prevention and punishment of crime, the preservation of our lives and property, and to insure that our ballot boxes shall hereafter express the actual and unforged will of a majority of our citizens; and we do bind

ourselves each unto the other by a solemn oath to do and perform every just and lawful act for the maintenance of law and order, and to sustain the law when faithfully and properly administered. But we are determined that no thief, burglar, incendiary, assassin, ballot box stuffer, or other disturber of the peace shall escape punishment, either by the quibbles of the law, the insecurity of prisons, the carelessness or corruption of the police, or the laxity of those who pretend to administer justice.[31]

Politics was in the forefront of the committee's concerns from the moment of its organization. But first the person who had called it into being, James P. Casey, had to be dealt with. This presented something of a problem, since the sheriff had reinforced the guard at the county jail. Although many members of the volunteer military companies had deserted the jail and gone over to the vigilance committee, the sheriff had managed to secure a number of guns from the various armories of the city. He issued a call for able-bodied persons to aid him, and by the time the committee had completed its organization, he had mustered roughly one hundred armed men, including some of the most prominent lawyers in the city, to guard the jail and the prisoner.[*32]

When the governor of the state, Know-Nothing J. Neely Johnson, received word from Van Ness that the city was dividing into two armed camps, he hurried down from Sacramento. He and Sherman, who had recently been appointed major-general of the Militia, went to the committee's headquarters where they met late Friday night, May 16, with William T. Coleman, who was, literally, Number One. According to Sherman's later recollections, Coleman said, "Governor, we are tired of having our people shot down in the streets." When Johnson acknowledged that he was not happy about it either, Coleman began to relax a bit. Then the governor, attempting to forestall vigilante action, offered a deal. He guaranteed that Casey would not escape from jail. He promised that if King died, Casey would immediately be indicted by a grand jury. He said that the courts would drop all other business to try Casey. If Casey was convicted, he promised that he would not employ executive action to lighten any sentence the courts might impose. In other words, the governor was practically promising the execution of Casey if the committee stayed put.[*33]

This was not enough for the vigilantes. At the end of the meeting, Johnson was forced to accept an arrangement that allowed the committee to post a guard inside the jail, to make certain on their own account that Casey did not escape. At about 11:00 A.M. on Sunday morning, May 18, Johnson was handed a curt note: "We beg to advise you that we have withdrawn our guard from the County Jail. By order of the Committee, 33 SECRETARY." Johnson hurried to the roof of a hotel near the jail where he, Sherman, and Mayor Van Ness watched helplessly as a crowd of three thousand vigilantes marched on the jail. The leaders of the group wheeled a cannon up to the front of the building and pointed it at the sheriff. David Scannell had not risen to the position of sheriff by indulging in any martyr complexes, so he quickly released Casey and Cora to the committee. The two were driven to vigilante headquarters, where they were tried by the executive committee. While the trials were under way, King died. A visitor recorded the public reaction in the city. He wrote, "The flags of the city and of the shipping were displayed at half mast, the bells all tolled and many of the buildings were hung in mourning."[34]

Thursday, May 22, was a typical late spring day in San Francisco: misty fog and cool in the morning, but clear, breezy, and pleasant by afternoon. While the fog still shrouded the city, Father Michael Accolti entered Fort Gunnybags—the vigilante headquarters—and witnessed the formal marriage of Charles Cora and Arabella Ryan. By the time the fog had burned off, King's funeral cortège was winding its way through the city to Lone Mountain cemetery, and the bodies of Casey and Cora were hanging from the second-story windows of the vigilante headquarters. Loyall Farragut, son of the naval commander, was visiting the city that day. He later recalled, "It was a most weird sight. All the streets approaching the fort were guarded by the cavalry uniformed and we could not approach very near. An immense mass of people stood in the vicinity, but what rendered the scene very impressive was that people were so quiet. Everyone seemed to be speaking in whispers."[35]

Casey and Cora out of the way, the committee swiftly turned to its important task. In short order, a number of Broderick's political operatives found themselves surrounded on the streets by squads of armed vigilantes and hustled to the waiting executive committee. They were tried for a variety of offenses, mostly relating to political fraud and ballot box stuffing. After conviction, which was virtually automatic, they were hurried off for deportation on ships that were already in the process of clearing the harbor. Billy Mulligan, whom King had wanted hanged, was one of those deported. Others were Martin Gallagher and Billy Carr, who were boatmen in the heavily Democratic first ward, and Bill Lewis, another first ward operative, who had on several occasions destroyed some ballots there. Yankee Sullivan and Terence Carr, who had managed Casey's election as supervisor, were also deported, and so, too, were Charles Duane, a power in the Fire Department, and James Cusick and James Claughey, who had served as Democratic election inspectors. Whether by coincidence or not, former Mayor Garrison decided that the time was ripe for a long business trip to New York, and Democratic Judge Alexander Campbell could not think of a better time to pay a visit to the Sandwich Islands.

For a heady instant, the committee even considered arresting Broderick himself, but it decided instead to ask him to appear and answer some questions. Had Broderick been a man given to irony, he would have appreciated the situation, for, at the time of his execution, Casey was allied with the Chivalry, and not the Tammany, wing of the party. Broderick got the message anyway, and literally headed for the hills. That turned out to be his advantage. He was able to employ his organizing abilities in the interior of the state, and the upshot was a legislature that, as its first order of business, sent him to the Senate. In San Francisco, however, the vigilance committee quite methodically and quite effectively destroyed his political organization.[36]

Most people knew that the committee generally went after Irish Democrats. The tone was set quite early. A *Bulletin* correspondent noted with horror that "hundreds" of Irish laborers had attended Casey's funeral. Since he thought that there was nothing about Casey that anyone could possibly admire, the only explanation that he could offer was that Father Gallagher had ordered his flock to appear as mourners. It was appropriate, the letter concluded, that "there were not over a dozen American born citizens" in Casey's funeral procession.[37]

It probably was appropriate, for the committee was dividing the city along just these lines, all the while denying that it was doing so. One resident wrote, "The Irish generally are down on the Vigilance Committee, and in fact charge them with murder—there may be some trouble with the Irish yet." In a dispatch to the Plymouth (Mass.) *Rock*, he reported, "Casey and Cora being Catholics, and as Casey and Sullivan were Irish, as well as most of those who are now in the hands of the committee, the ignorant lower classes of the Irish in this city are very jealous of the acts of the committee and easily excited on the subject." By the end of May, the committee's supporters found it necessary to try to correct "the impression that the action of the Vigilance Committee had been especially directed against the Irish population." The impression was a deep one, and the pro-vigilance *Bulletin* had to stoop to quoting Father Gallagher, of all people, to the effect that law-abiding Irish had nothing to fear from the committee. The impression nevertheless persisted, and in early June the *Bulletin* had to deny once again that "the Committee are opposed to foreigners generally, and the Irish in particular and the Roman Catholic religion."[38]

The impression persisted for good reasons. As the *Herald* noted, this year's vigilantes had been last year's Know-Nothings. Some actions of the committee indicated its consonance with the Know-Nothings. In June, for instance, the committee disarmed the Jackson Guards, a volunteer military company that had refused to side with it. Before it released the men, the committee attempted to make them take the following oath: "I do solemnly promise and swear, in the presence of Almighty God and these witnesses—by the hope of a future state—by the Blessed Virgin Mary and all the saints in the calendar, that I will not bear arms against the Vigilance Committee of San Francisco. So help me God and the Blessed Virgin." The members of the Guards, who were all Irish, "unanimously and indignantly," in their words, refused to take the oath. They regarded it as "composed of sectarian influence and intended to wound religious feelings."*[39]

The committee's applications for membership also underlined the fact that the vigilantes were out to get the Irish. Applicants had to state on the form their place of birth. Michael O'Sullivan, a plumber, wrote "citizen of the United States," and his application was accepted. William Turkington put down "England"; apparently on being questioned, he crossed that out and wrote "Ireland," but added "nearly seven years in this country." James Leighton Miller wrote "Londonderry, Ireland," so that he would not be confused with an Irish Catholic. For the same reason, Robert Moore, a baker, put down "Belfast." There was no doubt in the minds of these common folk which way the vigilance wind was blowing. Perhaps this was why, as one of the vigilantes later ruefully confessed, "The foreigners thought we were a mob" and "We had almost all the ministers in town on our side . . . except the Catholics and Dr. Scott [an Episcopalian]."*[40]

The committee was well launched on its program of political destruction within a few weeks after the execution of Casey and Cora, and it made tentative plans to adjourn on July 4, with an appropriate parade and party. Unanticipated events changed those plans. On June 3, the governor issued a proclamation from Sacramento declaring the county of San Francisco "in a state of insurrection," and commanding all persons in the volunteer military companies to report to Sherman for duty in the militia. The major-general was chagrined when only a few hundred persons responded to the summons, and appalled when these turned out to be people who did not share his social station. In short order he resigned after the commanding general of the Pacific division of the Army refused to supply him with arms. Sherman was also upset that a scheme of reconciliation he proposed was rejected by the governor. Sherman's plan involved withdrawal of the governor's proclamation, mutual disarmament of the committee and the law-and-order forces, and a promise by the committee not to resist any writs of habeas corpus that the courts might issue. The committee might have been willing to accept this, for it had pretty much sent away everyone it wanted.

Sherman's successor as militia commander, Volney Howard, finally did manage to pry some arms from the government arsenal at Benicia. As the weapons were being transported across the bay by schooner, the vigilance committee received word of what was taking place. It sent a force that intercepted the boat and seized the weapons. The executive committee, not satisfied with having the arms in its committee rooms, then decided to question the two men who had transported the arms across the bay and ordered their arrest.

A small squad of vigilante police caught up with the two in the office of the United States Naval Agent, a logical place for them to be, since government property had just been stolen on the seas. Symbolizing, perhaps, the web that the vigilantes termed "corruption," the office was immediately above Palmer, Cook, and Co. When the vigilantes moved in to make the arrests, they were brusquely ordered out by David S. Terry, an excitable judge of the State Supreme Court, who was for reasons known only to himself present at the scene. Terry, a Chivalry Democrat turned Know-Nothing, was a well-known law-and-order stalwart. His suggestion for solving the vigilante problem had been to "call the miners from the mountains who would sweep the damned pork sellers into the bay." The vigilantes retired to get help, and the group in the office decided to make a run for a nearby armory. The vigilante reinforcements intercepted them on the way. A scuffle resulted, and Terry stabbed one of the vigilantes, a Know-Nothing political operative named Hopkins. Terry was arrested by a larger force soon after.[41]

Having a state judge in their custody was a bit overwhelming even for the committee members, and they found themselves temporarily stymied. They could not let Terry go, for that would be an open confession of weakness. He was too important for them to deport casually, as they had deported the Irish ballot box stuffers, and they could hardly hang him because that would no doubt bring the state and federal authorities into action against them. They therefore charged him with a series of crimes, including resisting by force an officer of the committee, and kept him on trial for five weeks. Sherman was probably correct in his observation on the vigilantes at this time: he told his brother, "My own opinion is that the committee is tired of its position, but finds it difficult to withdraw from the complications in which they are involved." All they could do was to cross their fingers and hope that the city's doctors would be more successful in saving Hopkins than they had been in saving King. In the middle of August, Hopkins was declared out of danger and Terry was quietly released.[42]

The committee tried to put the best face on its defeat. While Terry was on trial, the vigilantes decided to charge Philander Brace, a minor political operative whom they were apparently planning to deport, with two murders which had taken place the previous year. He was found guilty and sentenced to death. And on July 24, a dispute in the lobby of the St. Nicholas Hotel over an unpaid debt led to the fatal shooting of a Dr. Andrew Randall by a man named Joseph Hetherington. The vigilantes, on the lookout for such an opportunity, seized Hetherington as a policeman was leading him to jail. The committee tried him and sentenced him to death. On July 29, to assuage the more excited members of the general committee who wanted blood, the executive committee hanged Brace and Hetherington. A week and a half later, at 2:00 A.M. on August 7, they released Terry, and on August 18 the committee held the parade and party it had promised itself for July 4. "GRAND FUNERAL PROCESSION OF VIGILANTS—2740 TRAITORS UNDER ARMS" was how the anti-vigilance *Herald* described it. The committee then adjourned.[43]

♦ II ♦

Just as the committee itself was much better organized than its 1851 counterpart had been, so the opposition to the committee expressed itself more fully than had the opponents of the earlier organization. The focus of the opposition to vigilance activities was the *Herald*. John Nugent, the paper's editor, was a native of Ireland who had worked for James Gordon Bennett on the *New York Herald* before coming to California. He had been a strong supporter of the 1851 committee, but proved himself just as strong an opponent of its successor. On the morning after the shooting of King, Nugent announced the position that he adhered to staunchly during the next months:

> An intense excitement was caused in this city last evening by the affray between Mr. James P. Casey and Mr. James King of William. Motives of delicacy, needless to explain, force us to abstain from commenting on this affair, but we could not justify ourselves in refraining from the most earnest condemnation of the mob spirit manifested last evening . . . we see that a number of highly respectable merchants—some of them our warm friends, have called a meeting of the old vigilance committee . . . we wish to be understood as most unqualifiedly condemning the movement. Much as we admire the acts of the vigilance committee, we have arrived at the conclusion that it cannot be revived except under the most extraordinary circumstances, and we declare that the time has not yet come.[44]

The morning on which the editorial appeared, the vigilance committee was in the process of organizing, and resolutions against the *Herald* were passed. Nugent, and the other editors of the city, quickly found out that the men of the vigilance committee meant business. During the course of that day, 212 persons canceled their subscriptions to the *Herald*; the auctioneers' association, under pressure from the importers, withdrew its advertising from the paper; and a group of merchants on Front Street, which contained a good number of the wholesale establishments in the city, collected as many copies of the *Herald* as they could find and burned them in the middle of the thoroughfare. The next morning, the *Herald* was only half its normal size and almost devoid of auction advertising.[45]

Although the *Chronicle*, which had begun by counseling restraint ("To the Courts we appeal"), got the point and declared its support for the acts of the vigilance committee, Nugent held firm. During the ensuing months, he opened his paper to criticisms of the acts of the committee. First of all, he reworked the arguments that had been employed against the 1851 committee and that he had rejected at that time—mostly to the effect that the committee, however laudable its professed aims and however solid its personnel, was setting a very dangerous precedent. For instance, he carried a letter denouncing the members of the committee for not putting all their energies into making the already existing government work, if they thought that things were so terrible. He agreed that the right of revolution did exist, but he insisted that the proper time for its exercise had not yet arrived: "In opposing the new regime erected in this city upon the ruins of the late constitution and government of California, we have acted in obedience to great public principles. We do not deny the right of revolution, but this right is the last-guard resort of an oppressed people. It is an august remedy to be reserved for an august occasion. . . . Forcibly to revolutionize a government because the laws are sometimes violated, or because an improper man is put or even swindled into office, is like amputating an arm because a wart is on the finger." With the overwritten pomposity that marked many of his editorials, he sneered, "For the signers of the Declaration of Independence and those revolutionary heroes we have hitherto revered, we are asked to substitute on our calendar of national saints the thirty-nine commercial gentlemen who hold their Sanhedrin on Sacramento Street."[46]

Nugent insisted that the present vigilantism was susceptible of later abuse: "You may not abuse the principle of power to bad uses, but will others be so nice and wise? . . . The directors of this movement are said to be humane, prudent, discreet and moderate men, and no doubt this inscription of this character of them has served greatly to compose the public mind in regard to their future action. But if they were as wise as Solomon, and as pure as Washington, this would not hurt our argument. No one is to be trusted with power to repeal the constitution." To him, the vigilance committee was simply another despotic power: "But criminals sometimes escape! So they do, and that is the distinguishing mark of a free government. In a despotism, the guilty never escape, because what the tyrant suspects, he condemns; but the free law acquits where it doubts." The despotic character of the committee could be seen, he asserted, in the domiciliary visits it practiced and in the way it tried to destroy his paper. (It ought to be pointed out, though, that no attempt was ever made to prevent the *Herald* from continuing to publish during the time that the vigilance committee held power in the city.)[47]

In addition to these civil liberty arguments, the *Herald* and the other opponents of the committee tried several other approaches. Nugent, not very wisely, tried to use the Know-Nothing temper of the committee for his own purposes and to denounce the committee within its own rhetorical terms. Though this was hardly sensible because, as a correspondent to the *Herald* observed, the vigilance committee was composed of those who had been Know-Nothings in 1854 and 1855, Nugent pursued the argument. He called attention to the numbers of French and German persons associated with the committee and said, "This admixture of an alien element in the ranks of the rebellious band" was "the worst feature of this organized defiance of the ministers of the law." He warned that such behavior would not go unpunished: "Men will hereafter tell the unwelcome story how by and of German bayonets and French guns, the Constitution of this great Republic, the Constitution of this free Commonwealth, were trampled underfoot—how by the same aid, American laws, framed by American freemen, were set at naught."[48]

More to the point, Nugent argued that behind all the talk of reformation lay a foray into politics. In June, he shrewdly predicted that the ultimate aim of the committee was "The resignation of the county and state officers, and the election of the prominent members of the vigilance committee to the offices thus rendered vacant." He went on, "The heads of the movement will thus have an opportunity to make good their losses, but what have the rank and file to expect? . . . The thanks of the Executive Committee of the Committee of Vigilance! This will, no doubt, be a very substantial reward for their services, and will be treasured up and handed down to their posterity, while the members of the executive committee will hand down something more tangible in the shape of large fortunes, acquired in the public offices to which they expect to be elected." In the same vein, the major general of the state militia wrote, "No one who has closely observed the proceedings of the vigilance committee for the past few days [after the arrest of Terry], can doubt it has sunk into a mere political machine. . . . They think they see in it a patent lever for controlling the elections in California."[49]

Besides politics, the opponents of the committee also argued that another factor motivating it was business. Nugent had originally asserted, before the executions of Casey and Cora, that the disruption of commercial affairs that would result from the merchants organizing a vigilance committee would harm business in the city. "A lynch law execution now would be a lasting detriment to the character of our city," he declared. "It would destroy all confidence abroad, and indirectly retard immigration and the investment of capital." He also warned that San Francisco would lose what was an early version of the tourist trade. A fleet of whaling ships had been expected to put in at San Francisco during the fall, but, according to him, "The owners . . . will never order their ships to put in at a place where there is no law and no government." Through May and June, Nugent continued to point out that the vigilance committee was run by businessmen, and he reminded them again and again that the longer they stayed away from business, the more they would be cutting their own throats: "It is well known to every person of intelligence that since the commencement of the present excitement very little business has been done in this city. This is a fact that will be duly weighed at the East . . . a total of a million and a half dollars wasted within the last month." On the other hand, he observed, failure might be just what some of the merchants deserved, since the men who had organized the vigilance committee were the very speculators who were constantly trying to corner the market in some commodity or other and thereby raise prices for the consumers. A correspondent of the *Herald* asked, "Did they [the vigilance committee members] not in the winter of 1852–1853 create a monopoly of flour and put it up to famine prices? . . . Is it a greater crime to cheat at elections by stuffing ballot boxes than to cheat and poison people by selling bad provisions?"*[50]

Similar characterizations were made by others. The *Democratic State Journal* called the vigilantes "The Sour Flour and Soft Pork Aristocracy." The Southern-born son of one of the Land Commissioners sneered that the committee was run by "Boston men and that ilk," whom he privately labeled as "the stranglers of Sacramento and Front Streets." And the *Sun* quipped that the committee was nothing more than a "hodge-podge of potato-vendors, small beer politicians and flour speculators."[51]

By the end of June, however, the *Herald* had adjusted its perspective. Nugent began to argue that "bad business" was exactly what the vigilance committee had been after all the time. This had first been suggested by General Volney Howard in a report to the governor. Speaking of the well-known practice of evading jury duty, Howard argued that, had the city's businessmen discharged their legal obligations as good citizens, there would have been no necessity for any vigilance committee. Furthermore, he continued:

> Neither can these men escape scrutiny into their motives. They are not purely those of the public good. There are in the vigilance committee some merchants of wealth and integrity. There are a host of others on the verge of bankruptcy. There are men unable to make their remittances before this commotion began, and who are now urging its prolongation, because it affords them a plausible excuse for not sending per mail funds which they are unable to remit. No one wishes to take out an attachment or foreclose a mortgage against an influential member of the vigilance committee. As to him, the courts are practically closed.[52]

Nugent picked up this argument, for it provided the perfect answer to the question that had been puzzling him so deeply: why were so many businessmen neglecting business? He argued that the vigilance committee was not just interested in canceling the immediate remittances that some businessmen were perhaps unable to meet. In his eyes, the committee had a more important goal:

> An intelligent and valued correspondent suggests that when the news reaches the city of New York of the state of things existing in this town, shippers will hesitate to ship large consignments as heretofore

to this place, and the comparatively smaller shipments will cause a rise in the price of many articles of merchandise. Will not many of the so-called Committee in that event reap a monstrous profit on various descriptions of goods which they may have in store? It is well known that a majority of the "Executive" represent the mercantile interest in the country. Is there not a species of selfishness underlying this bold movement of the committee?[53]

In the middle of July, noting that the flour speculation of the spring "fell through," Nugent presented his seasoned view of the 1856 vigilance committee:

Several clipper fleets have arrived at this port within the past three months. . . . There was no market for them previous to the commencement of the insurrection of this city. The immediate effect of recent events will be to destroy the confidence of foreign merchants. . . . Few will be ready to credit merchants doing business in a city where all law and civil rights have been subverted. Shipments will cease, and as a natural consequence the stock of necessaries now on hand will go up and the mercantile Diet who now sit in such state on Sacramento Street will realize large profits upon their wares. . . . The immediate results of the present movement will be that prices will be inflated, and those who have a large stock of those articles on hand will realize a fortune. Who will suffer? The people. By them the bills will have to be footed.

In other words, the portrait of the 1856 vigilance committee that was drawn by its most vocal opponent was that of a collection of financially insecure merchants who hoped to salvage profit from their declining fortunes by curtailing the shipment of merchandise to San Francisco, and who intended to seize political power in the upcoming election.*[54]

So far as I have been able to discover, no answer to Nugent's charges was ever forthcoming from the vigilance committee, either in public or in private. This law-and-order view, however, does have certain things to recommend it. Most importantly, it takes into account the primary commercial fact of the day—the San Francisco market, in May of 1856, was terribly overstocked. The importers of the city were well into their third year of this condition, with no relief from ordinary sources in sight. Vigilance in 1851 had been followed by a good business year in 1852, and, although there may not have been a demonstrable connection, it did happen. Also, the law-and-order view would account for the quick organization of the committee. Unless one is willing to attribute superhuman powers of practical organization to the merchants who formed the committee, one must account for the fact that thousands of men were mobilized into an effective military and police force within three days. It is plausible, as Olmsted suggests, that at least some of the details were worked out in advance, and that the men who comprised the core of the executive committee were awaiting an opportunity to act. James King of William obliged them by providing, in his death, an opportunity that more than met the need. And most importantly, whether or not all the charges leveled by Nugent and Howard were accurate, it was certainly true that politics was very much on the committee's mind.[55]

As I have indicated, driving out Broderick's operatives was the initial phase of the committee's political work. Within three days after Casey and Cora had been hanged, the executive committee began to discuss the possible ways of removing from their positions the existing city and county officers. It finally decided that the committee itself, since it was interested in gaining broad support throughout the city, would not be directly involved in this sort of activity. The members of the executive committee feared that if their political purposes became known, they would lose the considerable backing they expected to maintain so long as they themselves remained publicly "nonpartisan." In this pose, they demonstrated their debt to the tradition of the nonpartisan businessmen-reformers of 1851–53. So it was decided that the vigilance committee as such would remain in the background and that a series of public meetings would be fronted. These "spontaneous" gatherings of citizens were to handle the strictly political aspects of vigilance.[56]

Accordingly, a public meeting was held in front of the Oriental Hotel on June 14. Former city attorney Bailie Peyton was in charge. The anti-committee *Sun* needled, "Bailie commenced by saying that it was unnecessary for him to rehearse the causes which had given birth to the inquisition, and notwithstanding this preface, continued for three-quarters of an hour to 'rehearse'!" The famous false-bottomed ballot box was displayed to the crowd and appropriate resolutions were passed sustaining the work of the committee. But when a resolution was offered by William Sharon (later of Bank of California fame) to the effect that the preceding election had been rigged and therefore had not been an accurate reflection of public opinion, Peyton ruled it out of order. The meeting then broke up in a squabble. (Peyton, a Know-Nothing, had been elected city attorney in 1855, and did not take kindly to these aspersions upon the legality of his election.)[57]

The vigilance men realized that if they stayed too far in the background, nothing might be accomplished. At the next meeting of the executive committee the president, William T. Coleman, introduced resolutions that the executive committee should appoint a subcommittee to inquire into the conduct of the incumbent officials and report upon which of them ought to be invited to resign. The Terry business intervened, and the report was not ready for another month. When it had been completed, another mass meeting was called, this time more carefully staged—Peyton was not the presiding officer, and Sharon was one of the vice-presidents. A long document, entitled "Official Corruption," which had been drawn up by the subcommittee of the executive committee appointed on June 15, was read and adopted. That done, the meeting obediently adjourned.[58]

The report repeated standard businessmen-reformer and Know-Nothing themes. It attacked the expenses that the city and county governments had run up since 1851. The report complained that city warrants had depreciated to roughly half their values and that officials had adopted the practice of issuing warrants for twice the amount necessary, to enable the recipient to recover all the money marked on them. Needless expenses had been burdened on the taxpayers:

> The county has been grossly and continually swindled. Bills for carriage hire of grand juries, fees of coroner and sheriff, charges for stationery, travelling expenses of members of the Board of Supervisors, fees in criminal cases, appropriations and expenses for county roads, bridges, and jobs done without the authority of law, at the instance of individual members of the Board, printing bills, expenses of elections, furniture and other charges—some of which have been gratuitously allowed—have been presented for double and treble the amount due, to enable the holder to realize case value.

The report attacked the fee system and the practice of loading down offices with all sorts of clerks and deputies (i.e., patronage). It concluded by "urging the permanent importance of securing the sacred right of our elective franchise." Finally, it urged the resignations of the Board of Supervisors, the district attorney, the county judge, the county clerk, the recorder, the treasurer, the assessor, the coroner, the surveyor, and the county superintendent of schools—virtually everyone.[59]

The officials were quick to respond. With the exception of the school superintendent and one supervisor, who said they were willing to resign if everyone else did, the officials refused. A sample reply came from the sheriff: "In answer to a communication made to me this morning . . . requesting me to resign the office of sheriff of this county, I respectfully beg leave to inform you that I most positively decline to comply with your request."[60]

The vigilance committee probably expected the refusals and most likely only wanted to put the present officials on record as defying the clear will of the "people." The committee then moved into the second phase of its political operations and arranged another mass meeting for August 11. As it had done at the first mass meeting, the committee tried to stay formally in the background. As a result, the meeting almost broke up in confusion, after the person chosen to preside announced that he really did not know what was going on. Finally, however, the meeting ratified the selection of a committee of twenty-one to present a slate of candidates for offices at the upcoming elections. A month later, on September 11, the committee announced its choices, which were duly ratified at another mass meeting. When Broderick's forces showed what was considered to be surprising strength in a Democratic county primary, the ticket was modified slightly. The tickets were presented with the standard nonpartisan and Know-Nothing rhetoric about these men not having sought office, but rather the offices having sought them. Nugent could not resist: "Oh, no! The offices have been running after them, and judging from the caliber of the ticket we are inclined to think that the offices must have had a hard run of it, considering the by-ways and alleys through which they have been obliged to scamper."[61]

There is no doubt that the vigilance committee did affect the political climate of the city. First, the anti-Democrats presented for office a very high proportion of political novices. As one paper noted, "A number of the tickets are NEW MEN, never heard of before." Twenty-three out of the twenty-five People's Party candidates (92 percent) had not run for office in San Francisco between 1851 and 1855. One of the previous candidates had been an unsuccessful Whig candidate for assistant alderman in the seventh ward. The other had run for the Assembly in 1854 as a Know-Nothing and won. A separate Know-Nothing slate was even more heavily stocked with new faces. It contained only one person who had sought elective office before—a man who had run for the Assembly, as a Whig, in 1853, and had been a Know-Nothing candidate for inspector of elections in 1855. Over the preceding five years, using 1851 as a base, the various anti-Democratic parties had offered 200 men for 227 offices. That meant that about 88 percent of their candidates had been, at the time they ran for office, "new men." The 92 percent of the People's Party slate and the 96 percent of the Know-Nothing ticket topped the previous anti-Democratic performances. The vigilantes had indeed brought more new faces into politics.

The Democratic experience was even more pronounced. Only two of their candidates had stood for office before: one had run for fifth ward assistant alderman in 1855, and the other had not sought office since 1852, when he was the party's candidate for alderman in the same ward. The thirty-one new people out of thirty-three candidates added up to 96 percent of the ticket. Over the preceding five years, reflecting the fact that the Democrats had been more stable than their opponents, 83 percent of the party's candidates had been "new men." The eleven-point jump in 1856 offers very strong evidence that the vigilance committee did in fact drastically disrupt the politics of San Francisco.[62]

An examination of the occupations of the candidates who can be identified adds more evidence along the same lines. The most striking instance was the slate that the People's Party finally settled upon. Almost half (48 percent) of the candidates were merchants of one sort or another. This broke down into two (8 percent) who were importers, and ten (40 percent) who were merchants of a more general type. Up to 1856, the various anti-Democratic political groups in the city and county had presented tickets consisting of a total of 10.1 percent merchants and 14.8 percent importers, for a total of 26 percent in these two categories. The political opposition to the Democrats had always been business oriented; the vigilance committee completed the work that the Know-Nothings had begun and decisively broke through the reluctance of businessmen to stand for public office. Richard Maxwell Brown comments that the People's Party slate was "chosen very carefully so as to give full representation to the business enterprises, trades, and professions of San Francisco." This was true, for the ticket was quite a broad one. It contained, as I count them, three shipmasters, two real estate agents, three builders, two lumber dealers, two physicians, one dry goods dealer, one manufacturer of chemicals, one livery stable keeper, one produce dealer, one iron founder, and one insurance agent among its members.[63]

The other tickets also reflected the mercantile dominance that had been ushered in by the activities of the vigilance committee. Five men (19 percent) on the Know-Nothing slate were merchants, almost twice the anti-Democratic proportion that had been established in the five preceding years. Two Republicans were merchants and two were importers (18 percent each). These figures placed that young party in the position of also being more merchant-studded than had been their anti-Democratic predecessors.

The Democrats recognized the direction in which the wind was blowing. For president of the Board of Supervisors (the position under the Consolidation Act that was roughly equivalent to mayor), they nominated the president of the auctioneers' association, Thomas J. Poulterer. They filled 19 percent of their ticket with individuals from the combined merchant-importer sector. Since, up through 1855, the Democrats had presented slates that totaled only 8.5 percent merchant and 7 percent importer, their 1856 ticket was more heavily stocked with these types than had been their custom.

But this Democratic ticket did share something in common with its predecessors. From 1851 to 1855 fully a third of the Democratic candidates cannot be identified from the city directories. In 1856 this figure declined just a bit, to 28 percent. Since the directories were business and commercial directories, the relatively large number of unidentified candidates most likely indicates that the Democratic ticket continued to contain men from a broader spectrum of the city than the opposition ticket did.

The vigilance antipathy to the legal profession was also reflected in the composition of the People's Party ticket. Only two of those on the ticket were lawyers, meaning that the slate as a whole contained merely 8 percent lawyers. This figure was less than half the pre-1856 anti-Democratic proportion of 17.1 percent. In this respect, at least, the Republicans and the Know-Nothings fielded more "traditional" anti-Democratic tickets, with 19 percent and 18 percent, respectively, of their tickets being lawyers. The Democrats did not change their attitude to lawyers on the ticket. In fact, their slate was slightly more stocked with members of the legal profession than had been their average up to then. The figure in 1856 was 21 percent, as compared with the pre-1856 figure of 17 percent.[64]

The voting on election day proceeded in an orderly fashion. The pro-vigilance press stated that this was because the vigilance committee had expelled the troublemakers from San Francisco, and because the polls were patrolled on election day, not by firemen, but by vigilante military companies. But as I have demonstrated earlier, orderly elections were the rule, not the exception, in pre-vigilante San Francisco.

The vigilance committee scored a stunning victory. The coalition of Republicans and the People's Party carried all its candidates for the legislature and for local offices in all the districts of the city except the first. Buchanan did carry the city, but he had the good fortune to be running against John C. Frémont, whose successful speculation in Mexican estates had given him an unsavory reputation in California. The reeling San Francisco Democracy, whose strategy was to emphasize national, not local issues, paraded through the streets bearing placards with such charming slogans as "FREMONT—FREE NIGGERS AND COPPER CENTS" and "FREMONT—FREE NIGGERS AND FRIJOLES." But it was for nothing, as the vigilance committee assumed political control of the city and county of San Francisco. They also began the process of winning the legitimacy they were to enjoy for almost a century. At one of the theaters, a celebrated actress, Miss Mary Provost, moved audiences to tears with her song on the death of James King. With the stage "festooned with black and white muslin," Miss Provost sang out such verses as "he died at his post doing his duty."[65]

♦ III ♦

There are few natural beginnings or ends in history, but the election of 1856 is a good place to end this account and take our leave of San Francisco's first generation of merchants. They were, by the rules of the quest that had brought them to the Golden Gate, failures. The California gold rush, for all the hopes it inspired across the land, was not the time or place in which large fortunes were to be made. Riches, power, and national influence appeared only when a succeeding generation of San Francisco entrepreneurs learned to control the western transportation revolution and to extract silver from the eastern side of the Sierra. In nineteenth-century California, much that glittered, but nothing that profited, was gold.

Admitting defeat has never been easy for most people, and it certainly was not easy for these merchants. They truly believed that American expansion meant the opportunity for the acquisition of personal wealth. Adversity rarely pushes true believers to recantation; rather, it usually stimulates them to redouble and expand their efforts. Since they had been unable to do a profitable business in the city, they broadened their horizons and attempted, as vigilantes, to remake the entire city in the image of the commercial success that had eluded them. Denied the achievements that alone would have served to make their treks to the West worthwhile, they created another kind of success, another form of status. One of their opponents sensed this when he wrote, "God knows that we have had enough captains, majors, colonels, and such among us, but this late organization has created so many that you are at a loss to know how to address the gentleman you knew yesterday as plain 'Mr.,' for fear he may consider himself insulted by not giving him the title he has so lately acquired." Personal failures as businessmen, they became crusaders of a then-peculiar sort: crusaders for organization. The proudest time of their lives, the only time that served to redeem the failure of their dream, was a time of collective and impersonal action: those brief periods in the summers of 1851 and 1856 when each of them had been known, not by name, but by rank and serial number.[66]

After the 1856 elections, a San Francisco resident sarcastically wrote, "The Republicans combined with the Vigilantes carried the city for all our local offices, and I am informed that we are to have a grand reform." On the basis of their performances over the preceding years, it was clear what sort of principles would guide any government that these men would try to put together. Coleman stated the matter in a nutshell when he reminisced in the 1880's. "The People's Party," he said with satisfaction, "gave the city the delightful novelty of an honest, nonpartisan, and economical government."[67]

The People's Party government remained, as its name implied, formally nonpartisan until it merged with the Republicans in 1865: James King of William had at least that posthumous satisfaction! The party ruled San Francisco until 1867, and for all that time it served as the political arm of the vigilantes. It was, in fact, the successful political culmination of all the "nonpartisan" movements of the previous five years: the 1851–53 independents, the 1851 vigilance committee, the Know-Nothings, and the 1856 vigilance committee. It operated in the fashion of these predecessors. For instance, the party did not hold primary elections. Instead, a secret "Committee of Twenty-One," successor to the executive committee of the committee of vigilance, met in the late summer or early fall before each election and announced the ticket. The names of those who served on the group remain unknown, but there seems no doubt that they were of the same type, character, and occupation as the vigilante leadership. In 1860, for example, at the same time in which he was president of the Chamber of Commerce, Alfred A. Dibblee, no. 2584 in 1856, headed the Committee of Twenty-One. Members of the vigilance committees filled key offices in the People's Party over the term of its rule, and in 1856 the party installed former vigilantes in the offices of Chief of Police, Police Judge, Sheriff, and Treasurer. Also, all the men who served as San Francisco's mayors from 1856 to 1867 were either former vigilantes or closely associated with them.[68]

The People's Party never abandoned the nonpartisan language of disinterested public service. In his farewell address in 1867, retiring mayor H. P. Coon restated the principle that had animated the independent efforts from 1851 on. "I have been elected to office several times, and never by a party vote," he boasted to the Board of Supervisors. "I have never sought office on any occasion, and I am glad to say this because it accords with my own self-respect, and I would rather have made any sacrifice than not to have been able to say it, or to have obtained office in such a manner that I should forfeit the good opinion of my fellow citizens by accepting it." From the time of Sibley's abortive run for mayor in the spring of 1851, scores of political businessmen had been saying, or wanting to say, the same thing.[69]

The former vigilantes sought to keep this flame alive in the city's memory. Years later, Coleman, no. 96 in the 1851 committee and no. 1 in 1856, offered the same view. "I have never sought public prominence, never would accept any office, any emolument, have never been a seeker of place nor of preferment of any kind," he inaccurately recalled. "But happening to be where trouble arose, where danger existed, I have, in a plain way, done what I could to better the condition of affairs." Altruistic and selfless public servants, Cincinnati of San Francisco—that was how the vigilantes wanted themselves remembered.[70]

The People's Party was nonpartisan in another way. Within a year after it took power, it abolished annual elections and thus attempted to reduce the importance of political organization and the likelihood of substantial political change. As one of the vigilantes later put it, "The People's Party realized that rotation in office was the primal cause of the adulteration of public virtue." John Adams and the earlier land for which he spoke may have had other ideas, but for the shapers of the land to come, where annual elections ended, there good government began.[71]

As Coleman stated, the government was economical, although the novelty was not nearly so stunning as he preferred to remember. In its first year in office, the People's Party reduced the municipal budget by 59 percent from the year before. But what Coleman and his friends never mentioned was that the pre-vigilante Democratic administration under Van Ness had itself reduced expenses 68 percent from what they had been under the preceding Know-Nothing government. As I have argued earlier, municipal expenditures were a function of the size of the population and of necessary public improvements such as the construction and grading of streets, the installation of water supplies and equipment, and the building of wharves. Expenditures inevitably declined after the banking failures of early 1855 had made it clear to even the most obtuse resident of the city that San Francisco's boom days were quite over.

The city's population remained fairly stable for the rest of the 1850's and business did not recover until 1861—after more importers had failed, after the Panic of 1857 had tightened credit in the East, after another real estate slump in 1858, and after the beginning of the Civil War, which, by steering the output of eastern factories into military channels, stimulated the growth of local manufacturing. City expenditures, which had declined drastically under Van Ness, therefore remained low from 1856 to 1860. During that period, they averaged $486,407 a year, whereas from 1849 through 1855 (including the 1855 retrenchment) they had averaged $1.2 million. Even the partisan Bancroft reflected, in a footnote, that the People's Party cutback might have been "too severe, for gas and other needfuls were stopped for a while, and streets, schools, etc., suffered somewhat."[72]

But the city was to grow in the 1860's, as population increased 160 percent and local manufacturing and interior agriculture, both of which sparked the economy, advanced. With population growth, expenditures inevitably increased. The 1861–67 average was $853,372, a 75 percent increase over the 1856–60 period. In 1867, its last year in office, the People's Party spent $1.3 million, higher than the average for the period of boom and perceived boom from 1849 to 1855. In short, the financial policies of the People's Party were never so novel as its adherents claimed. When it confronted economic decline, it continued the trend toward reduction its predecessor had initiated. When faced with the phenomenon of economic growth, it proved no more thrifty than the allegedly corrupt and venal administrations that had preceded it. The claims of People's Party frugality were a serious exaggeration.[73]

Yet much else in gold rush San Francisco was exaggerated also. The expectations that had propelled the pioneer merchants to the Pacific Coast were exaggerated. Their claims about the crime and political corruption that supposedly frustrated them were wildly enlarged. And they saw to it that the vigilantism through which they tried to recover their losses and their positions would be remembered in a similarly overblown fashion.

In 1867 the Democrats defeated the People's Party at the polls. Their victorious candidate, Irish-born Frank McCoppin, had not arrived in San Francisco until 1858 and he was thus untainted by the ghosts of Broderick, Casey, and Cora. But in his inaugural address, an obituary on the People's Party, he served notice that he would like to turn the clock back a bit to their time. He gave the most frankly political speech a San Francisco mayor had delivered in a dozen years. Reminding his listeners that, during his own service on the Board of Supervisors, he had been "always hitherto in a minority, politically speaking," he promised an administration that, while not based on a "narrow, partisan spirit," would nevertheless be "in consonance with the noble party that elected me." Broderick, Garrison, and Van Ness would have felt right at home.[74]

Defeated by business in the 1850's and out of political steam in the 1860's, the vigilantes turned to the one area in which they would triumph. They beat a strategic retreat into history. Typically, their history was a history of exaggeration. They constructed a picture of themselves that was overdrawn and legendary. They invented a golden age of contentment, whose decline had allegedly called them forth. The early days—the period of the first boom and excitement—had been, they claimed, a time of prosperity, a commercial Eden. Importer George Schenck, no. 72 in the 1851 committee, recalled: "From November 1849 to March 1850, everything seemed to be quiet here. There was little thieving going on, only an occasional instance of it. As a general thing, it seemed to be very safe, both for life and property." Charles V. Gillespie, no. 188 in 1851 and no. 3 and a member of the executive committee in 1856, painted a similar picture. "In 1848 when gold was first discovered, property of all kinds was very safe, there was no stealing," he stated. "Money could easily be earned, there was no want among the people, and no professional thieves had come." James D. Farwell, a navigator who became a merchant, had been no. 89 in 1851 and no. 6 and a member of the executive committee in 1856. He professed to remember, "When I first came here, I was surprised at the entire cordiality and friendship among the people; they seemed like members of one family and there was a good fellowship prevailing." James Dows, a member of the executive committee in both years, stated, "Along in 1849 and 1850 property was very secure, there was no stealing. A great deal of property was wholly unprotected." James Olney, who commanded the vigilante force that removed Casey and Cora from the jail, had not arrived in the city until 1853, but he claimed to have a similar recollection: "Another thing which struck me was the way in which property was exposed in the stores and streets all the time. Merchandise of all types might stand on the sidewalks all night unmolested."[75]

This legendary golden age (which is absolutely unsupported

by any contemporary evidence, including what the vigilantes themselves said at the earlier times!) had an important benefit for the former committee members: it increased the stature of both their adversaries and of themselves. To corrupt such an idyllic existence, both Australian criminals and Irish political ruffians had to be very powerful, a set of enemies not easily broken. "No perjury was too black, no murder too foul," former mayor Coon insisted. Clancey J. Dempster, a member of the 1856 executive committee, said, "Before the organization of the vigilance committee, society was completely disorganized. Property had no protection and life was insecure." Farwell chimed in with the claim that "the abuses were so great, political and physical too, as I may say, that they had become unbearable, and the life, property, and peace of the community were in danger. Gentlemen were liable to be knocked down in the street or if they went into the saloon to get a drink. The most quiet citizen was liable to be knocked down and stamped upon." John P. Manrow, no. 414 in 1851 and an 1856 executive committee member, stated, "All sorts of assaults, robberies, and other crimes were common." If all this sounds familiar, it should. The former vigilantes peddled their recollections to the Hittells, to Royce, to Bancroft, and the historians picked it up from there. The imitative phase of the historiography, which enshrined the vigilantes and shaped the way the city remembered itself, was off and running. San Francisco may well be the only city in the United States whose early history was written by the losers.[76]

By the 1870's, contemporaries knew that San Francisco had changed, that it bore scant resemblance to the siren that had summoned thousands of ambitious and eager young men west and had promised them instant wealth. The pioneer generation, those who had placed such hopes in the city's commercial possibilities in the late 1840's and early 1850's, were no longer the kingpins in the city by the bay. When he began his 1878 *History of the City of San Francisco*, John Hittell spoke of the "succession of rapid and startling vicissitudes" that that first group had experienced. Hittell composed almost a dirge on the death of their hopes: "Whatever misfortunes have overtaken the individual citizens, they have the consolation of seeing that California has advanced with a swift and grand prosperity, and that they have participated in one of the most imposing pageants ever enacted on the stage of universal history." Perhaps they were thus consoled. If so, it was because an unforgiving city had forced them to abandon their youthful dreams.[77]

Two decades later, in a biographical collection celebrating the citizens of the Golden State, W. F. Swasey returned to the same theme. Speaking of James Wadsworth, no. 44 and an executive committee member in 1851, he said, "Like many other old pioneers, Mr. Wadsworth has met with many reverses." Again, Swasey reported that Alfred J. Ellis, no. 129 and also a member of the esteemed executive committee in 1851, "was at one time rich, but died several years ago very poor."[78]

By the time Hittell and Swasey wrote, San Francisco was a city of big business and corporate wealth. The men of influence were those like Leland Stanford, who had been a run-of-the-mill merchant in Sacramento in 1856 and who, on June 20 of that year, had to supply two references, just like anyone else, before the merchants of San Francisco would consent to enroll him in their vigilance committee. The booming metropolis of the later nineteenth century retained one element of the 1850's shell from which it had emerged: it continued to deny the hopes and defy the expectations of most of the gold rush merchants.[79]

Most of them, together with those with whom they lived and worked and competed and fought in early San Francisco, dropped from sight, like Harvey Lamb before them. But we can glimpse some of them as they moved through the city and state and nation after the vigilance committee had adjourned. A few final glances can serve to close this account.

Milton Latham found for a time that politics continued to be rewarding. He was elected governor in 1859, and still holds the distinction of being the state's shortest-term chief executive: five days after he took the oath of office, he was elected by the legislature to fill Broderick's unexpired term in the United States Senate. Failing in 1863 to be reelected, he returned to San Francisco and engaged in banking and speculation. In 1867 he was named head of the California Pacific Railroad. But he suffered financial reversals in the 1870's, and by 1880 he had gone back to New York City, where his contacts landed him an administrative position with the Mining and Stock Exchange. He did not manage to recover all his earlier losses before he died in 1882. At his request, his body was returned to the place that had given him the greatest success in life: he was buried in San Francisco's Lone Mountain cemetery.[80]

William Daingerfield got his wish in 1854 when Governor John Bigler made him a judge, but he had to be content with the Fourth Judicial District in the remote northern part of the state. He filled that position, without becoming either rich or renowned, for the next ten years. In 1864 he returned to the city in which he had placed such great hopes in 1853, and he practiced law successfully for another decade. Forming a partnership with a retired judge of the state supreme court, he became a moderately successful San Francisco attorney. He returned to the bench in 1875, in a position more consistent with his earlier hopes: Judge of the Twelfth Judicial District, which comprised San Mateo and San Francisco counties. But he served for only five years. He died while hearing a case in 1880.[81]

Henry M. Naglee continued in the banking business in San Francisco until the Civil War. The lure of battle beckoned the old soldier back east and he served in the Union army in some campaigns in Virginia and the Carolinas. In 1864, frustrated and embittered because he had not been promoted as rapidly as he thought he deserved, he resigned his commission and returned to California. But the booming city of San Francisco was not the place for him. He had had enough of the turbulence and uncertainty that was life in the port. So he settled in the Santa Clara valley and, as a contemporary put it, attended to "the culture of the grape." He became a local authority on the production of wines and brandies and died a respected member of the smaller and less hectic San Jose society. A street in that city still bears his name.[82]

George Oakes, who rang the bell for the trial of Jenkins, died of natural causes in October 1851, soon after the committee he had summoned adjourned.[83]

Alfred A. Dibblee was one of the vigilantes who did find prosperity in San Francisco. After 1856 his importing and shipping business thrived, and he served as president of the Chamber of Commerce from 1859 to 1861. He was chairman of the executive committee of the Chamber in 1867 and a trustee of the group in the early 1870's. In the 1860's he bought estates around Monterey with W. W. Hollister and managed to become something of a land baron. He died a respected and successful citizen in San Francisco in 1895.[84]

For a time Sam Brannan did as well. He continued his real estate business in the city for the rest of the decade and successfully weathered the 1858 decline in land values. In 1863, together with former governor Peter Burnett, he organized the first chartered bank in the state. Five years later he bought the huge Stearns estate in southern California. But his luck soured. He bought land in Napa County around Agua Caliente (Hot Springs) and decided to make the place a California version of the famous New York resort at Saratoga. Lest anyone miss his intentions, he renamed the place Calistoga. Even though he was able to push a railroad connection from there through to San Francisco, Calistoga, like San Francisco before it, never quite lived up to his expectations and he lost heavily. In an attempt to recoup he organized a colonization project in Sonora, Mexico. He received a grant from the Mexican authorities but, unfortunately for him, the Yaqui Indians who lived on the land were not amused by his scheme. Their hostility made settlement impossible and he lost more money. Then his wife divorced him and he turned increasingly to the bottle. He died in poverty in Escondido in 1889.[85]

Frederick W. Macondray, who was twenty years older than most of the other pioneer merchants and a father figure to many of them, contracted severe asthma during the operation of the 1856 vigilance committee. He served out a term as president of the Chamber of Commerce but pretty much retired from business after that. He died in the early 1860's.[86]

Isaac Bluxome, who was "67 Secretary" in the 1851 committee and "33 Secretary" in 1856, continued his career as a merchant through the 1850's and 1860's, but he had mixed results. He was burned out a few times after 1856, and, as a contemporary noted, "The reverses which have caught so many of the early pioneers of the state seriously affected him." In the late 1870's he tried his hand at investing in mining in Amador County, but the return was mediocre. Telling and retelling stories of the old days to his children, he continued to live in the city until his death, a man for whom having been secretary to two vigilance committees was the high point of his life.[87]

William T. Coleman left San Francisco for New York in August 1856, after the committee had disbanded but before the elections that swept the People's Party to power. Tending his business and building his company into a solid trading firm, he spent most of the next fourteen years in the East. He returned to San Francisco in 1870 and built a modest mansion for himself on a hill that soon became known as Nob Hill when Leland Stanford, Mark Hopkins, and Charles Crocker decided to construct residential monuments to themselves nearby. Coleman headed the Chamber of Commerce in 1873 and four years later organized the "Pick-Handle Brigade," a coalition of merchants and shopkeepers who beat up a fringe group of Kearneyites near the waterfront. His sojourn in New York had given him something of a national reputation. In 1887 Charles Dana of the New York *Sun*, desperate for anyone but Grover Cleveland, floated a quickly withdrawn trial balloon touting him as the next Democratic nominee for President. A bit later he was one of the few Californians to be included in the *National Cyclopaedia of American Biography*. The end of his life was not tranquil. In 1888 a large investment in borax production in Death Valley failed, and William T. Coleman and Co. went bankrupt. Coleman, always the stubborn individualist, almost a throwback to the antebellum years, told a reporter, "I can take my coat off and go back to work again." By liquidating his property and assets, he eventually paid off his creditors in full. He died, no longer rich, but deeply mourned, in 1893.[88]

David C. Broderick was elected to the United States Senate in 1857. His known position as a Free Soil Democrat resulted in hostility to him on the part of the Buchanan administration. As a result, he was never able to control the patronage that his dominance of the state legislature would otherwise have given him. He voted with Stephen A. Douglas and against the administration on the question of the admission of Kansas and gained national attention by his reply to the "Cotton is King" speech of South Carolina Senator James Hammond. In that address Hammond had argued that Northern white laborers were just as much a "mudsill" in their society as the black slaves were in the South. Broderick dramatically pointed to the columns in the Senate chamber and said that his own father had sculpted them. The fact that he himself was now a senator, he passionately argued, proved the fallaciousness of Hammond's assertions. Broderick closed the reply with a denunciation of "the fading intellect, the petulant passion, and the trembling dotage of an old man on the verge of the grave"—President Buchanan!

Remarks such as these did not endear him to the South or to the Chivalry in California. During the 1859 campaign in California, former vigilante prisoner and current state supreme court justice David S. Terry made a speech at the Chivalry state convention in which he denounced Broderick and his allies: "Perhaps they do sail under the flag of Douglas, but it is the banner of the black Douglass, whose name is Frederick, not Stephen." The next day Broderick remarked to a group in San Francisco that Terry's speech was terribly ungracious, since he, Broderick, had spent a lot of money in 1856 subsidizing newspapers that called for Terry's release from Fort Gunnybags. He went on to say that he had once thought that Terry was the only honest man on the high court, but that he did not think so any more.

One thing led to another and, on September 13, 1859, Terry killed Broderick in a duel near Lake Merced. Nineteenth-century victims always seemed to have time to utter some dramatic final words, and Broderick's supposedly were, "I die because I was opposed to a corrupt administration and the extension of slavery." Because he had died in a duel, the Catholic authorities refused to let him be buried at Mission Dolores. So what was reputed to be the largest crowd in the history of San Francisco escorted his body to Lone Mountain, where James King had been interred thirty-nine months before.[89]

Terry was not renominated in 1859 by the Chivalry Democrats for the state supreme court. After the duel with Broderick he headed for the Comstock Lode in Nevada to practice law. His brother was killed early in the Civil War and he then returned to Texas to fight in his place. He served in the Confederate forces for the duration of the conflict. Then he became involved in an abortive colonization scheme in Mexico. He finally settled in Stockton and by the end of the 1870's he was a figure in the local Democratic party. He served as a delegate to the 1879 California constitutional convention, but his political star set the following year, as he failed in an attempt to be chosen a presidential elector.

So he returned to the practice of law. As an attorney he entered the celebrated litigation between Sarah Althea Hill and William Sharon, former People's Party organizer, silver baron, and United States senator from Nevada. Hill claimed that Sharon had secretly married her. In the course of the tangled proceedings, as U.S. Supreme Court Justice Stephen J. Field, sitting on circuit, was reading a decision adverse to Sarah, she became agitated and Field ordered her out of the courtroom. When a marshal approached to remove her, Terry punched him in the face. For doing so, he was sentenced to six months in jail.

In August 1889—a year later—Terry and Justice Field happened to be on the same train heading from Fresno to San Francisco. On August 14, when the train stopped for breakfast at Lathrop, near Stockton, the two men discovered each other and words ensued. In an instant, a deputy marshal accompanying Field, David Neagle, claiming that Terry was about to stab Field, killed Terry with two shots. The sheriff of Stockton arrested Neagle and the case ended only when the United States Supreme Court found in Neagle's favor. So David Terry survives now as the answer to a law school trivia question: who was the disappointed litigant whose violence led to the broad definition of implied powers in the case *In Re Neagle*?[90]

J. Neely Johnson's political career in California ended with his opposition to the 1856 vigilance committee. In 1858 he invested unsuccessfully in mining in Trinity County, and two years later he started a reverse migration that would last for the rest of his life. He moved to the Washoe Valley in Nevada, was a delegate to the Nevada constitutional convention in 1863 and served as its president the next year, and then sat for four years on the Nevada Supreme Court. After that he moved to Salt Lake City, where he intended to practice law. But he died in 1872, before he had got well started. His Carson City, Nevada, residence, called Governor's House, is now a tourist attraction.[91]

C. K. Garrison returned permanently to the East in 1859. Investing in gas companies, steamships, and railroads, he became a regular figure in New York's financial circles. In 1876 he was named president of the Missouri Pacific Railroad, and later he was a part owner of the first elevated railroad constructed in New York City. He suffered a series of financial losses in the late 1870's, and he managed to recover only some of them before his death in 1885.[92]

James Van Ness found it difficult to resume a law practice in San Francisco after he left city government, so in 1861 he moved south, settling in San Luis Obispo and dabbling in agriculture. In 1871 he reentered politics as a state senator, but he died at the end of the following year. His children, though, remained connected to the city their father had governed. His daughter married Frank McCoppin, the first Democrat after Van Ness to be elected mayor. And, after studying at Santa Clara College, his son became a prominent San Francisco attorney, who specialized in insurance matters and scrupulously avoided criminal law.[93]

Billy Mulligan did not have a pleasant end. As Broderick had known, he was unstable, and his banishment from the city by the vigilantes did not change his condition. He arrived in New York by the end of 1856 and spent the next few years picking fights with, among others, former vigilantes who happened to be visiting the Empire City. He was finally sentenced to Casey's old residence, Sing Sing, but he got himself released on bail pending interminable appeals. He married in the early 1860's, but the union lasted only briefly. He returned to San Francisco in early 1864. A year later, claiming that the old vigilantes were still out to get him, he barricaded himself in a room at the St. Francis Hotel and started shooting out the window. He killed a friend of his who tried to calm him down and another passerby on the street below. The authorities surrounded the place, and police sharpshooters quickly ended his life.[94]

David Scannell, one of King's many candidates for the hangman's noose, remained in San Francisco after his term as sheriff expired. He devoted himself to the Empire Engine Co. No. 1, the organization that Broderick had started, which was renamed the Broderick No. 1 after the senator's death. In 1861, Scannell was elected chief engineer of the volunteer fire department and composed crisp, businesslike reports for his former adversaries in the People's Party government. In the 1870's, he served as head of the paid fire department. He never married. A contemporary remarked, "No one can ever remember of his having a sweetheart." When he died in 1893, the fire department gave the man they affectionately called "The Chief" a large and dignified funeral.[95]

Edward McGowan fled San Francisco soon after Casey shot King and spent the summer dodging vigilante informers and sympathizers in so many alleged places that he got the nickname "ubiquitous." He was finally tried for complicity in the murder of King in Napa in 1857. He was acquitted and shortly after published his memoirs. The next year he started a newspaper, *The Phoenix*, in Sacramento. He spent the next decade and a half wandering around the western United States and Canada.

By 1875 he was back in San Francisco. He and Coleman squared off in a series of newspaper articles in 1884, but, at the same time, they seem to have become personally friendly. Usually wearing a large white hat as he promenaded through the city, McGowan became by the end of his life a local character. One of the former vigilantes reflected that "without being absolutely wicked, he yet glories in a reputation for vice." He became a favorite of local reporters eager to enliven their historical sketches with lore from the gold rush period, and even Bancroft, who called him a "jolly villain," seems to have fallen under his spell. He died in December 1893, savoring what was for him the great pleasure of outliving Coleman by two weeks.[96]

Appendix

Some Notes on the Historiography of Early San Francisco

Because they were connected with such dramatic and public events, the vigilance committees served as the focus around which much of the history of the gold rush port was written. History is a collective enterprise, as each writer tries to build on the insights of predecessors. The historiography of early San Francisco has consisted of two broad phases. The first, the phase of imitation, began shortly after the 1856 committee disbanded, and it lasted for about a century. The second, the phase of analysis, began in the 1960's and has continued until the present.

A remark by a close observer serves to delineate the contours of the imitative phase of the scholarship. Of the more than 50,000 residents of San Francisco during the 1850's, the man who was to become the best-known national figure in later nineteenth-century America opposed the formation of the committee of vigilance in 1856. William Tecumseh Sherman had been a banker in the gold rush city, and when he came to write his *Memoirs* a quarter-century after his California sojourn, he said of the vigilantes, "As they controlled the press, they wrote their own history." His largely accurate comment serves to underscore the close relationship throughout the first phase of the historiography between what gold rush San Franciscans said about the vigilantes ("the press") and what later writers recorded ("history"). In fact, for almost a century, many historians of gold rush San Francisco seemed intent on standing Santayana's celebrated axiom on its head: the more they studied the past, the more they tended to repeat it.[1]

The imitative phase involved three movements, and, by the time it was over, it had come full circle. First, from the 1860's to the 1920's, during the period of California historiography that Gerald D. Nash has labeled the pioneer era (1850–90) and the romantic era (1890–1920), many early historians of the city sought to justify the vigilantes. Some actually seemed to be taking up residence in the vigilante headquarters, Fort Gunnybags, and establishing themselves as head cheerleaders for Judge Lynch. For the most part, their commentaries echoed what the pro-vigilance *Chronicle* and its allies had thundered in 1856, "This community must be purged from its dregs, the creatures, whoever they are, who have poisoned the fountains of society and made the place as loathsome as a charnel house." These historians outdid one another in describing how terrible life had been in the gold rush port, how the sober citizens took it for as long as they could, and how, when all other remedies had been exhausted, they finally came to the difficult conclusion that they had to take the law into their own hands if the city were to be saved. Second, around 1920, beginning the historiographical period that Nash termed the age of realism (1920–45), the hurrahs began to be toned down. Following the lead of people like Sherman, historians increasingly began to question the long-range utility of casting aside the law even for allegedly noble purposes. Finally, around 1950, the actions of the committee became increasingly condemned. The remarks of the anti-vigilance *Herald* came into vogue: "We rest now beneath the shadow of a vast and ominous tyranny. We have had extended over us, in time of profound peace, an unquestioned military tyranny." And so the circle closed, with the men of the committee more humbled than exalted.[2]

The initial movement of the imitative phase formally started in 1866, with the publication of Franklin Tuthill's *The History of California*, which Kevin Starr has correctly termed "California's first mature work of history." Tuthill adopted the vigilantes' own justification for their behavior. According to this version of events, by the spring of 1856, San Francisco was controlled by an interlocking directorate of crime and political corruption. With appalling regularity, a group of unscrupulous men stuffed the ballot boxes and filled the public offices with their cronies. Once elected, these "bad men," who "had things very much their own way," milked the public treasury and protected the criminals who had placed them in office. As a result, Tuthill claimed, the city became unlivable: "San Franciscans, after dark, instinctively avoided a crowd; and if they had occasion to go into the sandy or chaparral-covered suburbs after nightfall, they felt they neglected their duties to themselves and to their families unless they took a revolver." Since "rowdies, gamblers, state prison convicts, and 'Sydney ducks' could in ten minutes after the polls were closed make any majority for the side they wanted," ordinary political opposition to the thugs was useless, and extralegal activity offered the only possible solution. Tuthill conceded that the legal rights of some individuals were violated by the vigilantes, but he insisted that the committee was "a reign of terror only to evildoers." He argued that the work of the committee was fundamentally conservative: "They broke up the combination of the lawless and set law in an honored seat again." While admitting that there was a "political concern" in the work of the committee, he denied that the men of the committee sought any selfish objectives. They aimed only at the purification of the electoral process. Having achieved this limited goal, the vigilantes "drew a long breath and felt a grateful sense of relief to retire again into their private pursuits."

In other words, Tuthill thought that the vigilance committee had been an unqualified success because it brought a stunning cleansing of the city's political and civic life. And as a result of this justified cleansing, he wrote, "The people rule San Francisco, and, in consequence, it has the reputation of being the best-governed city in the Union."[3]

Over the next century, the main outlines of Tuthill's drama were widely accepted and repeated by writers on San Francisco history. Stephen P. Webb was one such writer. In 1874 he wrote an essay entitled "A Sketch of the Causes, Operations, and Results of the San Francisco Vigilance Committee of 1856." Webb had served for a time as mayor of Salem, Massachusetts, in the 1840's before coming to San Francisco in 1853. In 1854 he ran for mayor on the Know-Nothing ticket and was elected and served one year. He eventually returned to Salem, where he was elected mayor again in the early 1860's. The essay of 1874 is based on recollections of a city he had known in its early days and had long since left. Webb followed Tuthill in arguing that pervasive political corruption was the major cause of the formation of the committee. He asked himself a standard question, and he was content with a standard answer: "When a community had lapsed into a condition in which the bad element has become dominant and has succeeded in paralyzing or perfecting law and justice so that brute force and violence have full sway and life and property are entirely insecure, [is] there any other conceivable mode which the well-disposed, industrious, and orderly can assert their rights and secure their liberty than the one adopted by the San Francisco Vigilance Committee in 1856? No other was suggested at the time, nor, so far as the writer knows, has been since."

Webb did not entirely accept the contention that the political system of the gold rush city was hopelessly corrupt (he himself had been mayor, after all!), but he more or less supported the charge of apathy, especially on the part of the men who became vigilantes in 1856. They were too carried away by the get-rich-quick mania of the gold rush: "Confident that a short time would enable them to realize their great object of making a fortune and then leaving the country, the better portion of the community abandoned the control of public affairs to whoever might be willing or desirous to attempt it." The effect of Webb's strictures was to dim, ever so slightly, the glitter of the vigilantes. At the same time, Tuthill's basic division, good citizens versus criminals, was left intact.[4]

The first full-scale history of San Francisco was published in 1878. It was written by John S. Hittell, a journalist who had lived in the city during the 1850's. Like Webb, Hittell accepted the Tuthill notion that an unholy alliance between criminals and corrupt politicians had left the decent citizens no choice but to resort to vigilantism, but he deemphasized the alleged prevalence of street crime in the city. In his view, the main objective of the committee had been "to secure political justice." He stated categorically, in a judgment that was to be repeated often and examined rarely by subsequent historians during the imitative phase, "The American political system had in 1855 reached a greater depth of corruption in San Francisco than in any other part of the United States." He argued that the cause of this deplorable state of affairs was not the apathy of respectable citizens but their virtuous disinclination to "bribe conventions and descend to low associations." Politics had become so foul that the stench repelled good men. (Of course, this begged the question of just how politics had been allowed to become so foul.) So, in 1856, "Quiet men said that either they or the scoundrels must leave San Francisco."

Even though he wrote within Tuthill's framework, Hittell did make four important contributions to the historiography of vigilantism. The first, which I have already noted, was his emphasis on the political orientation of some of the committee's acts. The second was that he attempted to relate the formation of the vigilance committee in 1856 to a business recession that he said had begun in 1854. In his chapter on the committee, "The Golden Years in Decline," he sketched out the elements of a "serious depression" and "the decay in business" that hit the city in the mid-1850's. He viewed the years 1854–60 as a period of commercial adversity that attended the shift from gold to silver as the source of mining wealth. Though he did not elaborate the specific connection between recession and vigilance, his juxtaposition of the two was a reminder that the men of the committee had done more in San Francisco than run away from criminals and feel powerless before hordes of political bullies. He began to sketch, in very rough outline, a social context for San Francisco vigilantism.

Third, he called attention to the Consolidation Act, passed by the legislature in the spring of 1856. This statute merged the city and county governments and put a lid on the amount of money the consolidated government could spend. The People's Party government that was elected after the vigilante victory in 1856 drastically cut the municipal budget and claimed that fiscal conservatism was one of the tangible results of vigilance. Yet, at least some of the savings resulted from the Consolidation Act's explicit strictures concerning the budget and from its merging of some overlapping city and county administrative agencies. Finally, Hittell claimed that James King, the shooting of whom had sparked the formation of the 1856 committee, had been something less than a saint. Hittell said of King's paper, the *Bulletin*, "Many of its attacks on individuals were not sustained by proof, or even plausible testimony, and others were unjust or even inexcusable." There was something of a personal element in this criticism, dating from a quarrel between Hittell and King in the 1850's; King, a person of strong evangelical leanings, made no secret of his dislike of the freethinking Tom Paine Society, of which Hittell was secretary. Even so, the historian's negative appraisal of the editor was important, for King more than any other contemporary had popularized the image of innocent San Francisco in the grasp of political thugs that had served Tuthill and Webb so powerfully. Hittell's work meant that a slight revision of the justification interpretation would be necessary.[5]

Josiah Royce, in his 1886 work *California*, undertook this revision. For Royce, the city was indeed a moral theater, but the cast of characters was very different from the one sketched by Tuthill and his followers. When those writers had spoken of corruption, they had referred almost exclusively to the political arena. Royce argued that the whole city suffered from a deep-rooted corruption to which most of the citizens contributed; it was guilty of a "great social sin"—the lack of a "true public spirit." Royce saw signs of this sin in the existence of many phenomena that San Francisco shared with other frontier cities: gambling, prostitution, political chicanery, shady business dealings, and large indebtedness. But whereas Tuthill, Webb, and Hittell had made a distinction between good citizens and criminals, Royce believed that everyone in the city was to blame for "social apathy" and "treasonable public carelessness." Royce followed Hittell in claiming that business reversals in 1854 and 1855 were connected with the formation of the vigilance committee, and he was more explicit about the nature of the connection. He argued that they made manifest this "social corruption that had been growing but had previously been hidden." He dismissed Hittell's strictures against King ("Nobody cares now how far King's personal hatreds were well founded") but credited the journalist for his "denunciation of the whole social condition."

Royce always viewed San Francisco through moral lenses. The committee was an expression of the "depth and bitterness of the popular repentance" for the errors of the past. It signaled a "reformation" in which the people were "converted from their sins." Since he regarded San Francisco as "unpurified," he was able to ask, in explicitly scriptural terms, "What but a revolution could deliver the community from the body of this death?" The vigilante activity heralded the "conversion of honest men to a sensible and devout local patriotism." Royce concluded that the formation of the committee was probably "inevitable," an example of the workings of "the great law that people who forget the divine order of things have to learn thereof anew some day, in anxiety and in pain."

Royce's greatest contribution was his insistence that the vigilance committee must be understood in reference to the entire social history of the city, and his elaboration of the argument that the vigilantes were at least partly responsible for the evils of which they complained. He also called attention to the mercantile character of the executive committee of the committee of vigilance and labeled the entire committee a "Business Man's Revolution." In 1856, John Nugent, the editor of the anti-vigilance *Herald*, had branded it a "mercantile junta" and a "commercial diet," but this point had been obscured in the writings of Tuthill, Webb, and Hittell. Royce was sometimes imprecise. He believed in California history as a "parable of social philosophy," to use Earl Pomeroy's phrase, and he was interested in the subject not for its own sake but for the lessons he thought it could teach an increasingly industrialized America on the topic of human community. So he did not clutter his book with detail, and he ruled out of consideration incidents he judged to contain merely "adventurous interest." He probably ruled out too much. He did not investigate the business system in any detail, nor did he examine the way in which the recession of 1854–55 affected the businessmen who ran the revolution. Though he noted the importance of businessmen in the vigilance committee, he failed to investigate that importance closely.[6]

Royce's book was followed a year later by Hubert Howe Bancroft's two-volume *Popular Tribunals*. In this work, Bancroft broke little new ground, and his approach was decidedly apologetic. (The dedication to volume 2 reads: "To William T. Coleman, Chief of the greatest Popular Tribunal the world has ever witnessed.") Like his predecessors, Bancroft ascribed the formation of the committee to pervasive crime and political corruption (he emphasized the point by including an engraving of a phony ballot box). In his view, extralegal remedies were necessary to bring stability and order: "Attempts to purify society through the citizens' right of suffrage was applying to politics the Rosicrucian method of greasing the weapon while binding the wound." He continued, "Corruption propagated. Rascality bred rascality, and the reign of crime seemed self-perpetuating." The root of the evil, according to Bancroft, was the "politico-ruffian element" headed by Democratic chief David Broderick, which the committee attacked and defeated; and if civil liberties were violated, that could not be helped. The extreme state of emergency that prevailed in the city in the spring of 1856 was no time for quibbling over "legal technicalities," and he challenged those who disapproved of the committee to "first provide a substitute which promises protection."

Though by 1887 all this was quite standard, Bancroft did make an important, if perhaps unwitting, peripheral contribution when he rendered explicit the ethnic dimension of the committee. He fumed over the "impudent assumption of political power by foreign cutthroats" on which he blamed many of San Francisco's ills, and he was frankly disgusted that the United States had "opened the doors for the refuse of Europe to come in and govern us." Bancroft's greatest contribution, however, was the caliber of his scholarship. With the help of his staff, Bancroft examined all the available newspapers of the period, and the oral reminiscences he collected from many of the surviving vigilantes enriched the narrative account with color and spice. John Walton Caughey has written that the work is a "monograph of unusual merit," and Roger Olmsted has remarked that "it is unlikely that Bancroft's account can ever be topped as sound *narrative*." I tend to agree with both judgments.

Nonetheless, though *Popular Tribunals* is attractive for its narrative vividness, it fails to discuss questions that might have necessitated a revision of the justification interpretation. Preferring to remain with the conventional law-abiding citizen versus criminal dichotomy, Bancroft barely acknowledged the commercial backgrounds of most of the men on the executive committee and did not seriously discuss Nugent's "mercantile junta" charge. Similarly, even though he regarded politics as the committee's major concern, he did not investigate the political system. Together with many other genteel American historians in the late nineteenth century, he could see little but corruption and thievery emanating from urban and immigrant political organizations. His stridency in defending the work of the committee sometimes led him into curious inconsistencies. For example, he was absolutely convinced that Charles Cora was guilty of the murder of the marshal, Richardson, in the fall of 1855. Bancroft was apparently not bothered by the fact that Richardson was armed and that, even though public sentiment in the city had been inflamed against Cora, a jury of admittedly respectable citizens could not agree on a verdict (which as

David A. Williams was to point out, might be regarded as speaking well for the city's administration of justice). He even had some posthumous advice for Cora: "He could have walked away and Richardson would not have slain him. There was not the slightest danger of it." He concluded that, even if Cora had been killed as he was walking away, "I had rather be a murdered man than a murderer." Noble sentiments indeed, but never offered to the vigilantes! Again, Bancroft at one point argued that the fundamental nobility and virtuousness of the vigilantes were evident in their refusal to accept public office. "Had they wished to rule," he opined, "they might have easily made themselves governors, legislators, and judges, in the legitimate way, and without resorting to violence." If this indeed had been possible, then it undercut the argument that formed the backbone of the work, that extralegal activity was the only way to restore integrity to the political process.[7]

Bancroft's massive tomes were joined ten years later by another multivolume effort, Theodore H. Hittell's *History of California*. Like Bancroft, Theodore Hittell accepted the standard pro-vigilante arguments of crime and corruption, and, like Bancroft, his interpretive framework was unoriginal. He simply repeated John S. Hittell's statement that there had never been as much political corruption anywhere in the United States as there had been in San Francisco in the 1850's, and he continued the Hittell tradition of offering little evidence for that judgment. However, as had Bancroft, Hittell made an important peripheral contribution to the study of San Francisco vigilantism. Bringing together a number of events and interpretations, he attempted to present in a systematic way the causes of the allegedly deplorable state of the city in the spring of 1856. In the first place, he blamed the newness of the city and "the unsettled conditions of society and business" for frustrating the establishment of order. Nugent had argued along similar lines in a *Herald* editorial on May 26, 1856. Hittell also called attention to the gold rush and, with Webb, traced public apathy to a feverish desire for wealth. He also pointed a finger at the structure of the political system. Reflecting the values of the burgeoning progressive movement, he argued that any political system that depended upon patronage and party loyalties inevitably produced corruption and bad government. He also stated that "the gambling of over-speculation and the decline of the placer mines after 1853" also contributed to the social unrest in the city, but he left the question of the precise way in which these developments related to the vigilance committee unasked and unanswered. However, his treatment was the most systematic and thorough to date of the components of the situation Royce had branded "social corruption."[8]

The effect of the massive labors of Bancroft and Theodore H. Hittell was to establish almost a dogmatic and standard interpretation of the San Francisco vigilance committee of 1856. In broad outline, this interpretation was that crime and corruption were widespread and were patiently endured by the better class of citizens for too long a time; then a prophet appeared, exposing corruption and urging the citizenry to action, but it took the shock of his cold-blooded murder to produce results; men reluctantly took the law into their own hands, cleansed the city, selflessly renounced power after their noble tasks were completed, and left San Francisco a model city. This interpretation appears in full dress in a 1911 biography of Broderick by Jeremiah Lynch entitled *A Senator of the Fifties*. In his two chapters on the committee, Lynch mentioned Broderick's name only once—that being a grudging admission that, yes, the attorney E. D. Baker who defended Cora in court in 1855 and 1856 was the same E. D. Baker who delivered the stirring eulogy over the slain Senator Broderick in 1859; "What will lawyers not do for money?" Lynch inquired. Lynch took the rather startling view that the vigilance committee was not involved in politics at all. Though he conceded that it went after some of Broderick's "errant followers," he effectively—and quite inaccurately—tried to separate Broderick from all vigilance-related activity.[9]

The emergence of the committee as a sacred cow signaled defeat for writers who had written in opposition to the committee. In 1857 Judge Edward McGowan, an ally of Broderick, wrote a personal account that was one of the first published attacks on the committee. As with many nineteenth-century memoirs, the gist of McGowan's account can be gleaned from the full title: *Narrative of Edward McGowan, Including a Full Account of the Author's Adventures and Perils While Persecuted by the San Francisco Vigilance Committee of 1856*. McGowan had been accused by the committee and indicted by a grand jury of complicity in the shooting of King. He barely managed to escape from San Francisco, and most of the book deals with his escapades in flight from the vigilantes. He denied that he was part of any conspiracy to kill King, although he admitted that he had been aware that Casey was planning to shoot it out with the editor. McGowan's work is not much more than an unconvincing personal defense, but it was at least an indication that the opponents of the committee were attempting to put their own case on record.[10]

A more sustained attack on the committee appeared in 1858, in an unsigned pamphlet entitled *Judges and Criminals*. The author, generally thought to be Henry M. Gray, did for the opponents of the committee, who called themselves the "law and order" group, what Tuthill was to do for the vigilantes in 1866: he faithfully took up their arguments. His main attack was on the unconstitutional nature of the vigilance committee, its suppression of civil liberties, the secrecy of its proceedings, and its establishment of what he thought was a dangerous precedent. Gray admitted that social and political conditions in San Francisco were unsettled in 1856, but he insisted that whatever evils existed were of a long-term nature and were not susceptible to solution through lynch law. The federal government, he argued, had not protected lives and property at the beginning of the American occupation, and this neglect would take time to overcome. He attributed the lack of peace and quiet in the city to the presence of a large number of footloose former soldiers and also to the get-rich-quick mentality of the gold rush; the extreme heterogeneity of San Francisco's population complicated the establishment of a stable society, and the apathy of the leading citizens in the town greatly facilitated the breakdown of order. Gray made the interesting suggestion that the men of the committee might have had some ulterior motives—specifically, some of the vigilantes, he said, wanted to bring the courts into public disrepute, since the judges had handed down some legal decisions "adverse to some of the existing bogus titles to real estate," which, presumably, the vigilantes held. Further, he claimed that "anything which would occur by which the Democratic party could be broken up would be a godsend to numerous political vultures," who, presumably, were the vigilantes.

The strength of Gray's essay was his attempt to place the formation and acts of the committee within the context of life in gold rush San Francisco. But his failure to substantiate many of the numerous charges he tossed around made it easy for later pro-vigilance historians to ignore most of the issues he raised.[11]

The *Memoirs* of General William T. Sherman, which were published in 1875, were the first public statement of any importance after Gray's anonymous pamphlet to raise serious questions about the vigilance committee. Sherman accused the committee of having set a very dangerous precedent, for "who is to say that the vigilance committee may not be composed of the worst, instead of the best elements in the community?" He admitted that there was a certain amount of political corruption in San Francisco, but he joined Gray in assigning the primary responsibility to apathy. "The better classes," he remarked, "avoided the elections and dodged jury duty."[12]

Since Sherman was by 1875 a national figure, pro-vigilance historians were quick to attack the reliability of his version of events. Royce scoffed that Sherman's memory "was hardly meant by the Creator for historical purposes, genial and amusing though its productions may be," and Bancroft sneered that the California sections of the *Memoirs* were "a marvel of error and prejudice." It is true that there are minor errors of fact in the *Memoirs*, but it is also true that Sherman's general evaluation of the committee in the *Memoirs* was consistent with his public stand in 1856. A few weeks after the committee had been organized, he wrote to a newspaper, "It is pretty well known to this community that I am opposed to the action of the Vigilance Committee." As he was to do two decades later, Sherman denounced public apathy and stated that the situation in the city was not nearly so bad as the vigilantes claimed. Charging that "the amount of crime has been exaggerated," he declared that all the time he had been in California he had never had to carry a weapon, except in hostile Indian country, and that he had never been molested. He maintained that "the condition of society has been gradually improving and that if one-tenth the money had been expended, or one-tenth the effort been exerted, to sustain the courts as to overthrow them, our city would be as well governed as any in America." Though Sherman's *Memoirs* did not add much in the way of a positive contribution to the study of San Francisco vigilantism, they were an accurate reflection of the position of a major banker to the actions of the committee and they still serve as a continuing reminder of the imprecision of Royce's term, "Business Man's Revolution."[13]

In 1887, James O'Meara, a Democratic journalist who had worked in San Francisco in 1856, published an anonymous pamphlet entitled *The Vigilance Committee of '56*. In a complaint that reflected the dominance of the pro-vigilance school of Tuthill, John Hittell, Bancroft, and Royce, O'Meara observed that all the written accounts of the vigilance committee that he had seen were "partial," and he attempted to redress the balance. For instance, he painted flattering pictures of the persons who had been attacked by the committee: Charles Cora was "reserved and quiet in his demeanor; and his manner and conversation were those of a refined gentleman"; Casey was "a young man of bright, intelligent, and prepossessing face, neat in his person, inclined to fine clothes, but not flashy or gaudy in his attire."

Many of O'Meara's substantive arguments were repetitions of what had been offered by Gray some thirty years earlier. He too condemned mob rule and emphasized the avoidance of politics by too many men in the city. He denied that public life was as corrupt as the vigilantes had argued, and stated that the courts, in particular, discharged their duties fairly well. With Sherman, he denied that a serious crime problem existed in the city, and he asserted, "The administration of the law was better then in general criminal procedure than it is now." He also argued that the men of the committee had been on the giving as well as the receiving end of what crime and corruption had existed. Finally, he insisted with Nugent that there had been a sharp political focus to the work of the committee, noting that, with only a handful of exceptions, the men arrested by the vigilantes were "all Democrats, devoted to Broderick." The strengths and weaknesses of O'Meara's approach closely paralleled those of Gray. He did present a fuller picture of the social and political life of the city than had the writers who attempted to justify the committee, yet his charges were too diffuse, many of them were unsubstantiated, and he could not delineate the precise social and political forces that led to the formation of the committee.[14]

O'Meara's pamphlet was one of the last serious attacks on the committee during the first movement of the imitative phase of the scholarship. The writings of Bancroft and Theodore Hittell, which justified the work of the committee, held virtually unchallenged sway into the first two decades of the twentieth century. When that orthodoxy was contested, the impetus came from a collection of after-the-fact doubts from some historians who nevertheless composed accounts of the committee that were, on the whole, favorable.

The second movement of the imitative phase appeared in 1921, when Mary Floyd Williams published her authoritative account, *History of the San Francisco Vigilance Committee of 1851*. Williams did not treat the 1856 committee extensively in this work, and her treatment of the 1851 committee was favorable, but the closing chapter, entitled "In Retrospect," signaled an important shift of thinking: echoing Royce, she argued that the 1851 committee had been a "confession of failure." Although there was much to the committee's credit, she noted, "It was not a beacon on the pathway of constructive reform." She deplored the "lawlessness and danger of its methods" and the "destructive measures" that it employed. She insisted that "the structural weakness and consequent breakdown of a social system" ought to be closely studied if the impetus to extralegal organization was to be understood and avoided in the future.[15]

Williams's own refusal to engage in the elaborate rhetoric of justification that Bancroft had favored and her measured *caveats* on the subject of vigilantism were to have important consequences, but not for some time. A year after the publication of Williams's work, Robert Glass Cleland offered once again the standard picture of crime and corruption, and he applauded the work of the committee, "this over-riding of law to save law." In 1929 Gertrude Atherton joined the club with her lively *California: An Intimate History*. In this volume, the "grim, sober, and indignant citizens" of San Francisco joined to wrest control of the city from "crooks and criminals, and thieves, looters, and murderers as thick as fleas in the sand." Atherton's prose was vigorous enough, as in her description of the general state of voter intimidation: "Honest men learned to avoid going to the polls, gangs of bullies being on hand to relieve the political organization from the embarrassment of honest men's votes . . . the ballot boxes were stuffed . . . there was always the chance that a few honest men might get by and cast their votes." Still, one rather gets the impression that for Atherton the greatest outrage that called for the formation of a vigilance committee was that, as she pictured it, the judges "chewed and expectorated in court, sat on the bench in their shirt sleeves, swore and shouted, and even cut their corns."[16]

In 1936, some fifteen years after Mary Floyd Williams's work, Stanton A. Coblentz's *Villains and Vigilantes* interpreted the 1856 committee in much the same way in which Williams had treated the 1851 committee, with a rather general approval and some significant criticisms. Coblentz adopted the Bancroft-Hittell framework of crime and corruption, and became something of a full-fledged California historian by quoting Theodore Hittell to the effect that there had never been any American city so corrupt as gold rush San Francisco. The committee, he said, acted "in the spirit of righteous wrath against organized wrongdoing," and it was "a mass revolt against vice and iniquity." But he agreed with Williams in her criticism of the committee's methods, and even went so far as to say that perhaps the San Francisco vigilantes did "more damage than good in the long run." He argued that vigilante groups in San Francisco "lent themselves to imitation in their worst features," and ultimately declared that he was unable to render a final judgment on the committees.[17]

The Williams-Coblentz skepticism did not affect James A. B. Scherer's laudatory biography of William T. Coleman in 1939, but it made its way into the textbooks in 1940, with the appearance of John Walton Caughey's *California*. Caughey accepted the standard picture of political corruption and argued, "Wise and high-minded leadership kept the second vigilance committee from extremes, and its work was well done in the face of great opposition." He also contended, like Royce, that everyone in the city was responsible for the corruption that did exist, and he agreed with Webb and Theodore Hittell that the gold rush contributed to a "lapse of civic duty." But he followed Williams and Coblentz in qualifying his generally favorable opinion of the committee: "Admittedly it is dangerous to flout the regular avenues of justice and turn to extralegal means. . . . In theory and in practice there is much to be said for the Law and Order distrust of extralegal procedures."[18]

Alan Valentine's *Vigilante Justice* (1956) was also essentially laudatory, but with qualifications. It accepted Royce's view of "social corruption" and "public indifference" and praised the "nobility of motive and restraint" displayed by the vigilantes, but at the same time it noted that the committee actions raised important issues concerning "the social problems of a free government," issues whose importance was presumably not diminished by Royce's reluctance to confront them. From Williams to Valentine, a new orthodoxy had arisen. The story of the committee, based on nineteenth-century secondary sources that were themselves highly laudatory, was still rousing and favorable, but it was joined to a set of formalized, Monday-morning-quarterback doubts about the propriety of vigilantism and the lasting value of extralegal procedures (which in no way affected the tone or the telling of the story).[19]

Doubts have a way of growing, and the third movement of the imitative phase appeared when the doubts found their way into the mainstream of the accounts, and writers' evaluations of the committee were accordingly revised downward. This third movement was presaged in the 1930's in a series of unpublished essays by Peter T. Conmy on the political aspects of the committee. Conmy, arguing that considerable evidence existed that San Francisco possessed a fairly efficient government, came to the conclusion that the committee "overstepped its bounds . . . its existence was a menace to organized government."[20] Conmy's essays, and Walter Van Tilburg Clark's powerful novel *The Ox-Bow Incident* (1940), which is about the lynching of three innocent men by Nevada vigilantes, were both signs of an expanding awareness of what the vigilantes really were. In 1950, William Henry Ellison, in his influential *A Self-Governing Dominion*, condemned the 1856 committee lock, stock, and barrel as a flagrant violation of civil liberties unjustified by the rise in "social and personal crime" after the disbanding of the 1851 committee. In general, his objections followed the lines that had been emphasized by all anti-vigilance writers since Nugent and Gray and had formed the kernel of doubt in the qualified approval extended the committee by those writers who followed Mary Floyd Williams. Ellison branded the committee "a dictatorial body engaged in rebellion." Its executions of Casey and Cora were unjustified, for "it is certain that unbiased courts would not have produced identical verdicts nor imposed the same penalties." Ellison accepted Royce's phrase "Business Man's Revolution," but he was much less sanguine about the effects of the revolution. For him, some of the activities of the committee were "sadistic" and involved "an orgy of emotionalism." He joined Sherman in deploring the precedents established by the committee, and joined Conmy in calling it a "menace to organized society." His conclusion, that the 1856 committee was "a confession of failure such as practically always comes to a society that is theoretically democratic but in which business and other leaders bent on personal gain are blind to civic responsibility," is reminiscent of Royce. But Ellison parted from Royce in estimating the effects of vigilance. For him, little good came from an organization that, "acting arbitrarily and emotionally, built a house of fear on shifting sands, which soon disintegrated."[21]

Prompted by Ellison's highly critical account of the committee, and by contemporary events, Caughey in 1957 published a major essay in which he reappraised his position. In this essay, "Their Majesties the Mob," Caughey drew a parallel between the committee's violations of civil liberties and those of what he called the modern vigilantes, the McCarthyites and segregationists of the 1940's and 1950's. The pro-vigilante tone of much of the historical literature could, he felt, be used to legitimize the activities of these modern vigilantes, and for that reason he attempted to set the record straight. With Conmy, he emphasized that the San Francisco vigilance committee acted not in the absence of a system of functioning courts, but in "defiance" of one. Even though the "dignity and decorum" of the committee "symbolized the fair trial that it sought to give," the defendants it brought before it were not accorded "due process as the courts and legal profession construe it." These same arguments appeared in more fully developed form in Caughey's book, *Their Majesties the Mob* (1960). Here, Caughey flatly called the committee a "civil insurrection and military occupation," but his main arguments, as before, were directed against the committee's suppression of civil liberties.[22]

In the mid 1960's this Ellison-Caughey interpretation was used in biographies of two men who had opposed the committee. John Myers's biography of McGowan (1966) followed Ellison and Caughey in condemning the committee's disregard of civil liberties, and (like Caughey) attacked those historians who had justified the actions of the committee. It also took a less apocalyptic view of the allegedly pervasive political fraud in the city, claiming that all the political organizations in the city were guilty of "some rough stuff and over reaching." Myers, following Gray and O'Meara, made the point that understanding gold rush San Francisco involved more than postulating a simple distinction between the forces of light and darkness ("Some of the feuding sprang from the clumsy wording of election laws in a town which hadn't yet found its political feet") but instead of developing these points he chose to ride with McGowan through the hills and valleys of the state. Clifford M. Drury's favorable biography of Episcopalian minister William Anderson Scott, who was one of the few Protestant clergymen in the city to preach against the committee, appeared in 1967 to swell the anti-vigilante literature. Scott had sided with Nugent in tracing what evils there were in the city to "the neglect of public affairs" indulged in by too many citizens; his position, summed up in the subtitle of one of his sermons, was: "Education, not punishment, the true remedy for the wrong doings and disorders of society." (He was hanged in effigy for sentiments of this sort.) Drury supported Scott's charge that it was "perfectly preposterous to contend that the many thousands of men and money wielded by the committee could not have assured in a lawful manner the purity of our elections and the faithful execution of the laws." Drury followed Ellison and Caughey in branding the committee an example of "mob rule."[23]

The same view found its way into the textbooks in 1968, with the appearance of Walton Bean's important *California: An Interpretive History*. In this work, Bean launched a full-fledged attack on San Francisco vigilantism, which, like Ellison and Caughey, he condemned for its disregard of civil liberties. He introduced psychological motives associated with the "strange air of righteous solemnity" affected by the committee, and he suggested that the men of the vigilance committee were "inwardly tortured by assorted feelings of guilt." For instance, Sam Brannan's fortune was built on embezzled church property and tithes, and Bean suggested that Brannan was "subconsciously seeking freedom from his own guilt in arrogating to himself the punishment of others."

Bean went beyond the Ellison and Caughey accounts in analyzing not just the tone but the substance of vigilantism. He agreed with Royce that the committee might be termed a "Business Man's Revolution," but he failed to discern the elegance Royce had apparently found in that event. The committee, Bean argued, was attempting "an application of private enterprise to the administration of justice," and the philosophy of the committee leadership "reflected a set of attitudes characteristic of most early California businessmen and some later ones—their dislike and distrust of government and public officeholders, and their contempt for politicians as an inferior class." He admitted that there was some corruption in the city government, but he agreed with O'Meara that "the charge that the legally constituted courts had been corrupt is in general not true." He concluded by deploring the "vicious, dangerous, and persistent tradition of contempt for the normal processes of government," which he saw as the legacy of the committee. Bean's major contribution was in calling attention once again to the commercial orientation of the committee. Unlike most of his historical predecessors, Bean made a serious attempt to relate the businessmen's revolution to the needs, desires, and attitudes of the city's men of commerce.[24]

With Ellison, Caughey, and Bean, the imitative circle closed, and the stage was set for new approaches to investigating the gold rush port and its vigilantes. These new approaches witnessed the appropriation into the historical writings on early San Francisco of themes that concerned American historians in general during the 1960's: an effort at comparison, an attention to social tensions, an interest in the social and political uses of violence, and an attempt at quantitative precision.

This second phase, which I am calling the phase of analysis, began in 1968 with a dissertation at the University of California, Davis. In "Associational Life on the Urban Frontier: San Francisco, 1848–1856," Bradford Luckingham viewed the 1856 vigilance committee as one instance of the myriad voluntary associations that were so pronounced a feature of antebellum life throughout the United States. Luckingham impressively catalogued the existence of scores of voluntary associations—cultural, educational, religious, social—in the first decade of the history of San Francisco.

Although Luckingham's approach was to some degree imitative in that he tended to accept the crime and corruption model of the justification historians, he also called attention to the highly organized structure of the vigilance committee. He insisted that the committee should be looked at not just as a reaction to corruption but as the culmination of the very manifest urban tendency of associational activity. Speaking of the leaders of the committee, Luckingham says, "Unable to envision violent mob action, and unable to rely on corrupt city officials, they met the problem in the only way they knew how: they formed an association." Luckingham's impressive catalogue of voluntary associations in gold rush San Francisco and his insistence that the vigilance committee should be examined in this context invited historians to look beyond fragmentary crime statistics and occasional political brawling for clues to the impetus for extralegal organization.[25]

In the next year Richard Maxwell Brown, in two important essays, offered a new interpretation of the 1856 committee.[26] Brown placed San Francisco vigilantism in a comparative and national context. Drawing on his study of the 326 known vigilante movements in American history, he generalized that "the main thrust of vigilantism was to establish in each newly settled area the conservative values of life and property, law and order." For Brown, Royce's phrase "Business Man's Revolution" described more than just San Francisco vigilantism: "Vigilante movements were usually led by the frontier elite. This was true of the greatest American vigilante movement—the San Francisco Vigilance Committee of 1856—which was dominated lock, stock and barrel by the leading merchants of the city." Brown argued that the typical American community in the nineteenth century was marked by a threefold social structure. On top was the local elite of successful businessmen, eminent professionals, affluent farmers, and so on. In the middle were the average farmers, traders, and craftsmen, and on the third level were the honest poor. Below this third level were the "lower people," the "ne'er-do-well, shiftless poor whites," who were "not outlaws, but often tended to lawlessness and identified more with the outlaw element than the law-abiding members of the community." According to Brown, the local elite provided the vigilante leadership, the middle level filled the vigilante rank and file, and the lower people served as vigilante targets. Brown also called attention to what he called an "ideology of vigilantism" widespread in nineteenth-century America. This ideology included a pervasive doctrine of "vigilance" in all things and a philosophy that was compounded of the right of self-protection, the right of revolution, and the notion of popular sovereignty. The final element in the ideology was an economic rationale that emphasized that vigilante justice tended to be cheaper than regular justice. Brown also distinguished vigilantism in situations in which the regular system of law and order was absent and in which it was functioning effectively. Following Caughey, he placed the 1856 committee in the latter category, calling it "vigilantism as a parallel structure."

When he turned his attention specifically to San Francisco, Brown joined Sherman and others in claiming that there was no "crime wave" in 1856. He stated, "A survey of the police news column in the *Bulletin* and *Town Talk* [both of which supported the committee] during the fall, winter, and spring of 1855–1856 has convinced me that the San Francisco crime problem was under control." So he looked elsewhere and presented an ethnic explanation for the formation of the committee. A close analysis of some 2,500 applications for membership in the committee that survive at the Huntington Library enabled Brown to form a more precise picture of the composition of the committee than any previous writer. He reported that the vigilance committee was "composed of young men in their twenties and thirties." These men were of virtually every ethnic strain, but the bulk of the American membership was "from the northeastern United States from Maine to Maryland"; in other words, they tended to be old-stock Yankees. Brown further noted that there were few Irishmen in the committee. He reported that "the vigilantes came largely from the ranks of the city's merchants, tradesmen, craftsmen, or their young employees." On the basis of these findings, he attempted to relate the vigilance committee to "tensions" in the city between "upper and middle class, old American, Protestant merchants" and "a political faction based on Irish Catholic lower class laborers." He agreed with Gray and O'Meara that the basic goal of the committee had been the destruction of the Democratic political organization led by Broderick, and he offered a novel explanation for the existence of this goal. He related the formation of the committee to a mercantile desire for "fiscal reform at the municipal level." In this view:

> The mercantile complexion of the vigilance committee is the key to its behavior. The merchants of San Francisco were dependent on Eastern connections for their credit. Like most businessmen, the San Francisco merchants had a consuming interest in their own credit ratings

and the local tax rate. In the eyes of Eastern businessmen, San Francisco's economic stability was being jeopardized by the soaring municipal debt, rising taxes, and approaching bankruptcy under the Broderick machine. The spectre of municipal bankruptcy made Eastern creditors fearful that the city was on the verge of economic chaos. The restoration of confidence in San Francisco's municipal and financial stability was a *sine qua non*. It had to be accomplished—and in such a way that would let Easterners know that conservative, right-thinking men had definitely gained control. Fiscal reform at the municipal level was thus basic to the vigilante movement. But in order to bring about fiscal reform it was first necessary to smash David C. Broderick's machine.[27]

According to Brown, the precision of the committee's attacks, directed almost exclusively against Irish Catholic henchmen of Broderick (this had already been noted by O'Meara), made the 1856 vigilance committee a "pivot" between "old" and "new" styles of American vigilantism. The old vigilantism was directed "mainly at horsethieves, counterfeiters, outlaws, bad men, and lower people." The new vigilantism, which became important at the end of the nineteenth century, "found its chief victims among Catholics, Jews, immigrants, Negroes, laboring men and labor leaders, political radicals, and proponents of civil liberties." Brown's judgment was that the 1856 committee "represented a blending of the methods of the old vigilantism with the victims of the new."[28]

Brown's major contributions to the study of San Francisco vigilantism were his insistence on looking at the city as a whole, his detailed research on the composition of the committee, and his attempt to work the ethnic and political aspects of the committee's work, already noted by others, into a coherent framework. His was the most sophisticated account to date of the 1856 committee.

In the same year in which Brown's important essays appeared (1969), David A. Williams published a biography of Broderick. Following O'Meara, Williams emphasized the political nature of the committee's work. "In effect," he said, "the committee became a 'political engine' which was utilized by some of its members to strike at Broderick and his associates." Where Brown had attacked the "crime wave" justification of the committee, Williams went after the "political corruption" charge. Not only were many members of the committee old political enemies of Broderick but also the committee failed to produce any hard evidence of political fraud against Broderick or most of his cronies. He concluded: "The failure reflected the paucity of evidence, for much of what the committee's investigators assembled was faulty, insignificant, or not related to Broderick."[29]

In 1970 Roger Olmsted also took up the question of vigilantism, noting, with a mixture of truth and exaggeration, that the committees "have never been vigilantly examined by western historians in terms of their social context." Following Hittell and Royce, Olmsted argued that the economic slump after 1854 was related to vigilantism, and he added a twist that sought to make that relationship more precise: "When everyone is getting rich, municipal corruption is often the object of a kind of rueful civic pride. Such was the general attitude of the citizens of San Francisco until the bubble burst. Then suddenly the unmerited affluence of fraudulently elected officials became an affront increasingly hard to put up with." In other words, the depression did not so much reveal corruption, as Royce had argued; rather it made political corruption an object of distaste and jealousy on the part of the city's hard-pressed businessmen. In terms that were also reminiscent of Royce, Olmsted argued that "the deep-rooted corruption of San Francisco politics was more a function of popular psychology than individual depravity" and that the committee's "exposure" of this corruption was its chief work. Though it shared much with the justifying writings of the imitative phase, Olmsted's account demonstrated the effect that the analytical phase was having on the literature. Even a writer who generally approved of the committee could no longer accept the vigilantes' own self-estimate without serious qualification.[30]

Kevin Starr, in his wide-ranging *Americans and the California Dream*, discussed the 1856 committee only briefly, but in an interesting way, in a chapter entitled "City on a Hill" that dealt with the New England ministers who arrived in California with the intention of transforming Eldorado into a "Puritan commonwealth." The ministers fought slavery, gambling, prostitution, and lack of observance of the Sabbath, and they were very prominent in the establishment of San Francisco's public school system. Their efforts eventually failed, because, among other things, "the Roman Catholic presence was too strong." Echoing Nugent, Starr saw a connection between the Know-

Nothing activity in San Francisco in 1854–55 and the vigilance committee in 1856. In Starr's view, they were both accounted for by "anti-foreign reformism on the part of outraged businessmen." Since the design of his work took him elsewhere, Starr did not attempt to describe the practical effects of "the Catholic presence" or the components of "reformism." But his introduction, albeit brief, of religion so centrally into the picture was entirely new and highly imaginative.[31]

In 1974, San Francisco historiography took an enormous step forward with the appearance of Roger Lotchin's detailed and comprehensive study of the early city, *San Francisco, 1846–1856: From Hamlet to City*. Topical in organization, Lotchin's study is a generally successful attempt to insert the early history of San Francisco into the mainstream of American urban history. For example, an early contest between San Francisco and Benicia over which would become the bay's major port occurs in a chapter entitled "Urban Rivalries," thereby putting it in the context of other commercial rivalries between sets of American cities. Schools are treated in a chapter entitled "Urban Institutions," and there are also chapters on government, labor, politics, and so on. Lotchin's book is undoubtedly the best account of the early American period.

Lotchin deals with the 1856 committee in a chapter entitled "The Revolution of 1856." He does not accept what he called the "deterioration-tyranny" thesis that the city was in the grip of crime and corruption. With John S. Hittell, he points to the enactment of the Consolidation Act and to the fact that the confused real estate titles were being straightened out by the courts as indications that things were looking up in the city at the beginning of 1856. He makes the point that electoral violence was on the wane and that Broderick's political power was tenuous at best, and concludes that there was simply no insoluble crisis that explained the formation of the vigilance committee.

He suggests three main causes leading to the organization of the committee: "spouses, spatial relationships, and spurious sensationalism." The sensationalism was that of King, whom Lotchin regards as having "ignited a class struggle of sorts, though not of the European variety involving the classic duality of working class and middle class." Rather, King appealed to those who regarded themselves as "an all-embracing alliance of worthy citizens that cut across the categories of upper, middle, and lower orders." In this light, Lotchin maintains, "The upheaval of 1856 was pre-eminently a revolution of the legitimates." The spouses, according to Lotchin, were the ones who were responsible for the "moral fervor" of the vigilance struggle (and not, as Bean had suggested, guilt feelings). King, in championing "family and home interests in the metropolis against gamblers, prostitutes, and their allies," gave voice to female concerns. And the spatial relationships in the city, Lotchin says, gave these concerns their intensity and guaranteed the continuing urgency of the values King was defending. Relying on his own detailed study of the residential and commercial patterns of land use in the early city, Lotchin argues that the period under investigation witnessed "a decentralization of economic and residential patterns . . . considerable specialization of land use . . . and greater concentration of the various categories within each." While the business section of the city remained downtown, "the middle classes moved west and the separation of places of home and work unfolded." As a result:

> Men worked downtown and lived on the heights; but in between these two areas and to an extent mixed in with them was a large concentration of sin, especially along Dupont and cross streets between there and Stockton. Many middle-class people still lived on Dupont; and even those who did not were thrown into proximity with this vice street, whose inhabitants were entrenched upon the access routes to downtown. A trip to the dentist, the doctor, the milliner, the husband's office, and sometimes even to church kept the situation explosive by renewing the contact between the housewives and harlots.

The shooting of King sparked "institutional form to these frustrations," namely the vigilance committee, which, Lotchin says, was "a species of urban revolution against the Gold Rush status quo": "The colorful, lawless metropolis had often been exciting, and many would remember it affectionately. Yet contemporaries had seen enough of it." As a result of the activities of the vigilance committee an "ideology of community," which stressed the importance of local issues and the malevolence of politicians, crystallized.

For the most part, Lotchin downplays the more traditional foci of discussion, but where he does touch on them, he tends to side with the opponents of the committee. He joins Webb and others in excoriating public apathy, and remarks that in pre-vigilante San Francisco it was not so much that democracy failed as that it was never tried. He denies with Ellison and Caughey that any "regeneration or purification" resulted from the vigilante action: "San Francisco in 1857 did not differ markedly from what it had been in 1855." He agrees with David A. Williams that there was little specific evidence for contending that "fraud carried the day in San Francisco elections."[32]

In 1978 extensive quantification finally appeared in the historiography of San Francisco with the publication of Peter R. Decker's *Fortunes and Failures: White Collar Mobility in Nineteenth Century San Francisco*, which covers the years 1848–80. Decker culled his data on occupational mobility from the State Census of 1852, the city directories, and the credit reports of R. G. Dun and Co. Too frequently in American quantification history, insight and argument are lost in impenetrable prose, but Decker's findings are a happy exception, and he presents his sophisticated findings on San Francisco in clear, readable, and disarming fashion.

Decker's main argument is that in the gold rush city there were "distinct gradations within the merchant occupation." At the summit were "commission merchants, importers, wholesalers (including those who combined wholesaling and retailing), and jobbers"; at the next level were "general retail merchants"; and "petty merchants: the retail shopkeepers, dealers, traders, grocers, and peddlers" were "lowest on the occupational scale." He makes the point that the gold rush economy, like most American economies, was cyclical: "By 1858, San Francisco had experienced four major business cycles, all quite independent of the national economy: June 1848–January 1850—boom; February 1850–April 1852—recession; May 1852–December 1853—boom; January 1854–January 1858—depression." He follows John S. Hittell in arguing that "the oversupply of goods in the San Francisco market was the single most important factor that fueled the excessive business cycles." While some groups, such as German Jewish merchants, fared better than most, during the 1850 decade "the rate of failure was probably somewhere between half and two-thirds of all merchants." All in all, the 1850's were "a decade of economic loss rather than profit." In particular, "The high status merchants, those who owned the commission houses, wholesale outlets, and import firms, found it difficult . . . to maintain their occupational status." By 1860, Decker says, less than half of this group had managed to stay at the level at which they had begun their mercantile careers in San Francisco.

Like Hittell, Royce, and others, Decker attempts to relate the 1856 vigilance committee to this context of business uncertainty. With a few reservations, he generally adopts Brown's interpretation that the businessmen wanted to "protect both their individual credit ratings and the general fiscal reputation of the city." The merchants, according to him, attempted by vigilance "to halt the corrosive effects of economic recession" that was affecting them so adversely. Though the vigilance committee may not have done very much for the city as a whole, it did benefit the merchants who organized it: "Taking all committee members who held either civil or military executive positions in the vigilance committee, 70 percent of whom were either high status general merchants, importers-wholesalers, bankers, brokers, manufacturers, or professionals, over 80 percent either maintained or improved their occupational status. They did, in fact, outperform the merchants and general population of the city in the years 1852–1860."[33]

R. A. Burchell's *The San Francisco Irish, 1848–1880*, which appeared in 1980, was the first work to deal exclusively with the urban Irish during the gold rush period. It revolves around what the author terms "two themes": the major theme is "the local circumstances that produced . . . feelings of satisfaction" on the part of the city's Irish; the minor theme involves "the host culture's at best ambivalence, at worst hostility, to the immigrant presence." Most of the book centers on the major theme, and Burchell argues that the San Francisco Irish fared rather well during the period he investigated. He argues this major theme so strenuously, in fact, that he occasionally has to interrupt the presentation and caution the reader not to get the wrong idea—as in this comment that occurs at the beginning of one chapter: "It may appear, though it is not its purpose to do so, that this study argues in some rightly suspicious and peculiar way that all members of the Irish were satisfied with their lives in San Francisco. This was hardly the case." But the thrust of the book revolves so definitely around the major theme of a favorable environment for the Irish in San Francisco that Burchell, in the last paragraph, feels it necessary to add "a final caution": "It is not argued that the Irish performed as well as the native stock in San Francisco. The point is that, given the time, the mid-to-late nineteenth century; the place, the United States; and the group, the Irish, their history in San Francisco was, by contrast with that elsewhere, comparatively successful and fortunate."

Burchell attempted to do for the San Francisco Irish what other historians during the 1970's had done for the blacks and other minority groups: to present them not only as historical victims but as historical actors. And in that task he was eminently successful. Following Luckingham, he presents a very complete account of the host of voluntary associations which the Irish formed and directed. He argues that the Irish family in the city was more stable than the native stock family, that "the occupational status of the Irish-born males improved slowly but surely until after 1870," and that the second-generation Irish were "marginally in front of the total community" in job status. Although the vigilance committee and the Civil War, in weakening the Democratic party, did diminish Irish political power in the city, he says, the weakening was temporary and did not consign the Irish to a "permanently secondary role in San Francisco politics."

Burchell's discussion of the 1856 vigilance committee tends, like Decker's, to follow the broad outline of Brown's argument. He agrees with David A. Williams and Brown that the committee attacked Broderick men, and he terms the committee's acts "a very neat surgical operation on the body politic." But since his focus is almost exclusively on the Irish, he does not speculate at any length on the reasons for the formation of the committee or on the functions of nativism in the city.[34]

In my study, I have tried to combine the two phases that I have outlined above. On the one hand, I think that the writers of the imitative phase were correct when they accorded vigilantism a central place in their histories of the gold rush period. Some of the analytical writers who treat vigilantism as an aspect of a larger process such as urbanization or social mobility tend to remove themselves a bit too much from the texture of life as it was lived in the 1850's. San Franciscans of that period did not think of themselves as urbanizers or the like, but they *did* think of themselves as vigilantes or law and order people. I have attempted to be critical and yet to tell their story in terms that they would have understood. History involves entering worlds in which we might feel as strangers or out of place.

On the other hand, the analytical writers have brought great sophistication to the study of the early city, and I have availed myself of some of their insights. For I agree, as the present study makes clear, with the thrust of their writings.

Notes

The following abbreviations are used in the Notes:

AHR	*American Historical Review*
AJD	Andrew Jackson Davis Papers, New-York Historical Society, New York
AQ	*American Quarterly*
CC	San Francisco Chamber of Commerce Papers, California Historical Society, San Francisco
CH	*California History*
CHQ	*California Historical Quarterly*
CHSQ	*California Historical Society Quarterly*
CPD	Charles P. Daniell Papers, Huntington Library, San Marino
FDA	Faxon D. Atherton Papers, California Historical Society, San Francisco
HL	Harvey Lamb Papers, Beinecke Library, Yale University
JBC	Joseph B. Crockett Papers, Bancroft Library, Berkeley
LF	Lammot Family Papers, Bancroft Library, Berkeley
LS	Lura Smith Papers, Huntington Library, San Marino
MH	Milton Hall Papers, Bancroft Library, Berkeley
MVHR	*Mississippi Valley Historical Review*
PH	*Pacific Historian*
PHR	*Pacific Historical Review*
RSB	Roger Sherman Baldwin Papers, Sterling Library, Yale University
SCQ	*Southern California Quarterly*
TTS	Thomas T. Seward Papers, California Historical Society, San Francisco
VC	Papers of the Vigilance Committee of 1856, Huntington Library, San Marino
WKW	William K. Weston Papers, California Historical Society, San Francisco
WMQ	*William and Mary Quarterly*

CHAPTER 1

1. These four accounts are culled from the contemporary newspapers and from Hubert Howe Bancroft's two-volume work, *Popular Tribunals* (San Francisco: History Co., 1887).

2. Kathleen P. Hext, "Eastern Opinions of the San Francisco Vigilance Committee of 1856," Stanford University, seminar paper, winter 1964; Richard Maxwell Brown, *Strain of Violence: Historical Studies of American Violence and Vigilantism* (New York: Oxford University Press, 1975), pp. 95–103, 305–19.

3. See, e.g.: David Lindsey, "The Reign of the Vigilantes," *American History Illustrated* 8, no. 3 (1973): 22–35; C. W. Harper, "Committees of Vigilance and Vigilante Justice," *Journal of the West* 17 , no. 1 (1978): 3–7; J. A. B. Scherer, *The Lion of the Vigilantes: William T. Coleman and the Life of Old San Francisco* (Indianapolis: Bobbs-Merrill, 1939); Gunther Barth, *Instant Cities: Urbanization and the Rise of San Francisco and Denver* (New York: Oxford University Press, 1975), pp. 203–4; William P. Wood, "The Committee of Vigilance: Justice and Legal Order," *California State Bar Journal* 53, no. 3 (1978): 154–59.

4. U.S. Bureau of the Census, *Historical Statistics of the United States, From Colonial Times to the Present* (Washington: Government Printing Office, 1960), p. 14.

5. Daniel Boorstin, *The Americans: The National Experience* (New York: Random House, 1965), pp. 115–23; Carl Abbot, *Boosters and Businessmen: Popular Economic Thought and Urban Growth in the Antebellum Middle West* (Westport, Conn.: Greenwood Press, 1981); Charles N. Glaab and A. Theodore Brown, *A History of Urban America* (2nd ed.; New York: Macmillan, 1976), pp. 59–65; Earl Pomeroy, "The Urban Frontier of the Far West," in *The Frontier Challenge: Responses to the Trans-Mississippi West*, ed. John Clark (Lawrence: University Press of Kansas, 1971), pp. 7–29. On the notion of the West, the best place to start reading is still Henry Nash Smith, *Virgin Land: The American West as Symbol and Myth* (Cambridge, Mass.: Harvard University Press, 1950); also see Loren Baritz, "The Idea of the West," *AHR* 68 (1961): 618–40; and Howard Mumford Jones, "The Allure of the West," *Harvard Library Bulletin* 28 (1980): 19–32.

6. For differing views on this complicated question see, on the one hand, Kenneth Lockridge, *A New England Town: The First Hundred Years* (New York: Norton, 1970); J. E. Crowley, *This Sheba, Self: The Conceptualization of Economic Life in Eighteenth-Century America* (Baltimore: Johns Hopkins University Press, 1974); James Henretta, "Families and Farms: *Mentalité* in Pre-Industrial America," *WMQ* 35 (1978): 3–32; Lewis O. Saum, *The Popular Mood of Pre-Civil War America* (Westport, Conn.: Greenwood Press, 1980); on the other hand, Charles S. Grant, *Democracy in the Connecticut Frontier Town of Kent* (New York: Columbia University Press, 1961); James T. Lemon, *The Best Poor Man's Country: A Geographical Study of Early Southeastern Pennsylvania* (Baltimore: Johns Hopkins University Press, 1972); Car-

ville Earle, "Comment," *AHR* 83 (1978): 1206–9; attempts at syntheses include Joyce Appleby, "Liberalism and the American Revolution," *New England Quarterly* 49 (1976): 3–26; Ralph Lerner, "Commerce and Character: The Anglo-American as New Model Man," *WMQ* 36 (1979): 3–26; and especially Rowland Berthoff, "Independence and Attachment, Virtue and Interest: From Republican Citizen to Free Enterpriser, 1787–1837," in *Uprooted Americans: Essays to Honor Oscar Handlin*, ed. Richard L. Bushman, Neil Harris, David Rothman, Barbara Miller Solomon, and Stephen Thernstrom (Boston: Little, Brown, 1979), pp. 99–126.

7. *Daily Alta California* (San Francisco), May 12, 1851; Frank Soulé, John H. Gihon, and James Nisbet, *The Annals of San Francisco* (New York: D. Appleton and Co., 1855), pp. 489–90; John P. Young, *San Francisco: A History of the Pacific Coast Metropolis*, 2 vols. (San Francisco: S. J. Clark Publishing Co., 1912), 1:489–90; Gunther Barth, *City People: The Rise of Modern City Culture in Nineteenth-Century America* (New York: Oxford University Press, 1980), p. 35; Glaab and Brown, *History of Urban America*, pp. 230–32.

8. Christine Fischer, "Women in California in the Early 1850's," *SCQ* 60 (1978): 231–53.

9. *Alta*, Mar. 25, 1851.

10. *San Francisco Daily Herald*, May 17, 1851; *Alta*, July 8, 1851; on the Chinese see Ping Chiu, *Chinese Labor in California, 1850–1880: An Economic Study* (Madison: Historical Society of Wisconsin, 1963); Stuart C. Miller, *The Unwelcome Immigrant: The American Image of the Chinese, 1785–1822* (Berkeley and Los Angeles: University of California Press, 1969); Alexander P. Saxton, *The Indispensable Enemy: Labor and the Anti-Chinese Movement in California* (Berkeley and Los Angeles: University of California Press, 1971); the blacks, a significant minority, are the subjects of Rudolph M. Lapp, *Blacks in Gold Rush California* (New Haven: Yale University Press, 1977), and Douglas Henry Daniels, *Pioneer Urbanites: A Social and Cultural History of Black San Francisco* (Philadelphia: Temple University Press, 1980).

11. Soulé, *Annals of San Francisco*, p. 173.

12. *Ibid.*, pp. 173–74, 219, 236, 300; Mary Floyd Williams, *History of the San Francisco Vigilance Committee of 1851* (Berkeley: University of California Press, 1921), p. 176; Roger Lotchin, *San Francisco, 1846–1856: From Hamlet to City* (New York: Oxford University Press, 1974), pp. 7, 8, 30, 37, 102, 104.

13. Soulé, *Annals of San Francisco*, p. 205.

14. *Ibid.*, pp. 245, 249; Robert S. Lammot to Daniel Lammot, Jan. 13, 1850, LF.

15. Soulé, *Annals of San Francisco*, pp. 183, 199, 264; Theodore H. Hittell, *History of California*, 4 vols. (San Francisco: N. J. Stone and Co., 1897), 3:337.

16. Soulé, *Annals of San Francisco*, p. 193; Lotchin, *San Francisco*, pp. 31–38; Paul W. Gates, "The Land Business of Thomas O. Larkin," *CHQ* 54 (1975): 335–37.

17. Williams, *San Francisco Vigilance Committee*, pp. 49, 98, 99, 100, 104, 112–13, 134, 165; Soulé, *Annals of San Francisco*, pp. 208, 219–20, 229–30, 237, 266, 272, 273, 326, 348, 350; David A. Williams, *David C. Broderick: A Political Portrait* (San Marino: Huntington Library, 1969), pp. 28–30; Susan M. Kingsbury, "The Municipal History of San Francisco to 1879," M.A. thesis, Stanford University, 1899; Earl Pomeroy, "California, 1846–1850: The Politics of a Representative Frontier State," *CHSQ* 32 (1953): 291–302.

18. Roger Sherman Baldwin to his mother, Mar. 19, Oct. 31, 1852, RSB.

19. Gerald McKevitt, S.J., *The University of Santa Clara: A History, 1851–1977* (Stanford: Stanford University Press, 1979), p. 7; Charles P. Daniell to Lucetta Daniell, Apr. 2, Dec. 9, 1850, CPD; Harvey Lamb to his mother, Feb. 6, 1852, HL; Andrew J. Davis to George Wright, Jan. 20, 1854, AJD.

20. Charles P. Daniell to his mother, June 14, 1851, CPD; Roger Sherman Baldwin to Elizabeth Wooster Whitney, May 31, 1852, Baldwin to his mother, June 29, 1852, RSB. For similar sentiments see John B. McGloin, S.J., *San Francisco: The Story of a City* (San Rafael, Calif.: Presidio Press, 1978), p. 35; J. S. Holliday, *The World Rushed In: The California Gold Rush Experience* (New York: Simon and Schuster, 1981), p. 396.

21. Joseph B. Crockett to his wife, May 1, 1854, JBC; William K. Weston to his father, Apr. 28, 1851, WKW; Roger Sherman Baldwin to his sister, May 30, 1851, RSB; John and Mary Banfield to mother, Feb. 10, 1852, Banfield Collection, New York Historical Society, New York.

22. Doris M. Wright, "The Making of Cosmopolitan California: An Analysis of Immigration, 1848–1870," *CHSQ* 19 (1940): 323–43. For the notion that California tended to attract a more reckless type of individual than Oregon did, see Dorothy O. Johansen, "A Working Hypothesis for the Study of Migrations," *PHR* 36 (1967): 1–12; and Gary G. Hamilton, "The Structural Sources of Adventurism: The Case of the California Gold Rush," *American Journal of Sociology* 80 (1978): 1466–90.

23. Henry Mellus to William Appleton and Co., Oct. 31, 1846, Mellus and Howard Co. Papers, Bancroft Library, Berkeley.

24. Andrew J. Davis, undated fragment, AJD; Ferdinand C. Ewer to his mother and sister, Oct. 31, 1849, Ferdinand C. Ewer Diary, California Historical Society, San Francisco; Charles P. Daniell to his mother, Dec. 9, 1850, CPD; Andrew J. Davis to George Wright, Nov. 10, 1853, AJD.

25. Charles P. Daniell to his mother, Nov. 15, 1853, CPD.

26. Roger Sherman Baldwin to his father, Feb. 28, 1853; Baldwin to his mother, Aug. 29, 1853, RSB.

27. The sketch of Coleman relies on the data presented in the hagiographic Hubert Howe Bancroft, *History of the Life of William Tell Coleman* (San Francisco: History Co., 1891), and the slightly more critical Scherer, *The Lion of the Vigilantes*.

28. The sketch of Folsom relies primarily on the data presented in

Soulé, *Annals of San Francisco*, pp. 754–57. Many of the depositions taken in the court cases that arose out of the Leidesdorff estate are preserved in the Joseph Libby Folsom Papers, California Historical Society, San Francisco.

29. The sketch of Broderick relies primarily on the excellent biography by David Williams, *David C. Broderick*; also useful is Lionel E. Fredman, "Broderick: A Re-assessment," *PHR* 30 (1961): 39–46.

30. Henry Haight to his father, July 17, 1850, Misc. papers, VC; W. W. Robinson, *Land in California* (Berkeley and Los Angeles: University of California Press, 1948), pp. 59–73; Bruno Fritzsche, "San Francisco, 1846–1848: The Coming of the Land Speculator," *CHSQ* 51 (1972): 18.

31. Young, *San Francisco*, 1:40.

32. Fritzsche, "San Francisco, 1846–1848," p. 20.

33. Geoffrey P. Mawn, "Framework for Destiny: San Francisco, 1847," *CHSQ* 51 (1972): 165–78; Hubert Howe Bancroft, *Chronicles of the Builders* (San Francisco History Company, 1882), 2:286–94.

34. William T. Sherman to Joseph L. Folsom, Mar. 29, 1848; Folsom to George Hyde, May 24, June 1, 1848, Joseph Libby Folsom Collection, Bancroft Library, Berkeley. The best introduction to the complex land questions is the series of articles by Paul Gates: "Adjudication of Spanish-Mexican Land Claims in California," *Huntington Library Quarterly* 31 (1958): 213–36; "California's Embattled Settlers," *CHSQ* 41 (1962): 99–130; "Pre–Henry George Land Warfare in California," *CHSQ* 46 (1967): 121–48; "The California Land Act of 1851," *CHSQ* 51 (1971): 395–430; "The Land Business of Thomas O. Larkin." On the enormous amount of speculation see Gordon M. Bakken, "The Development of the Law of Mortgage in Frontier California, 1850–1890. Part One: 1850–1866," *SCQ* 63 (1981): 48–50. The Thornton Papers, Nevada Historical Society, Reno, also contain some useful information, since Thornton was a Land Commissioner.

35. William Elton Franklin, "The Political Career of Peter Hardeman Burnett," Ph.D. dissertation, Stanford University, 1954, pp. 153–57; Peter Burnett to Horace Hawes, Feb. 8, 1850, Horace Hawes folder, California Historical Society, San Francisco.

36. Lotchin, *San Francisco*, pp. 144–46; California, *Statutes* (1851), chap. 41, pp. 307–10.

37. *Statutes* (1851), chap. 44, p. 311; Young, *San Francisco*, 1:153; Lotchin, *San Francisco*, pp. 143–48.

38. California, *Statutes* (1851), chap. 85, pp. 387–91.

39. Soulé, *Annals of San Francisco*, pp. 370–77; Milton Hall to his father, Dec. 18, 1854, MH, mentioned that these sales were still a topic of conversation and confusion at the end of 1854.

40. Lionel Fredman, "The Bigler Regime," M.A. thesis, Stanford University 1959, pp. 16–21; Roger Olmsted, "San Francisco and the Vigilante Style," *American West* 7, no. 2 (1970): 62.

41. California Assembly, *Journal* (1853): 21–24; Alexander B. Grogan to Faxon D. Atherton, Feb. 28, Apr. 16, 1853, FDA.

CHAPTER 2

1. Edward Pessen, "How Different from Each Other Were the Antebellum North and South?" *AHR* 85 (1980): 1130.

2. Edmund S. Morgan, *American Slavery, American Freedom: The Ordeal of Colonial Virginia* (New York: Norton, 1975), pp. 110–11; also see Carl Bridenbaugh, *Jamestown, 1544–1699* (New York: Oxford University Press, 1980). The literature on the gold rush is too enormous even to begin to list here. I shall simply record my own opinion that the place to begin studying it is the wonderful book by John W. Caughey, *Gold Is the Cornerstone* (Berkeley and Los Angeles: University of California Press, 1948); for the overland journey, see the equally wonderful book by J. S. Holliday, *The World Rushed In: The California Gold Rush Experience.* Armour is mentioned briefly in Harold M. Mayer and Richard C. Wade, *Chicago: Growth of a Metropolis* (Chicago: University of Chicago Press, 1969), p. 51.

3. Ralph Bieber, "California Gold Mania," *MVHR* 35 (1948): 6; Brian H. Smalley, "Some Aspects of the Maine to California Trade, 1849–1852," *Journal of the West* 6 (1967): 594; Gunther Barth, *Instant Cities*, passim; Roger Sherman Baldwin to Emily Perkins Hale, Jan. 30, 1853, RSB. Additional information on gold rush prices is conveniently brought together in many good histories; see, for instance, Jay Monaghan, *Australians and the Gold Rush: California and Down Under, 1849–1854* (Berkeley and Los Angeles: University of California Press, 1966), pp. 72–73.

4. Bessie L. Pierce, *A History of Chicago*, 3 vols. (New York: Knopf, 1937–57), 1:52; Journal of Captain J. Shepherd, Oct. 16, 1849, Papers Relating to the British Consulate at San Francisco, Borel Collection, Stanford University; this type of individual hustling was part of a more national phenomenon: Alfred Chandler, "Entrepreneurial Opportunity in Nineteenth Century America," *Explorations in Entrepreneurial History* 1 (1963): 106–24.

5. Edward T. Hosmer to his father, Feb. 25, Mar. 2, 1849, Hosmer Correspondence, Borel Collection, Stanford University.

6. "A California Commission Merchant," *Bulletin of the Business History Society* 5 (1931), no. 5: 7–11, and no. 6: 1–5; 6 (1932), no. 1: 7–11; List of Presidents of the San Francisco Chamber of Commerce, CC.

7. *Macondray and Co., Inc., 1848–1949: One Hundredth Anniversary* (n.p., n.d.), F. W. Macondray Papers, California Historical Society, San Francisco.

8. James W. White, "Great Expectations: The Business Correspondence of Gibbons and Lammot," *CHQ* 55 (1976): 294.

9. Joseph L. Folsom to General George Gibson, May 6, 1848, Folsom Collection, Bancroft Library, Berkeley.

10. Robert S. Lammot to William Lammot, Jan. 22, 1851, LF; Thomas T. Seward to Lucy Seward, Jan. 13, 1855, TTS; Alexander B. Grogan to Faxon D. Atherton, Dec. 19, 1855, FDA.

11. Joseph B. Crockett to his wife, Jan. 31, 1853, JBC.

12. William T. Sherman to John Sherman, Aug. 24, 1848, in *The Sherman Letters: Correspondence Between General and Senator Sherman From 1837 to 1891*, ed. Rachel Sherman Thorndike (New York: Da Capo Press, 1969), p. 42; N. S. B. Gras, "Business Letters from San Francisco Bay," *Journal of Business and Economic History* 1 (1929): 324–34.

13. Frank Soulé, *Annals of San Francisco*, p. 362; Charles P. Daniell to his father, Sept. 14, 1853, CPD; Grogan and Lent to Faxon D. Atherton, Jan. 31, 1853, FDA; Andrew J. Davis, undated fragment (from internal evidence, probably 1852 or 1853), AJD; Moses Pearson Cogsell, "San Francisco in August, 1849," *PH* 10, no. 3 (1966): 14.

14. *Alta*, Sept. 11, 1851.

15. *Ibid.*, Jan. 31, 1853; Arbitration Award no. 7, San Francisco Chamber of Commerce, Nov. 25, 1852, CC.

16. Charles Hosmer to his parents, Jan. 8, 1851, Hosmer Correspondence, Borel Collection, Stanford University; Isaac Annis to Nancy Russell, Aug. 31, 1849, Item 2773, New York Historical Society, New York; Robert Lammot to E. I. Du Pont de Nemours and Co., Apr. 11, 1850, in White, "Great Expectations," p. 294; Charles P. Daniell to his father, July 17, 1850, CPD; Roger Sherman Baldwin to his father, Mar. 31, 1851, RSB; *Alta*, Mar. 19, 1851; "Trade with California in the Fifties," *Bulletin of the Business History Society* 5 (1931): 9.

17. Macondray and Co. to W. F. Parrot, May 12, 1851, F. W. Macondray Papers, California Historical Society, San Francisco; Samuel Weston to his father, Feb. 14, May 16, 1851, WKW; Smalley, "Some Aspects of the Maine to California Trade," p. 599.

18. Robert S. Lammot to his mother, July 22, 1851; Lammot to his father, July 22, 1851, LF; Charles P. Daniell to his mother, July 31, 1851, CPD.

19. *Alta*, Sept. 15, 23, 1851; *Herald*, June 6, 1851.

20. Robert Kelley, *The Cultural Pattern in American Politics: The First Century* (New York: Knopf, 1979), p. 188; Robert S. Lammot to his father, Mar. 1, 1852, LF; Roger Sherman Baldwin to his mother, May 2, 1852, RSB; Charles P. Daniell to his father, July 14, 1852, CPD; *Pacific* (San Francisco), Sept. 3, 1852; Thomas T. Seward to his wife, Nov. 30, 1852, TTS.

21. Grogan and Lent to Faxon D. Atherton, Jan. 14, 1853; P. N. McKay to Faxon D. Atherton, Jan. 31, 1853; Grogan and Lent to Faxon D. Atherton, Mar. 31, 1853, FDA; William Sherman to John Sherman, June 3, 1853, in *The Sherman Letters*, ed. Thorndike, p. 53.

22. Charles P. Daniell to his father, Apr. 29, June 15, 1853, CPD; Grogan and Lent to Faxon D. Atherton, July 30, 1853, FDA.

23. Alexander B. Grogan to Faxon D. Atherton, Aug. 15, Sept. 15, 1853, FDA; Henry L. Leffingwell to his father, Nov. 14, 1853, Coe Collection, New York Historical Society, New York; Robert S. Lammot to Du Pont and Co., Dec. 15, 1853, in White, "Great Expectations," p. 300.

24. Thomas S. Berry, "Gold! But How Much?" *CHQ* 55 (1976): 253; Alexander B. Grogan to Faxon D. Atherton, Mar. 15, 1854, FDA; Lura

Smith to Helen Case Huntling, May 30, 1854, LS; Thomas T. Seward to his wife, June 1, 1854, TTS; Dwight L. Clarke, *William Tecumseh Sherman: Gold Rush Banker* (San Francisco: California Historical Society, 1969), p. 52; Andrew J. Davis to a friend, Nov. 15, 1854, AJD; David Lavender, *Nothing Seemed Impossible: William G. Ralston and Early San Francisco* (Palo Alto: American West Publishing Co., 1975), p. 79.

25. Alexander B. Grogan to Faxon D. Atherton, Mar. 15, 30, 1853, FDA; Joseph B. Crockett to his wife, Feb. 28, 1855, JBC; Grogan to Atherton, May 15, 1853, FDA. The decline in shipments can be inferred from the decline in revenue at the Customs House: Lionel Fredman, "The Bigler Regime," p. 62.

26. *Daily California Chronicle* (San Francisco), Aug. 27, 1855.

27. *Ibid.*, Jan. 9, 1856; *Herald*, Mar. 14, 1856; *San Francisco Daily Evening Bulletin*, Mar. 27, 1856.

28. *Bulletin*, Apr. 18, 1856; Alexander B. Grogan to Faxon D. Atherton, Apr. 4, 1856; *Herald*, Apr. 29, 1856; Grogan to Atherton, May 14, 1856, FDA.

29. *Alta*, Jan. 10, 1853; on the jobber, see Gerald Gunderson, *A New Economic History of America* (New York: McGraw-Hill, 1976), pp. 203–5, 208–10; on antebellum Western merchants in general, the basic work is Lewis E. Atherton, *The Pioneer Merchant in Mid-America* (Columbia: University of Missouri Press, 1939).

30. *Alta*, Oct. 17 and 24, Nov. 14, 1853.

31. Captain J. Shepherd to Rear Admiral Hornby, Dec. 24, 1849, Papers Relating to the British Consulate at San Francisco, Borel Collection, Stanford University; see also Charles P. Daniell to his father, Jan. 14, 1851, CPD.

32. *Alta*, Feb. 7, 1851; Henry D. Lammot to Daniel Lammot, Apr. 4, 1852, LF.

33. Alexander B. Grogan to Faxon D. Atherton, Feb. 23 and Apr. 16, 29, 1853, FDA.

34. *Chronicle*, Mar. 21, May 16, 1854.

35. *Ibid.*, Jan. 4, 1855; Alexander B. Grogan to Faxon D. Atherton, Feb. 28, 1855, FDA; *Chronicle*, Apr. 13, June 28, Aug. 3, 1855.

36. *Alta*, Jan. 7, 1853; Alexander B. Grogan to Faxon D. Atherton, Mar. 31, 1853, FDA: *Chronicle*, Apr. 30, 1855.

37. *Chronicle*, Apr. 18, Nov. 22, 1855.

38. Pierce, *History of Chicago*, 1: 129; Stuart Bruchey, *The Roots of American Economic Growth, 1607–1861: An Essay in Social Causation* (New York: Harper & Row, 1965), pp. 44–48.

39. Grogan and Lent to Faxon D. Atherton, July 30, 1853, and Jan. 31, 1854, FDA; *Chronicle*, June 16, 1854.

40. *Chronicle*, July 25, 1855.

41. Alexander B. Grogan to Faxon D. Atherton, Feb. 15, 1855, FDA; Edwin M. Lewis to Rodman Price, Oct. 29, 1854, Rodman Price Papers, Bancroft Library, Berkeley; Thomas T. Seward to his wife, Feb. 9, 1855, TTS.

42. Roger Sherman Baldwin to his sister, Jan. 14, 1853, RSB. See

also Harvey Lamb to his mother, Dec. 31, 1852, HL; Charles P. Daniell to his mother, Jan. 15, 1853, CPD.

43. *Chronicle*, Jan. 18, 1855.

44. *Alta*, Mar. 8, 1851, and Oct. 10, 1853; Alexander B. Grogan to Faxon D. Atherton, Nov. 30, 1853, and Jan. 31, 1854, FDA.

45. *Chronicle*, Aug. 1, 1845. See also Kelley, *The Cultural Pattern in American Politics*, p. 188.

46. Robert Albion, *The Rise of New York Port, 1815–1860* (New York: Scribner's, 1939), pp. 276–80.

47. Peggy Robbins, "Levi Strauss," *American History Illustrated* 5, no. 5 (1971): 34; *Alta*, June 6–9, 1853. The Strauss case might in itself be representative of the Jewish mercantile experience in San Francisco, for, according to Peter Decker, Jewish merchants did better in San Francisco than their non-Jewish counterparts: Decker, "Jewish Merchants in San Francisco: Social Mobility on the Urban Frontier," *American Jewish History* 68 (1979): 402.

48. *Chronicle*, Nov. 29, 1854; see also *Alta*, Mar. 1, 1853.

49. *Chronicle*, Nov. 16, 1854. On "steamer days" along the Ohio see Paul Kramer, "The River Cities," in *The City in American Life: From Colonial Times to the Present*, ed. Paul Kramer and Frederick L. Holborn (New York: Capricorn, 1970), p. 101.

50. See Alexander B. Grogan to Faxon D. Atherton, Sept. 15, 1853, and Mar. 30, 1855, FDA; *Alta*, Mar. 5, 6, 1853.

51. California, *Constitution* (1849), art. 4, sec. 5; Bayrd Still, "California's First Constitution: A Reflection of the Political Philosophy of the Frontier," *PHR* 4 (1935): 221–34; Bayrd Still, "An Interpretation of the Statehood Process," *MVHR* 23 (1936): 189–204. On the importance of credit nationally see James D. Norris, *R. G. Dun and Co.: The Development of Credit Reporting in the United States* (Westport, Conn.: Greenwood Press, 1978). See also Ira B. Cross, *Financing an Empire: The History of Banking in California*, 4 vols. (San Francisco: S. J. Clark Publishing Co., 1927), 1: 74.

52. For the material on banking, where not otherwise specified, I am relying on Cross and on Benjamin C. Wright, *Banking in California* (San Francisco: H. S. Crocker Co., 1910). For the similar development of banking in another regional emporium see Pierce, *History of Chicago*, 1: 124, 157–59.

53. John D. Carter, "The San Francisco Bulletin, 1855–1865: A Study in the Beginnings of Pacific Coast Journalism," Ph.D. dissertation, University of California, 1941, pp. 1–16; Charles Milton Lane, "James King of William and the San Francisco Bulletin," Master of Journalism thesis, University of California, 1958, pp. 17–30; Henry Cohen, *Business and Politics from the Age of Jackson to the Civil War: The Career Biography of W. W. Corcoran* (Westport, Conn.: Greenwood Publishing Co., 1971), p. 123.

54. Clarke, *Sherman*, pp. 161–65; Dwight L. Clarke, "Soldiers under Stephen Watts Kearny," *CHSQ* 45 (1966): 133–48; John S. Hittell, *The Commerce and Industries of the Pacific Coast of North America* (San Francisco: A. L. Bancroft and Co., 1882), p. 127.

55. The attempt to keep Page, Bacon, and Co. afloat is related in the Diary of F. W. Page, California Historical Society, San Francisco; and in Joseph B. Crockett to his wife, Feb. 23, 26, 28, and Mar. 9, 1855, JBC.

56. Donald C. Biggs, *Conquer and Colonize: Stevenson's Regiment and California* (San Rafael, Calif.: Presidio Press, 1977), pp. 111–12; T. H. Hittell, *History of California*, 3: 708. Naglee was reported as "universally despised" in A. M. Van Nostrand to Mrs. R. M. Price, Mar. 10, 1850, Rodman Price Papers, Bancroft Library, Berkeley.

57. Quoted in John D. Unruh, *The Plains Across: The Overland Immigrants and the Trans-Mississippi West* (Urbana: University of Illinois Press, 1979), p. 65.

58. William Daingerfield to his mother, July 14, Aug. 13, Sept. 1, 1853, and Apr. 1, 1854, Daingerfield Family Letters, Borel Collection, Stanford University.

59. George Doherty to Rev. John Nobili, June 6, 1852, Nobili Collection, University of Santa Clara, Santa Clara.

60. Harvey Lamb to his mother, Feb. 6, Apr. 29, Sept. 15, Oct. 18, Dec. 31, 1852, HL.

CHAPTER 3

1. *Herald*, May 2, 1851; *Alta*, May 5, 1851.

2. *Alta*, Feb. 5, Sept. 29, 1851.

3. *Alta*, July 26, 1851; *Bulletin*, Apr. 15, 1856. A random sampling of typical complaints can be found in *Alta*, July 30, Aug. 1, Sept. 27, Oct. 30, 31, 1851.

4. Roger Sherman Baldwin to his sister, Nov. 14, 1852, RSB; W. Van Voorhies to Col. J. D. Stevenson, July 25, 1856, Papers Relating to Ballot Box Stuffing, VC.

5. Richard C. Hammond to Beverly C. Saunders, July 16, Aug. 4, 1853, CC.

6. Milton S. Latham to Secretary Guthrie, Sept. 25, Oct. 4, 17, 1855, Milton S. Latham Letter Book, VC.

7. Robert S. Lammot to his father, Dec. 29, 1852, LF.

8. *Chronicle*, June 7, 1855, and Feb. 7, 22, 27, 1856; *Bulletin*, Feb. 6, 1856; Rough Minutes of a meeting of the Chamber of Commerce, Aug. 11, 1855, CC.

9. Rodman W. Paul, "The Origins of the Chinese Issue in California," *MVHR* 25 (1937): 181–96. McGowan was later pursued by his erstwhile mercantile allies when they formed the 1856 vigilance committee. His exploits were narrated in a book entitled *Narrative of Edward McGowan including a full account of the author's adventures and perils while persecuted by the San Francisco Vigilance Committee of 1856* (San Francisco: the author, 1857).

10. California Assembly, *Journal* (1856), pp. 321–22; *Bulletin*, Oct. 19, 1855; *Colville's San Francisco Directory for the Year Commencing October 1856* (San Francisco: S. Colville, 1856); *Herald*, Mar. 3, 1856. Sr. M. Celeste Standart, O.P., "The Sonora Migration to California, 1848–1856," *SCQ* 58 (1976): 333–57, shows that country

merchants also tended to oppose this type of legislation; in the same vein, see Cheryl L. Cole, "Chinese Exclusion: The Capitalist Perspective of the Sacramento *Union*," *CH* 57 (1978): 8–31.

11. Frank Soulé, *Annals of San Francisco*, p. 231; *Alta*, Oct. 16, 20, 1851.

12. A Committee of the Chamber of Commerce to Paul K. Hubbs, Mar. 1, 1852, CC.

13. California, *Statutes* (1852), chap. 39, pp. 91–92, 94–95.

14. California, *Statutes* (1853), chap. 167, p. 237; *Statutes* (1854), chap. 63, p. 91.

15. California, *Statutes* (1852), chap. 3, p. 35; *Statutes* (1853), chap. 167, p. 244; *Statutes* (1854), chap. 63, pp. 97–98.

16. California, *Statutes* (1852), chap. 3, p. 39; *Statutes* (1853), chap. 167, pp. 243–44; *Statutes* (1854), chap. 63, pp. 95–96.

17. Committee of Chamber of Commerce to Hubbs, Mar. 1, 1852, CC; California, *Statutes* (1853), chap. 167, p. 245; *Statutes* (1854), chap. 63, pp. 97–99; John P. Young, *San Francisco*, 1: 344.

18. California, *Statutes* (1853), chap. 167, pp. 242–43; *Statutes* (1854), chap. 63, p. 96.

19. Grogan and Lent to Faxon D. Atherton, July 30, 1853; Alexander B. Grogan to Faxon D. Atherton, Aug. 15, 1853, FDA.

20. Roger Lotchin, "San Francisco: The Patterns and Chaos of Growth," in *Cities in American History*, ed. Kenneth T. Jackson and Stanley K. Schultz (New York: Knopf, 1972), p. 151.

21. Soulé, *Annals of San Francisco*, pp. 329–33; M. F. Williams, *San Francisco Vigilance Committee of 1851*, p. 164; John B. McGloin, S. J., *San Francisco: The Story of a City*, pp. 68–75; F. W. Macondray and Co. to W. F. Parrot, May 12, 1851, F. W. Macondray Papers, California Historical Society, San Francisco; Samuel Weston to his father, May 8, 1851, WKW; Robert S. Lammot to his father, May 11, 1851, LF; Leo Deuel, *Memoirs of Heinrich Schliemann: A Documentary Portrait from His Autobiographical Writings, Letters, and Excavation Reports* (New York: Harper & Row, 1977), p. 74; George Doherty to Rev. John Nobili, June 26, 1851, Nobili Papers, University of Santa Clara, Santa Clara.

22. Charles P. Daniell to his mother, Dec. 9, 1850, CPD; Andrew J. Davis to a friend, Nov. 15, 1854, AJD.

23. H. Eastman to a friend, June 29, 1851, Eastman Papers, Bancroft Library.

24. Carl Bridenbaugh, *Cities in the Wilderness: The First Century of Urban Life in America, 1625–1742* (New York: Knopf, 1955), p. 57; Sylvia Doughty Fries, *The Urban Ideal in Colonial America* (Philadelphia: Temple University Press, 1977), pp. 79–107; Sidney I. Pomerantz, *New York, An American City, 1783–1803: A Study of Urban Life* (New York: Columbia University Press, 1939), pp. 297–300.

25. Bridenbaugh, *Cities in the Wilderness*, p. 97; Wade, *The Urban Frontier* (Cambridge, Mass.: Harvard University Press, 1959), pp. 91–92, 292; Bessie Pierce, *A History of Chicago*, 1: 219; 2: 313; Robert Albion, *The Rise of New York Port, 1815–1860*, p. 261.

26. *Alta*, Jan. 1, Feb. 18, 21, 1851; *Herald*, May 12, 1851.

27. Williams, *San Francisco Vigilance Committee*, p. 113.

28. Gary B. Nash, *The Urban Crucible: Social Change, Political Consciousness, and the Origin of the American Revolution* (Cambridge, Mass.: Harvard University Press, 1979), p. 314; Pomerantz, *New York*, pp. 297–300; Robert Ernst, *Immigrant Life in New York City, 1825–1863* (New York: King's Crown Press, 1949), p. 39; Frank Browning and John Gerassi, *The American Way of Crime* (New York: Putnam, 1980), pp. 148–51.

29. Wade, *Urban Frontier*, pp. 123–24; Leonard L. Richards, *Gentlemen of Property and Standing: Anti-Abolitionist Mobs in Jacksonian America* (Oxford: Oxford University Press, 1970); Pierce, *History of Chicago*, 1: 127.

30. Kai T. Erikson, *Wayward Puritans: A Study in the Sociology of Deviance* (New York: John Wiley and Sons, 1966), pp. 161–82; Browning and Gerassi, *The American Way of Crime*, p. 10.

31. Sherman L. Richards and George M. Blackburn, "The Sydney Ducks: A Demographic Analysis," *PHR* 42 (1973): 20–31; Bridenbaugh, *Cities in the Wilderness*, p. 59.

32. Jay Monaghan, *Australians and the Gold Rush*, pp. 91–95, 121; Milton S. Latham to his aunt and uncle, May 12, 1850, Milton S. Latham Correspondence and Day Book, Borel Collection, Stanford University.

*33. Richards and Blackburn, "The Sydney Ducks." This essay is based on the 1852 state census figures, which are not strictly applicable to 1851; but they are the only figures we have. Further, the two authors treat only those persons "who listed Sydney as their last place of residence" (p. 24). Since it is obvious, from even a cursory reading of the sources, that "Sydney" was a generic, rather than a strictly geographical term in San Francisco in the 1850's, the authors do not really treat all the "Sydney Ducks" as San Franciscans used the term. Complementary figures for the Irish-born are given in R. A. Burchell, *The San Francisco Irish, 1848–1880* (Berkeley and Los Angeles: University of California Press, 1980), p. 73; other figures are in Burchell, "The Gathering of a Community: The British-born of San Francisco in 1852 and 1872," *Journal of American Studies* 10 (1976): 279–312.

34. *Alta*, Feb. 25, Mar. 13, 1851; *Herald*, May 12, June 3, 1851.

35. Richards and Blackburn, "The Sydney Ducks," p. 31; Paul, "The Origins of the Chinese Issue in California"; Leonard Pitt, "The Beginnings of Nativism in California," *PHR* 30 (1961): 23–38; J. S. Holliday, *The World Rushed In*, p. 116; Lawrence Ferlinghetti and Nancy Peters, *Literary San Francisco: A Pictorial History from its Beginnings to the Present Day* (San Francisco: City Lights and Harper & Row, 1980), p. 18; Charles P. Daniell to his mother, July 29, 1850, CPD; Richard H. Peterson, "Anti-Mexican Nativism in California, 1848–1853: A Study of Cultural Conflict," *SCQ* 62 (1980): 309–27; Edwards Phillips, "Seeing the Elephant," *PH* 18 (1974): 12–30. The phrase "seeing the elephant" did not always or necessarily imply racism; but, like so much else in the 1850's, it could.

36. Ping Chiu, *Chinese Labor in California 1850–1880*, p. 8; Roger

Olmsted, "San Francisco and the Vigilante Style," *American West*, 7, no. 1 (1970): 7.

37. Olmsted, "San Francisco and the Vigilante Style," p. 62, has said, "It is unlikely that Bancroft's account can ever be topped as sound narrative." I agree. Therefore, for the bare facts of the 1851 vigilance committee, I am relying on Bancroft, *Popular Tribunals*; the first volume deals largely with the 1851 committee. I am also using M. F. Williams, *San Francisco Vigilance Committee*. Another fine account of this organization is George R. Stewart, *Committee of Vigilance: Revolution in San Francisco, 1851* (Boston: Houghton, Mifflin, 1964). Students of the 1851 committee are also fortunate to have three volumes of superbly edited primary sources available: Mary Floyd Williams, ed., *Papers of the San Francisco Committee of Vigilance of 1851: Minutes and Miscellaneous Papers* (Academy of Pacific Coast History Publications, vol. 4, Berkeley: University of California Press, 1919); Porter Garnett, ed., *Papers of the San Francisco Committee of Vigilance of 1851: Constitution and List of Signers. Book of Names Kept by the Sergeant-at-Arms* (Academy of Pacific Coast History Publications, vol. 1, Berkeley: University of California Press, 1910); Porter Garnett, ed., *Papers of the San Francisco Committee of Vigilance of 1851: List of Names Approved by the Committee on Qualifications* (Academy of Pacific Coast History Publications, vol. 2, Berkeley: University of California Press, 1911).

38. *Alta*, Mar. 10, 1851.

39. *Herald*, May 17, 1851; *Alta*, Apr. 1, May 19, June 2 and 8, July 8, 1851; Robert S. Lammot to his mother, June 3, 1851, LF; Williams, *San Francisco Vigilance Committee*, p. 181.

40. *Herald*, May 22, 1851.

41. James Neall, Jr., Statement, Bancroft Library. This is the clearest account of the organization of the committee.

42. Robert S. Lammot to his mother, June 11, 1851, LF; Charles P. Kimball, Statement, p. 14, Bancroft Library; on the notion of the ritual functions of vigilantism, see David A. Johnson, "Vigilance and the Law: The Moral Authority of Popular Justice in the Far West," *AQ* 33 (1981): 558–86.

*43. *Alta*, June 13, 14, 1851; *Herald*, June 14, 1851; Ferlinghetti and Peters, *Literary San Francisco*, p. 35. David A. Williams attributes Broderick's opposition to the lynching to "his principles" and "his deepest personal values" (*Broderick*, pp. 60, 63). This seems to be largely true, but opposition to vigilantism was probably for Broderick an instance in which principle was wedded to self-interest. For one thing, the San Francisco political scene prior to 1851 had propelled Broderick to the presidency of the State Senate, and he had no desire to see the scene disrupted. Also, he may well have doubted how energetic the newly elected Whig city administration would be in attempting to bring successful vigilantes to justice. Broderick was always quite sensitive to attacks on white immigrants, having lost a congressional election back in New York in 1846 partly because of the presence of a nativist candidate.

*44. M. F. Williams, ed., *Papers of the San Francisco Committee of*

Vigilance, pp. 825–27. The historiography of the 1851 vigilance committee is less extensive than that of its 1856 successor. Bancroft, in the first volume of *Popular Tribunals*, presented the committee as an instance of mining camp vigilantism writ larger. He argued that the committee was a justified response to a tremendous crime wave. In the absence of law and order, and with a criminal justice system that was too corrupt to be effective, the people legitimately took the law into their own hands. Mary Floyd Williams, in *History of the San Francisco Committee of Vigilance of 1851*, somewhat modified Bancroft's approach, pointing out that crime was not so pervasive as the more extreme vigilante claims asserted; but she still spoke of the "defiant triumph of lawlessness and crime" that justified the committee (p. 432). Williams's sensitive closing chapter, "In Retrospect," helped to change historical thinking about the 1856 committee, but for some reason, views on the 1851 committee remained largely unchanged. The only other full-length treatment, George R. Stewart's *Committee of Vigilance: Revolution, 1851*, closely follows Williams's, even to the extent of entitling the closing chapter "Retrospect"! Stewart praised the committee's "courage and moderation" and its "sense of responsibility for humanity and justice."

Contemporary writers continue to follow a crime and punishment approach. Lotchin, for instance, frames his treatment in these categories. He claims that the committee "eliminated a gang of robbers in 1851" (*San Francisco*, p. 195), but he is less sure than Bancroft about how successful the vigilantes were. He catalogues a series of spectacular crimes that occurred during the committee's tenure and after its adjournment and concludes, "It seems clear, therefore, that the Vigilantes' effectiveness has been overrated" (p. 197). Peter R. Decker follows a similar approach. Describing the public temper after the Jansen robbery, he writes, "It was clear that most citizens believed the civil authorities were unwilling to ensure the safety of law abiding citizens" (*Fortunes and Failures: White Collar Mobility in Nineteenth Century San Francisco*, Cambridge, Mass., 1978, p. 122). Through the vigilance committee, "the city's merchants gave clear warning that if the elected civil authorities could not keep social order, then the merchants would not only introduce order into the city, but maintain it through vigilante justice" (p. 123). Burchell argues that the committee had an "ethnic and political dimension," but he also claims that it was interested in "reforming and strengthening law and order in the city" (*The San Francisco Irish, 1848–1880*, p. 125).

My approach downplays the crime and punishment view for a number of reasons. First, I find it odd that the committee was not formed after some dastardly crime had been committed. Neither the Jansen robbery nor the May 4 fire (accepted, without much evidence, as arson) resulted in vigilantism. Second, I cannot find any proof of a "crime wave" in 1851. If one were to sit down and read the San Francisco newspapers for the spring of 1850, the spring of 1851, and the spring of 1852 without knowing which year was which, it would be difficult to say that one year had appreciably more crime than either of the others. Crime did not increase in the spring of 1851. What did increase were Australians, newspaper accounts of alleged (and mostly unsuccessful) incendiarism, and generalized denunciations of the allegedly worsening situation. Third, the committee existed only during the summer, during a lull in the trading season. Crime alone seems an insufficient explanation for the 1851 vigilance committee. A dull period in a trade that did not seem to be bouncing back to prosperity was quite as important.

45. Martin J. Burke, Statement, p. 4; Gerritt W. Ryckman, Statement, p. 5; James Dows, Statement, p. 10; George W. Frink, Statement, p. 21, Bancroft Library; Charles P. Daniell to his mother, July 14, 1851, CPD; Garnett, ed., *Papers . . . Constitution and List of Signers*; James M. Parker, *The San Francisco City Directory for the Year 1852–1853* (San Francisco: J. M. Parker, 1852); *A. W. Morgan and Co.'s San Francisco City Directory* (San Francisco: F. A. Bonnard, 1852).

46. M. F. Williams, ed., *Papers of the San Francisco Committee of Vigilance*, pp. 819–21.

47. Bancroft, *Popular Tribunals*, 1: 331–32.

48. *Ibid.*, pp. 323–24.

49. *Alta*, June 13, 18, 1851; Williams, *San Francisco Vigilance Committee*, p. 461.

50. The phrase "the general insufficiency of the laws and their present maladministration" was used on the committee's membership certificate. One such certificate is in the Charles H. West Papers, California Historical Society, San Francisco; *Herald*, July 14, 17, 1851; Isaac Bluxome, Jr., Statement, p. 10, Bancroft Library.

51. *Alta*, June 23–25, 1851.

52. Robert S. Lammot to his father, July 22, 1851, LF.

53. *Alta*, Aug. 22, Sept. 8, 1851.

CHAPTER 4

1. See, for example, *Alta*, Feb. 27, Apr. 15, Aug. 17, Sept. 4, 1851.

2. *Ibid.*, Mar. 18, 1851. For other charges of public apathy and voting fraud see *ibid.*, Jan. 30, Feb. 27, 1851; Apr. 30, Aug. 18 and 26, Sept. 8 and 19, 1853; Sept. 6, 1855; *Herald*, Nov. 3, 1853; *Chronicle*, Sept. 7, 1854, and Apr. 6, 1855. These are only a sampling; they could be multiplied many times over in the gold rush press.

3. *Bulletin*, June 16, July 14, 1856.

4. Francis P. Farquhar, ed., *Up and Down California: The Journal of William H. Brewer* (Berkeley and Los Angeles: University of California Press, 1966), p. 449.

5. See William T. Sherman, *Memoirs of General Willic n T. Sherman*, 2 vols. (New York: D. Appleton and Co., 1875), 1: 131.

6. Barbara J. Fields, "Resurrecting Reconstruction," *The Nation*, Nov. 29, 1980, p. 583. For the paragraphs that follow, see *Alta*, May 1, 1851; *Herald*, May 3, 1851; *Alta*, Sept. 8, 1851, and Nov. 10, 1852; *Herald*, Nov. 7, 1852; *Alta*, Oct. 1, 1853, and Sept. 27, 1854; *Chronicle*, Sept. 26, 1854; *Alta*, June 7, 1855; *Herald*, June 7, Sept. 20, 1855.

7. *Alta*, Apr. 29, 1851.
8. Michael J. Feldberg, *The Turbulent Era: Riot and Disorder in Jacksonian America* (New York: Oxford University Press, 1980), p. 55.
9. *Chronicle*, May 29, 1855.
10. Feldberg, *Turbulent Era*, p. 58; Frank Browning and John Gerassi, *The American Way of Crime*, p. 146.
11. Malcolm J. Rohrbough, *The Trans-Appalachian Frontier: People, Society, and Institutions, 1775–1850* (New York: Oxford University Press, 1978), p. 393.
12. *Herald*, Mar. 28, Apr. 10, 1851; William K. Weston to his father, Apr. 29, 1851, WKW; also Robert S. Lammot to Daniel Lammot, Apr. 30, 1851, LF; Roger Sherman Baldwin to his father, May 1, 1851, RSB.
13. *Herald*, Aug. 8, 12, 1851.
14. *Ibid.*, Sept. 4, 1851; *Alta*, Sept. 4, 1851.
15. *Herald*, Nov. 3, 1852; *Alta*, Nov. 3, 1852. The independent slates of 1851–53 might have done better had they organized earlier than a few days before each election.
16. *Alta*, Aug. 8 and 22, Sept. 2, 1853.
17. *Ibid.*, Sept. 8, 1853; see also Alexander B. Grogan to Faxon D. Atherton, Sept. 15, 1853, FDA.
18. Peyton Hurt, "The Rise and Fall of the Know-Nothings in California," *CHSQ* 9 (1930): 29. The Democrats had been split informally for years; see *Alta*, Dec. 27, 1851.
19. *Herald*, Aug. 6, 7, 10, 18, 1854; *Chronicle*, Aug. 7, 10, 18, 1854.
20. *Herald*, Sept. 7, 1854; the election is also described in Alexander B. Grogan to Faxon D. Atherton, Sept. 15, 1854, FDA; the specifics of the 1854 violence are taken from Papers Relating to Ballot Box Stuffing and Fraudulent Elections and Files of the Investigating Committee, especially William Johnson to the Executive Committee of the Committee of Vigilance, July 15, 1856, VC; the feud between Garrison and the special policemen (Garrison threatened to "blow them to hell") is related in Thomas T. Seward to Lucy Seward, Sept. 10, 1854; on Garrison's background, see David Lavender, *Nothing Seemed Impossible*, pp. 64–96; and William F. Heintz, *San Francisco's Mayors, 1850–1880* (Woodside, Calif.: Gilbert Richards Publications, 1975), pp. 20–25.
21. *Chronicle*, May 18, 1855; Jan. 21, 1856.
22. *Herald*, May 29, 1855; *Chronicle*, May 29, Aug. 6, 22, 1855; *Alta*, Aug. 22, 23, 1855; *Herald*, June 16, 17, 1855; also Thomas T. Seward to his wife, May 31, 1855, TTS.
23. *Alta*, Sept. 6, 1855; *Chronicle*, Sept. 6, 1855.
24. A. Theodore Brown, *Frontier Community: Kansas City to 1870* (Columbia: University of Missouri Press, 1963), p. 136.
25. *Chronicle*, Sept. 7, 1854.
26. *Ibid.*, Sept. 18, Nov. 13, 1855; *Alta*, Sept. 19, 1855; James King of William referred to this instance in the editorial for which Casey shot him: *Bulletin*, May 14, 1856.
27. The quotes and accusations are all taken from Papers Relating to Ballot Box Stuffing and Fraudulent Elections, VC; the accusations

that the vigilance committee investigated were the ones that were current at the time.

28. *Alta*, Sept. 9, 1853; for a typical allegation, see *Alta*, Aug. 26, 1853.

29. *Herald*, Nov. 3, 1852; *Chronicle*, Sept. 6, 1855.

30. William T. Sherman to John Sherman, Aug. 19, 1856, in *The Sherman Letters*, ed. Thorndike, p. 62.

*31. *Herald*, Nov. 5, 1856. The full remarks of the paper were: "The vote of the entire city yesterday with Judges and Inspectors of Elections composed of our most respected citizens, was 12,152. Last year, the vote polled for Governor (the highest) was 12,251—a difference of 99 in favor of 1855. After this test, all that has been trumpeted forth to the world of ballot box stuffing falls to the earth. The city has not increased, we believe, in population since its extent has been abridged by the erection of the southern portion into the County of San Mateo. We will see what shifts will be resorted to now when this fact is established beyond all doubt. With officers at the polls whose integrity is beyond all blemish, the vote of the county is as large as it was in 1855, and more than it was in 1854. Did a hejira take place last election day, or are the charges of ballot box stuffing, like most of those made by the Vigilance Committee Reformers, without foundation?" The *Herald* was probably correct in saying that there had not been an increase in population in the past year. In March 1856, many prominent San Franciscans had sent a petition urging Congress to construct a wagon road to California, for the purpose of stimulating immigration; see *Bulletin, Herald,* and *Chronicle*, Mar. 26, 27, 1856; also *Bulletin*, Apr. 20, 1856; also D. A. Williams, *Broderick*, p. 143. In his investigation of the overland migration to the west, Unruh found that the number of people involved declined "considerably" in 1855 and 1856: John Unruh, *The Plains Across*, p. 86.

32. Lotchin's findings are presented most conveniently in "San Francisco: The Patterns and Chaos of Growth," in *Cities in American History*, ed. Jackson and Schultz, pp. 143–63; the material is also in Lotchin, *San Francisco*, pp. 3–30. Passages quoted in the text are taken from the essay, pp. 149–50, 155–56. A somewhat more impressionistic account of the location of the ethnic neighborhoods is Bradford Luckingham, "Immigrant Life in Emergent San Francisco," *Journal of the West* 12 (1973): 600–601. For a fine treatment of the changing location of the central business district see Martyn J. Bowden, "Downtown Through Time: Delimitation, Expansion, and Internal Growth," *Economic Geography* 47 (1971): 121–35; for location of the wards, see *Herald*, May 28, Sept. 6, 1855.

33. *Herald*, Feb. 4, 1856; R. A. Burchell, *The San Francisco Irish*, p. 39. Dupont Street was later renamed Grant Avenue.

34. Gunther Barth, "Metropolism and Urban Elites in the Far West," in *The Age of Industrialism in America*, ed. Frederick C. Jaher (New York: Free Press, 1968), pp. 157–87; Charles Lockwood, "Rincon Hill Was San Francisco's Most Genteel Neighborhood," *CH* 58 (1979): 48–61.

35. Kelley, *The Cultural Pattern in American Politics*, p. 5.
36. For comparisons, see Robert Ernst, *Immigrant Life in New York City 1825–1863*, p. 164; Mark L. Berger, *The Revolution in the New York Party Systems* (Port Washington, N.Y.: Kennikat Press, 1973), p. 48; Michael Holt, *Forging a Majority: The Formation of the Republican Party in Pittsburg* (New Haven: Yale University Press, 1969), pp. 75–77; Kathleen Neils Conzen, *Immigrant Milwaukee: Accommodation and Community in a Frontier City* (Cambridge, Mass.: Harvard University Press, 1976), p. 194; Grace McDonald, *History of the Irish in Wisconsin in the Nineteenth Century* (diss. Catholic University 1954; rpt. New York: Arno Press, 1976), p. 126; Jo Ellen McNergney Vineyard, *The Irish on the Urban Frontier* (diss., Michigan, 1972; rpt. New York: Arno Press, 1976), p. 241; Burchell, *San Francisco Irish*, pp. 116–17.

CHAPTER 5

1. Milton Hall to his father, Apr. 25, 1852, MH; Thomas T. Seward to his wife, Dec. 29, 1852, TTS; also Charles P. Daniell to his mother, Dec. 9, 1850. On boarding houses in general see John Modell and Tamara K. Hareven, "Urbanization and the Malleable Household: An Examination of Boarding and Lodging in American Families," *Journal of Marriage and the Family* 35 (1973): 467–79.
2. Roger Sherman Baldwin to his mother, Aug. 30, 1852, RSB; Andrew J. Davis to Bacon, fragment, AJD; Charles P. Daniell to his mother, June 14, 1851, CPD; Robert S. Lammot to Anna R. Lammot, July 30, 1851, LF.
3. Charles P. Daniell to his mother, July 31, 1851, CPD.
4. Charles Thompson to his uncle, Sept. 10, 1851, Thompson Collection, New York Historical Society, New York; Ferdinand C. Ewer to his mother, Sept. 21, 1851, Ewer Diary, California Historical Society, San Francisco; Alexander B. Grogan to Faxon D. Atherton, Feb. 15, 1855, FDA; Milton Hall to his father, Apr. 25, 1852, MH.
5. William K. Weston to his brother, Jan. 15, 1851, WKW; Andrew J. Davis to a friend, Jan. 15, 1854, AJD.
6. Alexander B. Grogan to Faxon D. Atherton, May 7, 1855, FDA; John Banfield to home, June 29, 1852, Banfield Collection, New York Historical Society, New York; Milton Hall to his father, Aug. 15, 1852, MH; also J. S. Holliday, *The World Rushed In*, p. 352.
7. Joseph B. Crockett to his wife, May 4, 1854, JBC; William K. Weston to his father, Apr. 28, 1851, WKW; Edward T. Hosmer to his father, Sept. 29, 1849, Hosmer Correspondence, Borel Collection, Stanford University; Lura Smith to Helen Case Huntling, Sept. 29, 1854, LS; William Thornton to Lucy Thornton, Feb. 14, 1852, Thornton Collection, Nevada Historical Society, Reno; Roger Sherman Baldwin to his father, Mar. 31, 1851, RSB.
8. Thomas T. Seward to Lucy Seward, May 15, 1853; Jan. 26, 1854, TTS.
9. Thomas T. Seward to Lucy Seward, July 15, 1853, TTS; Charles P. Daniell to his father, June 15, 1853, CPD; Roger Sherman Baldwin

to his sister, Dec. 27, 1851, and Dec. 31, 1852, RSB; Charles P. Daniell to his mother, Dec. 9, 1850, CPD. Longing for home and family by displaced Easterners may have been more extreme among San Franciscans because of the great distance from home, but it was a lament of all pioneers. See, for instance, Bessie Pierce, *A History of Chicago*, 1: 187; Richard Wade, *The Urban Frontier*, p. 218; Kathleen Conzen, *Immigrant Milwaukee*, p. 46. The fullest account of associational life in San Francisco is Bradford Luckingham, "Associational Life on the Urban Frontier: San Francisco, 1845–1856," dissertation, University of California, Davis, 1968; see also Luckingham, "Agents of Culture in the Urban West: Merchants and Mercantile Libraries in Mid-Nineteenth Century St. Louis and San Francisco," *Journal of the West* 17, no. 2 (1978): 28–35.

10. Lura Smith to Helen Case Huntling, Apr. 2, 1856, LS; Mary Banfield to Prudence Haddan Vanderbeck, Oct. 12, 1851, Banfield Collection, New York Historical Society, New York; Lura Smith to Helen Case Huntling, Dec. 26, 1854, LS.

11. *Alta*, Apr. 23 and 29, May 1, 1851; *Herald*, May 3, 1851; Parker, *San Francisco City Directory; A. W. Morgan and Co.'s San Francisco City Directory*.

12. M. F. Williams, ed., *Papers of the San Francisco Committee of Vigilance*, pp. 819–21; Parker, *San Francisco City Directory; A. W. Morgan and Co.'s San Francisco City Directory*.

13. *Alta*, Nov. 1, 2, 10, 1852; *Herald*, Nov. 7, 1852.

14. *Alta*, Aug. 22, Sept. 2, Oct. 1, 1853.

15. The election returns may be found in *Alta*, Sept. 8, 1851; *Herald*, Nov. 7, 1852; *Alta*, Oct. 1, 1853; the national analogue to all this is in Ronald P. Formisano, "Political Character, Antipartyism, and the Second Party System," *AQ* 21 (1969): 683–709.

16. David M. Potter, *The Impending Crisis, 1848–1861* (New York: Harper & Row, 1976), p. 44; Michael F. Holt, *The Political Crisis of the 1850's* (New York: Wiley, 1978), p. 102.

17. Edward Pessen, "How Different from Each Other Were the Antebellum North and South," p. 1140; Charles N. Glaab and A. Theodore Brown, *A History of Urban America*, p. 176; *Herald*, Nov. 1, 1852.

18. Gunther Barth, *Instant Cities*, p. 161.

19. Edward Pessen, "We Are All Jeffersonians, We Are All Jacksonians: or, A Pox on Stultifying Periodizations," *Journal of the Early Republic* 1 (1981): 20; Holt, *Forging a Majority*, p. 36; Pierce, *History of Chicago*, 1: 91, 114, 397.

20. A. Theodore Brown, *Frontier Community*, p. 84; Conzen, *Immigrant Milwaukee*, p. 211; Michael H. Frisch, *Town into City: Springfield, Massachusetts, and the Meaning of Community, 1840–1880* (Cambridge, Mass.: Harvard University Press, 1972), p. 43. San Francisco's debt quickly approached a million dollars: *Alta*, Jan. 22, 1851.

21. *Alta*, Aug. 6, 1854.

22. *Chronicle*, Sept. 6, 1854; Hurt, "The Rise and Fall of the Know-Nothings in California," pp. 28–29. On the national origins of the

Know-Nothings, the best brief treatment is Michael Holt, "The Politics of Impatience: The Origins of Know-Nothingism," *Journal of American History* 60 (1973): 309–31.

23. Charles A. Hosmer to George Hosmer, June 1, 1850, Hosmer Correspondence, Borel Collection, Stanford University.

24. Luckingham, "Immigrant Life in Emergent San Francisco," p. 605; William Hanchett, "The Blue Law Gospel in Gold Rush California," *PHR* 34 (1955): 363; Paul Boyer, *Urban Masses and Moral Order in America, 1820–1920* (Cambridge, Mass.: Harvard University Press, 1978), p. 6.

25. Potter, *The Impending Crisis*, pp. 241–42; William K. Weston to his father, Apr. 29, 1851, WKW; Henry D. Lammot to his mother, Apr. 31, 1851, LF.

26. Robert Ernst, *Immigrant Life in New York City*, p. 71; Stuart M. Blumin, *The Urban Threshold: Growth and Change in a Nineteenth Century American Community* (Chicago: University of Chicago Press, 1976), p. 87; Pierce, *History of Chicago*, 1: 180; 2: 151; Conzen, *Immigrant Milwaukee*, pp. 66, 74, 160, 164, 171; Brian McGinty, "The Green and the Gold: The Irish in Early California," *American West* 15, no. 2 (1978): 18–21, 65–69.

27. Lawrence J. McCaffrey, *The Irish Diaspora in America* (Bloomington: Indiana University Press, 1976), pp. 7, 63; Ernst, *Immigrant Life in New York City*, pp. 95, 98; Conzen, *Immigrant Milwaukee*, p. 88.

28. W. J. Rorabaugh, *The Alcoholic Republic: An American Tradition* (New York: Oxford University Press, 1979), p. 196; Ernst, *Immigrant Life in New York City*, p. 148; Frisch, *Town into City*, p. 38; McCaffrey, *Irish Diaspora*, p. 85.

29. Lura Smith to Helen Case Huntling, Aug. 12, 1854; Jan. 2, Apr. 2, 1856, LS.

30. *Chronicle*, Sept. 9, 1854; Thomas T. Seward to Lucy Seward, Jan. 13, 1855, TTS; Milton Hall to his father, Dec. 18, 1854, MH.

31. R. A. Burchell, *The San Francisco Irish*, p. 13.

32. *Ibid.*, p. 88; on the beginnings of Catholicism in San Francisco see John B. McGloin, *San Francisco*, pp. 37–44.

33. See Hofstadter's *The Paranoid Style in American Politics and Other Essays* (New York: Knopf, 1966), and Davis's "Some Themes of Countersubversion: An Analysis of Anti-Masonic, Anti-Catholic, and Anti-Mormon Literature," *MVHR* 47 (1960): 205–24, and "Some Ideological Functions of Prejudice in Antebellum America," *AQ* (1963): 115–26; also Davis, ed., *The Fear of Conspiracy: Images of un-American Subversion from the Revolution to the Present* (Ithaca: Cornell University Press, 1971).

34. Robert Francis Huetson, *The Catholic Press and Nativism* (diss., Notre Dame, 1972; rpt. New York: Arno Press, 1976), p. 38; Vincent P. Lannie and Bernard C. Diethorn, "For the Honor and Glory of God: The Philadelphia Bible Riots of 1840," *History of Education Quarterly* 8 (1968): 89.

35. Pierce, *History of Chicago*, 2: 360; Huetson, *The Catholic Press and Nativism*, p. 180; Joseph P. Chinnici, O.F.M., "Organization of the Spiritual Life: American Catholic Devotional Works, 1791–1866,"

Theological Studies 40 (1979): 229–55. The trustee issue was not merely one of power politics, for some lay people based their arguments on theological conceptions of the nature of the church; see, for instance, Patrick W. Carey, "John F. O. Fernandez: Enlightened Lay Catholic Reformer," *Review of Politics* 43 (1981): 112–29; on the trustee question and its re-emergence in the 1840's see James Hennesey, S. J., *American Catholics: A History of the Roman Catholic Community in the United States* (New York: Oxford University Press, 1981), pp. 95–105; also David J. O'Brien, "American Catholics and the Diaspora," *Cross Currents* 16 (1966): 307–24.

36. Holt, *Forging a Majority*, p. 324; Vincent P. Lannie, *Public Money and Parochial Education: Bishop Hughes, Governor Seward, and the New York School Controversy* (Cleveland: Press of Case Western Reserve University, 1968); Jay P. Dolan, *The Immigrant Church: New York's Irish and German Catholics, 1815–1865* (Baltimore: Johns Hopkins University Press, 1975), p. 164; Huetson, *The Catholic Press and Nativism*, p. 161.

37. See the following works by David Tyack: *The One Best System: A History of American Urban Education* (Cambridge, Mass.: Harvard University Press, 1974); "The Kingdom of God and the Common School: Protestant Ministers and the Educational Awakening in the West," *Harvard Educational Review* 36 (1966): 447–69; "Onward Christian Soldiers: Religion in the American Common School," in *History and Education: The Educational Uses of the Past*, ed. Paul Nash (New York: Random House, 1970), pp. 212–55.

38. Quoted in Vincent P. Lannie, "Alienation in America: The Immigrant Catholic and Public Education in Pre-Civil War America," *Review of Politics* 32 (1970): 509.

39. Lannie and Diethorn, "For the Honor and Glory of God," pp. 68, 87.

40. *Ibid.*, p. 94; Lannie, "Alienation in America," p. 515; Luckingham, "Immigrant Life in Emergent San Francisco," p. 612; Bradford Luckingham, "Religion in Early San Francisco," *PH* 17 (1973): 69; *Alta*, Feb. 21, 1851; John S. Young, *San Francisco*, 2: 785.

41. *Pacific*, Mar. 30, 1855. In a different context, R. Laurence Moore has recently speculated that Hughes adopted "the paradoxical strategy of pursuing the power of the 'insider' by keeping the stigma of outsiderhood constantly attached to the people he tried to lead." See Moore, "Insiders and Outsiders in American Historical Narrative," *AHR* 87 (1982): 390–412.

42. Mary McDougall Gordon, "Patriots and Christians: A Reassessment of Nineteenth Century School Reformers," *Journal of Social History* 11 (1978): 554–73; Carl F. Kaestle and Maris A. Vinovskis, *Education and Social Change in Nineteenth Century Massachusetts* (Cambridge: Cambridge University Press, 1980), p. 18; Pomerantz, *New York*, p. 423; Clifford M. Drury, "Church-Sponsored Schools in Early California," *PH* 20 (1976): 158–66; W. W. Ferrier, *Ninety Years of Education in California* (Berkeley: Sather Gate Book Shop, 1937), p. 18.

43. For the two paragraphs see Bancroft, *History of California*, 6:

717; Ferrier, *Ninety Years of Education*, pp. 17–26, 41–42; Roy W. Cloud, *Education in California* (Stanford: Stanford University Press, 1952), p. 29; *Alta*, Mar. 1, 4, 13, July 8, 1851.

44. *Alta*, Feb. 25 and 27, Oct. 10, 1851; Ferrier, *Ninety Years of Education*, pp. 38–39; Cloud, *Education in California*, p. 29; Nicholas C. Polos, "John Swett: The Rincon Period," *PH* 19 (1975): 135; Frank Soulé, *Annals of San Francisco*, pp. 681–85.

45. California, *Statutes* (1851), chap. 126, p. 499; *Statutes* (1852), chap. 53, p. 125; *Pacific*, Feb. 27, July 16, 1852.

46. California Senate, *Journal* (1853), doc. 61, app. 3, p. 27; doc. 61, p. 8; California, *Statutes* (1853), chap. 156, p. 231. This type of funding became quite controversial after the Civil War, but it was not unusual in the antebellum period; see Huetson, *The Catholic Press and Nativism*, pp. 174–77; Vineyard, *The Irish on the Urban Frontier*, p. 215; Holt, *Forging a Majority*, pp. 118, 132; Kelley, *The Cultural Pattern in American Politics*, p. 189. On Alemany see John B. McGloin, *California's First Archbishop: The Life of Joseph Sadoc Alemany* (New York: Herder and Herder, 1966).

47. Lee S. Dolson, "The Administration of the San Francisco Public Schools, 1847–1947," dissertation, University of California at Berkeley, 1964, p. 58; *Pacific*, May 4, 18, 1855. For a similar situation in Chicago see James W. Sanders, *The Education of an Urban Minority: Catholics in Chicago, 1833–1965* (New York: Oxford University Press, 1977), p. 22, see also Huetson, *The Catholic Press and Nativism*, pp. 174–77; Ernst, *Immigrant Life in New York City*, p. 140; Pierce, *History of Chicago*, 2: 379; Lannie and Diethorn, "For the Honor and Glory of God," pp. 48, 55, 82.

48. *Pacific*, Jan. 31, 1856.

49. Burchell, *San Francisco Irish*, p. 161; John Swett, *Public Education in California* (New York: American Book Co., 1911), p. 115; Dolson, "The Administration of the San Francisco Public Schools," p. 58; Ferdinand C. Ewer Diary, September and October 1855, p. 246, California Historical Society, San Francisco.

50. Dolan, *The Immigrant Church*, p. 105; *Pacific*, May 4, 1855; *Herald*, May 1, 1855; *Bulletin*, Nov. 27, 1855.

51. *Bulletin*, Dec. 19, 1855; *Pacific*, Mar. 24, 1854. The *Pacific* kept up a constant barrage against the division of the fund: see, as a sample, May 6, June 3, Aug. 19, 1853; Jan. 20, Feb. 10, Mar. 24, June 9, 16, 23, 1854; also Wesley Norton, "'Like a Thousand Preachers Flying': Religious Newspapers on the Pacific Coast to 1865," *CHQ* 56 (1977): 194–209.

52. California, *Statutes* (1855), chap. 185, p. 235; chap. 197, pp. 251–67; *Herald*, Sept. 20, 1855.

53. *Bulletin*, Nov. 24, Dec. 1, 5, 6, 21, 1855. The language describing the teachers is taken from the teaching certificate the Board issued. One such certificate is that of Miss Clara B. Walbridge, issued Aug. 8, 1853, Alfred A. Rix Collection, California Historical Society, San Francisco.

54. Ewer Diary, pp. 248–49, California Historical Society.

55. *Herald*, Jan. 11, 1856.
56. *Ibid.*, Mar. 25, Apr. 5, 1856; *Bulletin*, Apr. 8, 1856.
57. *Bulletin*, Apr. 20, 29, 1856; *Chronicle*, Mar. 20, Apr. 28, 1853.
58. William Barnaby Faherty, S. J., "Nativism and Midwestern Education: The Experience of St. Louis University, 1832–1856," *History of Education Quarterly* 8 (1968): 447–58. The literature on antebellum nativism is vast, but the basic work is Ray Allen Billington, *The Protestant Crusade, 1800–1860: A Study in the Origins of American Nativism* (New York: Macmillan, 1938).
59. *Bulletin*, Nov. 30, 1855.
60. *Ibid.*, Nov. 14, 27, 1855.
61. *Chronicle*, Apr. 27, 1855.
62. *Bulletin*, Nov. 24, 27, 1855; May 12, 1856.
63. *Ibid.*, May 12, 1856.
64. *Pacific*, Jan. 31, 1856.

CHAPTER 6

1. John D. Carter, "The San Francisco Bulletin"; C. M. Lane, "James King of William and the San Francisco Bulletin"; Stanton A. Coblentz, *Villains and Vigilantes: The Story of James King of William and Pioneer Justice in California* (New York: Wilson-Erikson, 1936); Edward C. Kemble, *A History of California Newspapers, 1846–1858*, edited and with an Introduction by Helen Harding Bretnor (Los Gatos, Calif.: Talisman Press, 1962).
2. Henry Cohen, *Business and Politics from the Age of Jackson to the Civil War*, p. 123; *Alta*, Jan. 15, 1851; California, *Statutes* (1851), chap. 88, pp. 387–91; *Alta*, June 15, 1851; *A "Pile," or, A Glance at the Wealth of the Monied Men of San Francisco* (San Francisco: Cooke and Le Count, 1851); M. F. Williams, *San Francisco Vigilance Committee*, p. 197; *Alta*, Aug. 27, 1851; Ira B. Cross, *Financing an Empire*, 1: 73.
3. *Alta*, Sept. 20, Nov. 29, Dec. 1, 2, 1853; *Herald*, Nov. 29, Dec. 1, 5, 1853.
4. Dwight Clarke, *William Tecumseh Sherman*, p. 44; *Alta*, July 13–20, 1855; *Chronicle*, July 18–20, 1855.
5. *Bulletin*, Oct. 12–13, 17, 1855.
6. *Ibid.*, Oct. 9, 1855.
7. *Ibid.*, Jan. 22, Apr. 3, 1856; *Chronicle*, Apr. 3, 1856.
*8. As part of his argument that "spouses, spatial relationships, and spurious sensationalism" were responsible for the formation of the vigilance committee, Lotchin places a great deal of emphasis on King's presentation of himself as the champion of home, women, and the family (*San Francisco*, pp. 255–58). But King was not the only San Francisco journalist who portrayed himself in that fashion. The notion that San Francisco was moving in a direction that would make it much like more settled eastern cities was present in the city from the beginning of the American occupation. And the notion that "respectable" women were in an important fashion the bearers of civilization, so that the presence of wives and potential wives was an index of any locality's progress in culture, was as standard along the

Pacific as it was along the Atlantic. The contemporary *Annals of San Francisco* (1855) affords many examples. Though the authors admitted, "There are known mistresses and common prostitutes enough to bring disgrace upon the place," they boasted of the "very many beautiful, modest, and virtuous women in San Francisco, fit friends and companions to honest men," whose "presence here confers inestimable blessings on society" (p. 503). The *Annals* also delighted whenever a "Miss" or "Mrs." delivered a "poetical address" upon the opening of a theater, the link between women and culture being fixed in the popular mind. In the same vein, an illustration of the Customs House in the same volume shows twenty people strolling or riding in the streets nearby. Of those, nine are women, and they all look, to my unpracticed eye, very respectable! Though this proportion was far in excess of the actual proportion of women in the city, the artist knew that this kind of crowd would make the city look more refined and cultivated. King had no monopoly on any of this. Further, it cannot be demonstrated that women read the *Bulletin* more than they read other papers, or that they urged their husbands on (Lotchin calls them the "shock troops" of the vigilante revolution). Even if more women did read King, the question would be, to which of his many crusades did they respond? The testimony of Ellen Ewing Sherman, not a typical woman but certainly no harlot, is probably closer to the mark than Lotchin's. Writing of King after Casey had shot him, she said, "King has dealt in false personal abuse of Fr. Gallagher, rector of the cathedral, and . . . strengthened his position by so popular an attack." Anna McAllister, *Ellen Ewing: Wife of General Sherman* (New York: Benziger Brothers, 1936), p. 150.

9. Charles Collins, Deposition to the Committee of Vigilance, July 19, 1856, VC; *Bulletin*, Dec. 22, 1856.

10. William T. Coleman, "San Francisco Committees of Vigilance," *Century Magazine* 43 (1891): 138.

11. Milton S. Latham to Secretary Guthrie, Oct. 4, 30, 1855; Latham to Dr. H. H. Toland, Nov. 3, 1855, VC; Ethel M. Tinneman, "The Opposition to the San Francisco Vigilance Committee of 1856," M.A. thesis, University of California at Berkeley, 1941. On the Sisters of Mercy see James Hennesey, *American Catholics*, p. 140; on cholera in the city see Soulé, *Annals of San Francisco*, pp. 305, 419; John P. Young, *San Francisco*, 1: 174; and Charles Hosmer to his parents, Nov. 15, 1850, Hosmer Correspondence, Borel Collection, Stanford University.

12. *Bulletin*, Mar. 19, 1856.

13. *Ibid.*, Apr. 7, 1856.

14. *Ibid.*, Apr. 8, 1856.

15. *Ibid.*, Apr. 9, 10, 12, 17, 1856.

*16. *Ibid.*, Dec. 28, 1855. In my judgment, Lotchin's point about King's "sensationalism" also needs qualification. Lotchin states that King was not "openly anti-Catholic, anti-Semitic, or anti-Quaker." That is true. But his further observation that King's "language skirted these sentiments so closely that the adherents of those faiths must have been uneasy" is seriously understated, at least so far as the Catholic part of it goes (*San Francisco*, p. 252). Especially after the *Bulletin* attained full size at the beginning of March 1856, a considerable amount of space was given to matters of religion, notably on school and hospital issues.

17. *Chronicle*, Feb. 26, Mar. 11, 1856; *Herald*, Mar. 30, 1856.

18. *Chronicle*, Apr. 3, 9, 1856; Alexander B. Grogan to Faxon D. Atherton, Apr. 4, 1856, FDA.

19. Alexander B. Grogan to Faxon D. Atherton, May 4 and 20, July 20, 1856, FDA.

20. Young, *San Francisco*, 1: 239.

21. Milton Latham to Secretary Guthrie, Apr. 4, 1856; R. Shoyer to the Executive Committee of the Committee of Vigilance, May 17, 1856, VC.

22. *Bulletin*, May 6, 8, 1856; Fredman, "The Bigler Regime," p. 54.

23. *Bulletin*, May 9, 10, 1856.

24. The May 11, 1856, issue of the *Times* is not extant. The account here is based on the following: William T. Sherman to Stephen J. Field, Feb. 25, 1868; Milton S. Latham to Secretary Guthrie, Jan. 14, 1856, VC; *Chronicle*, Jan. 14, 1856; *Herald*, May 12, 1856; C. Rivors, *A Full and Authentic Account of the Murders of James King of William, Dr. Randall, Dr. Baldwin, West, and Marion. The Execution of James P. Casey, Charles P. Cora, Philander Brace, and James Hetherington, by the Vigilance Committee of San Francisco* (Rochester, N.Y.: E. Darrow, 1858), p. 37.

25. *Bulletin*, May 15, 1856; *Herald*, May 15, 1856.

26. Walter Van Tilburg Clark, ed., *The Journals of Alfred Doten, 1849–1903*, 2 vols. (Reno: University of Nevada Press, 1973), 1: 273. For reasons noted earlier (in Chapter 3, n. 37), in my narrative of the activities of the 1856 vigilance committee, I am following Bancroft, *Popular Tribunals*; the second volume deals almost exclusively with the 1856 committee; other good accounts of the committee include one by former Mayor Webb: "A Sketch of the Causes, Operations, and Results of the San Francisco Vigilance Committee of 1856," *Essex Institute Historical Collection* 84, no. 2 (1948); an especially fine bibliography is in Doyce B. Nunis, ed., *The San Francisco Vigilance Committee of 1856: Three Views* (Los Angeles: Los Angeles Westerners, 1971). Also useful are Myers, *San Francisco's Reign of Terror*, and Alan C. Valentine, *Vigilante Justice* (New York: Reynal and Co., 1956).

27. *Herald*, May 15, 1856; L. Q. Washington to James Van Ness, May 15, 1856; Milton S. Latham to James Van Ness, May 16, 1856, VC; Thomas G. Cary, "The San Francisco Vigilance Committee of 1856," paper read before the California Historical Society, June 1, 1888, VC.

28. Bancroft, *Popular Tribunals*, 2: 73. Concern for the secrecy of the password is evident in an unsigned note dated June 28, 1856, in the files of the investigating committee, VC.

29. "Sherman and the San Francisco Vigilantes," p. 298; James Dows, Statement, p. 11, Bancroft Library; George Aikin to Lord

Crampton, May 21, 1856, Papers Relating to the British Consulate at San Francisco, Borel Collection, Stanford University; *Herald*, May 28, June 1, July 14, 1856. The commercial orientation of the committee was a major theme in Josiah Royce's treatment of it in *California, From the Conquest in 1846 to the Second Vigilance Committee in 1856: A Study of the American Character* (Boston: Houghton, Mifflin and Co., 1886).

30. *Herald*, June 12, 1856; Bancroft, *Popular Tribunals*, 2: 13; *Colville's San Francisco Directory, Vol. I, for the Year Commencing October 1856* (San Francisco: S. Colville, 1856).

31. Bancroft, *Popular Tribunals*, 2: 111–12.

*32. The seemingly endless land litigations, which I sketched in broad outline in Chapter 1, meant that there was a lot of business for attorneys in the gold rush port. As a group, they had little interest in seeing the city changed. As one lawyer wrote to his wife, "It seems to me that my whole character has changed since I have been in California, and I feel now the responsibilities of my position and more like a man of standing and character than I ever did before" (Joseph B. Crockett to his wife, Nov. 16, 1853, JBC). Legal opposition to both the 1851 and 1856 vigilance committees probably stemmed from a combination of interest and principle, with interest weighing the more heavily.

*33. The correspondence of Governor Johnson that deals with his activities concerning the committee is conveniently collected in Herbert G. Florken, ed., "The Law and Order View of the San Francisco Vigilance Committee of 1856. Taken from the Correspondence of Governor J. Neely Johnson," *CHSQ* 14 (1935): 350–74; 15 (1935): 70–87, 143–62, 247–65. Sherman's later recollection of the meeting is in William T. Sherman to Stephen J. Field, Feb. 25, 1868, VC; Coleman's even later recollection is in Coleman, "San Francisco Committees of Vigilance," pp. 140–41; as a public official, Johnson had to oppose the committee, regardless of his private opinion of it. He was in a position similar to that of Whig Mayor Brenham in 1851: he had a political affinity with the vigilante leadership. But whereas Brenham had issued the necessary proclamation and then remained relatively quiet for the summer, Johnson was more impetuous. He tried to strike a deal. Once Casey and Cora had been executed, he had no choice but to do what Governor McDougal had done, in 1851, to condemn the committee. But the same impetuousness that had led him to seek a deal in the first place, and his sense that he had been betrayed by the vigilantes, led him to make his own proclamation stronger than the 1851 declaration.

34. Clark, *Journals of Doten*, 1: 278.

35. Loyall Farragut, "Autobiography," VC.

36. Milton S. Latham to Secretary Guthrie, June 18, 1856, VC; Lavender, *Nothing Seemed Impossible*, p. 102; Edwin Lewis to Rodman M. Price, June 29, 1856, Rodman Price Papers, California Historical Society, San Francisco; *Bulletin*, May 30, 1856; *Herald*, May 18, 1856; D. Williams, *Broderick*, p. 126; James O'Meara, *The Vigilance*

Committee of 1856 (San Francisco: J. H. Barry, 1887), p. 27; Frank Meriweather Smith, *San Francisco Vigilance Committee of 1856, with Some Interesting Sketches of Events Succeeding 1846* (San Francisco: Barry, Baird, and Co., 1883), pp. 82–83; Gerritt W. Ryckman, Statement, p. 20, Bancroft Library; James O'Meara, *Broderick and Gwin* (San Francisco: Bacon and Co., 1881).

37. *Bulletin*, May 26, 1856. The allegation about Father Gallagher was denied in the *Herald*, May 29, 1856.

38. Clark, *Journals of Doten*, 1: 280, 286; *Bulletin*, May 29, June 9, 1856. In the *Bulletin* on June 12, 1856, another correspondent, who signed himself "Lately an Irishman, Now a Naturalized American," urged the Irish to recognize that "the American people are better educated and more enlightened than we are."

*39. *Herald*, June 19, 27, 1856; Henry M. Gray, *Judges and Criminals* (San Francisco: printed for the author, 1858), p. 67. Burchell says that the Irish were given the "role of scapegoats" (*San Francisco Irish*, p. 213). This was true only for lower class Irish Catholic Democrats, and it should be understood, as I have argued in Chapter 3, as the final result of a long mercantile search through the city for usable scapegoats.

*40. The places of birth are taken from the applications for membership, VC; James Dows, Statement, p. 7; George Frink, Statement, p. 10, Bancroft Library; on Scott, a leading minister in the city, see Clifford M. Drury, *William Anderson Scott: No Ordinary Man* (Glendale, Calif.: A. H. Clark Co., 1967). With all of this in the sources, it is difficult for me to understand why some scholars insist that Richard Maxwell Brown was off base in insisting on the importance of the committee's attacks on Irish Catholic Democrats. Lotchin concedes that "anti-Catholic feelings probably tainted many reformers," but he goes on to argue that he "found no such evidence" that would justify stressing the "fiscal-ethnic dimension" of the vigilante action (*San Francisco*, pp. 268, 384). Although I agree with Lotchin on the fiscal part, downplaying the ethnic dimension seems a little like discarding the baby with the bath water. Similarly, Decker argues that Brown "places too much emphasis on the anti-Irish bias of the 1856 vigilance committee. A few Irish merchants were members of the executive committee, and many more were enrolled in the full committee" (*Fortunes and Failures*, p. 301). This is true enough, but there were Irish and then there were Irish! Some had an identifiably Catholic background, and some did not. The applicants for membership in the committee thought that that distinction was more important than Decker does, and they were there. Finally, Burchell, though admitting that "the Irishness of the committee's targets cannot be disputed," faults Brown for "over-stressing the ethnic dimension" (*San Francisco Irish*, p. 213). But he does not detail why he thinks that Brown was incorrect. Overall, it seems clear, on the basis of the evidence that I have presented in this and the previous chapter, that anti-Catholicism was central to successful political reform in the city from 1854 to 1856.

41. A. Russell Buchanan, *David S. Terry of California: Duelling Judge* (San Marino: Huntington Library, 1956), pp. 20–71; William T. Sherman to Stephen J. Field, Feb. 25, 1868, VC. Hopkins was a Know-Nothing election inspector; see *Herald*, Sept. 20, 1855.

42. "Sherman and the San Francisco Vigilantes," p. 308.

43. *Herald*, Aug. 19, 1856.

44. *Ibid.*, May 15, 1856.

45. *Ibid.*, May 16, 1856.

46. *Chronicle*, May 15, 1856; *Herald*, May 18 and 23, June 13, 1856.

47. *Herald*, May 22–25, 1856.

48. *Ibid.*, June 4 and 19, July 8, 1856.

49. *Ibid.*, June 12, 25, 1856.

*50. *Ibid.*, May 16, 29, 1856. The accuracy of the speculation charge is uncertain, but some committee members were heavy speculators. One was James Dows, whose unsuccessful flour speculation is reported in P. N. McKay to Faxon D. Atherton, Jan. 31, 1853, FDA; *Herald*, June 4, 1856. Richard Maxwell Brown's argument that the vigilantes were trying to restore confidence in San Francisco's fiscal integrity must, it seems to me, be qualified. In *Strain of Violence* (p. 138), Brown cited the pro-vigilance *Town Talk*, which claimed on May 28, 1856, that the executions of Casey and Cora would have a good impact. The paper said, "The 'reign of terror' is working our redemption and California stocks will rise in the market when this news reaches the Atlantic." However, as the remarks by Nugent I have quoted show, even before the hangings, Nugent was arguing that the vigilance committee would hurt business with the East by its display of uncivilized behavior. *Town Talk* was most likely trying to answer these types of criticisms, and its editorial should not be read as a statement of the organizational aims of the vigilance committee. Also, as John S. Hittell pointed out long ago, the Consolidation Act, which did deal with fiscal reform, had been passed by the legislature by the time the committee was organized. This criticism, it should be clear, does not touch Brown's larger point that the 1856 committee was a pivot between older and newer forms of American vigilantism.

51. William Thornton to home, June 5 and 13, Aug. 25, 1856, Thornton Papers, Nevada Historical Society, Reno.

52. *Herald*, June 25, 1856.

53. *Ibid.*, June 30, 1856.

*54. *Ibid.*, July 12, 1856. Lotchin dismisses the *Herald* by saying that it "fanned every prejudice imaginable, particularly ethnic and regional ones" (*San Francisco*, p. 268). But even if one grants that Nugent was wrong much of the time, it does not follow that he could not have been right some of the time. Here, I think he was.

55. Olmsted first suggested this in "San Francisco and the Vigilante Style," p. 24.

56. T. H. Hittell, *History of California*, 3: 521.

57. *Sun* (San Francisco), June 16, 1856; *Bulletin*, June 14, 16, 17, 1856.

58. Hittell, *History of California*, 3: 635.
59. *Bulletin*, July 14, 1856.
60. *Ibid.*, July 15, 1856.
61. Hittell, *History of California*, 3: 638; D. Williams, *Broderick*, p. 141; *Herald*, Sept. 21, 1856.
62. *Herald*, Sept. 16, Nov. 4, 1856; *Bulletin*, Nov. 3, 1856; *Chronicle*, Nov. 8, 1856; Gerald Stanley, "Slavery and the Origins of the Republican Party in California," *SCQ* 60 (1978): 1–16.
63. Brown, *Strain of Violence*, p. 139.
64. My statistics in this section are based on the following: *Bogardus' San Francisco, Sacramento City and Marysville Business Directory For May and June 1850* (San Francisco: William B. Cooke, 1850); Charles P. Kimball, *The San Francisco City Directory* (San Francisco: Journal of Commerce Press, 1850); Parker, *The San Francisco City Directory for the Year 1852–1853*; *A. W. Morgan and Co.'s San Francisco City Directory; Le Count and Strong's San Francisco City Directory* (San Francisco: Le Count and Strong, 1854); *Colville's San Francisco City Directory, Vol. I, for the Year Commencing October 1856*.
65. *Herald*, Nov. 1, 1856; Gerald Stanley, "Racism and the Early Republican Party: The 1856 Presidential Election in California," *PHR* 43 (1974): 171–87; Lura Smith to Hèlen Case Huntling, Nov. 12, 1856, LS.
66. William M. Lent to Faxon D. Atherton, Aug. 3, 1856, FDA.
67. William M. Lent to Faxon D. Atherton, Nov. 29, 1856, FDA; Coleman, "San Francisco Committees of Vigilance," p. 145.
68. Dibblee's 1856 number appeared on the application of his warehouse keeper, Henry Burgess, for membership in the 1856 committee, VC; Bancroft, *Popular Tribunals*, 2: 113; *Bulletin*, Nov. 3, 1856. The People's Party mayors were E. W. Burr (1856–59), Henry F. Teschenmacher (1859–63), and H. P. Coon (1863–67). Burr was probably not a formal member of the vigilantes; since the People's Party was anxious to deflect charges that it was out for power, it most likely would not have nominated a former vigilante. Teschenmacher was no. 107 in 1851. M. F. Williams (*History of the San Francisco Committee of Vigilance*, p. 406) says that Coon was a member of the 1856 committee; Bancroft (*Popular Tribunals*, 2: 645–55) says that Coon was not a member, though he "sympathized" with it.
69. San Francisco, *Municipal Reports* (1867–68), p. 623.
70. Williams, ed., *Papers of the San Francisco Committee of Vigilance of 1851*, p. 807; Alonzo Phelps, *Contemporary Biography of California's Representative Men* (San Francisco: A. L. Bancroft and Co., 1881), p. 280. Coleman had been a candidate for the U.S. Senate in 1864; Bancroft, *California*, 7: 322.
71. Clancey J. Dempster, Statement, p. 17, MS. in Bancroft Library.
72. Bancroft, *California*, 6: 772.
73. San Francisco, *Municipal Reports* (1867–68), p. 544; Decker, *Fortunes and Failures*, pp. 147–51; Lewis Francis Byington and Oscar Lewis, *The History of San Francisco* (Chicago: S. J. Clarke Publishing Co., 1931), 1: 285–87; Young, *San Francisco*, 1: 233–42.

74. San Francisco, *Municipal Reports* (1867–68), p. 624.
75. The numbers of the 1851 members are in Williams, *Papers*, pp. 806–14; Gillespie's 1856 number is on E. D. Sawyer's 1856 application, VC; Farwell's is on Maine-born laborer Hartford Joy's 1856 application, VC; George Schenck, Statement, p. 22; Charles V. Gillespie, Statement, p. 4; James D. Farwell, Statement, p. 5; James Dows, Statement, p. 3; James Olney, Statement, p. 1, all MS. in Bancroft Library.
76. Bancroft, *Popular Tribunals*, 2: 4; Clancey J. Dempster, Statement, p. 20; James D. Farwell, Statement, p. 13; John P. Manrow, Statement, p. 2, all MS. in Bancroft Library.
77. John Hittell, *History of the City of San Francisco*, pp. 5–6.
78. W. F. Swasey, *The Early Days and Men of California* (Oakland: Pacific Press Publishing Co., 1891), pp. 245, 272.
79. Stanford's application is in VC.
80. Phelps, *Contemporary Biography of California's Representative Men*, pp. 156–60.
81. Oscar T. Shuck, *History of the Bench and Bar of California* (Los Angeles: Commercial Printing House, 1901), pp. 542–43.
82. Frederic Hall, *The History of San Jose and Surroundings* (San Francisco: A. L. Bancroft and Co., 1871), pp. 355–59.
83. M. F. Williams, *History of the San Francisco Committee of Vigilance of 1851*, p. 441.
84. Byington and Lewis, *History of San Francisco*, 3: 137–40.
85. Rockwell D. Hunt, *California's Stately Hall of Fame* (Stockton: College of Pacific Press, 1950), pp. 237–42; W. F. Wallace, *History of Napa County* (Oakland: Enquirer Print, 1901), pp. 248–49, 262.
86. Phelps, *Contemporary Biography*, pp. 173–76.
87. *Ibid.*, pp. 269–71.
88. J. A. B. Scherer, *The Lion of the Vigilantes*, is the most modern biography of Coleman.
89. David A. Williams, *David C. Broderick*, is an outstanding account of the Senator's political life.
90. Terry's later career is detailed sympathetically in A. Russell Buchanan, *David S. Terry*.
91. H. Brett Melendy and Benjamin F. Gilbert, *The Governors of California: Peter H. Burnett to Edmund G. Brown* (Georgetown, Calif.: Talisman Press, 1965), pp. 67–80.
92. Melvin G. Holli and Peter d'A. Jones, *Biographical Dictionary of American Mayors, 1820–1980* (Westport, Conn.: Greenwood Press, 1981), pp. 129–30; William F. Heintz, *San Francisco's Mayors, 1850–1880* (Woodside, Calif.: Gilbert Richards Publications, 1975), pp. 20–25.
93. Heintz, *San Francisco's Mayors*, pp. 30–35; *History of San Luis Obispo County* (Oakland: Thompson and West, 1883; rpt. Berkeley: Howell-North, 1966, with an Introduction by Louisiana Clayton Dart), pp. 381–82; Oscar Shuck, *Bench and Bar in California* (San Francisco: Occident Printing House, 1888), p. 301.

94. Bancroft, *Popular Tribunals*, 2: 604–8.
95. Doyce Nunis, ed., *San Francisco Vigilance Committee of 1856*, pp. 79–80; William Heath Davis Notes, VC.
96. McGowan's story is told in Myers, *San Francisco's Reign of Terror*.

APPENDIX

1. William T. Sherman, *Memoirs of General William T. Sherman*, 1: 159. I should note that I am not attempting an exhaustive bibliography of the literature dealing with the 1856 committee. I am rather concentrating on the works that, in my judgment, are important for the development of the historiography. The most complete bibliography up to 1971 is Doyce Nunis, ed., *San Francisco Vigilance Committee of 1856*, pp. 170–76.
2. *Chronicle*, May 16, 1856; Gerald D. Nash, "California and Its Historians: An Appraisal of the Histories of the State," *PHR* 50 (1981): 387–413; *Herald*, May 22, 1856.
3. Franklin Tuthill, *The History of California* (San Francisco: H. H. Bancroft and Co., 1866), pp. 430, 480, 500, 508, 510, 524; Kevin Starr, *Americans and the California Dream* (New York: Oxford University Press, 1973), p. 114.
4. Stephen P. Webb, "A Sketch of the Causes, Operations, and Results of the San Francisco Vigilance Committee of 1856," *Essex Institute Historical Collection* 84, no. 2 (1948): 100, 130.
5. J. S. Hittell, *A History of the City of San Francisco*, pp. 239–43, 252, 267; California, *Statutes* (1856), chap. 125; on Hittell, see Claude Petty, "John S. Hittell and the Gospel of California," *PHR* 24 (1955): 1–16.
6. Josiah Royce, *California, From the Conquest in 1846 to the Second Vigilance Committee in San Francisco: A Study of the American Character* (1886; rpt. Santa Barbara and Salt Lake City: Peregrine, 1970), pp. 328–66; Earl Pomeroy, "Josiah Royce: Historian in Search of Community," *PHR* 40 (1971): 1–20.
7. Bancroft, *Popular Tribunals*, 2: 7, 13, 16, 160, 242, 324, 391, 430, 559, 692; John Walton Caughey, *Hubert Howe Bancroft: Historian of the West* (Berkeley and Los Angeles: University of California Press, 1946), p. 245; Roger Olmsted, "San Francisco and the Vigilante Style," *American West* 7, no. 2 (1970): 62.
8. Theodore H. Hittell, *History of California*, 3: 460–62.
9. Jeremiah Lynch, *A Senator of the Fifties: David C. Broderick of California* (San Francisco: A. M. Robertson and Co., 1911), pp. 108–9, 141.
10. Edward McGowan, *McGowan vs. California Vigilantes* (1857; rpt. Oakland: Biobooks, 1946), pp. 1–4.
11. Henry M. Gray, *Judges and Criminals. Shadows of the Past. History of the Vigilance Committee of San Francisco, Cal., with the Names of Its Officers* (San Francisco: printed for the author, 1858), pp. 5–8, 11, 16, 19, 67, 98.

12. Sherman, *Memoirs*, 1: 118, 131.
13. Royce, *California*, p. 350; Bancroft, *Popular Tribunals*, 2: 289; *Herald*, May 31, 1856.
14. James O'Meara, *The Vigilance Committee of 1856*, pp. 8–9, 12, 24, 43, 46.
15. M. F. Williams, *History of the San Francisco Committee of Vigilance of 1851*, pp. 438–39.
16. Robert Glass Cleland, *A History of California: The American Period* (New York: Macmillan, 1922), p. 302; Gertrude Atherton, *California: An Intimate History* (New York: Boni and Liveright, 1929), p. 172.
17. Stanton A. Coblentz, *Villains and Vigilantes: The Story of James King of William and Pioneer Justice in California*, pp. 103–6, 248–49, 252.
18. J. A. B. Scherer, *"The Lion of the Vigilantes": William T. Coleman and the Life of Old San Francisco*; John Walton Caughey, *California* (New York: Prentice-Hall, 1940), pp. 351–52.
19. Alan C. Valentine, *Vigilante Justice* (New York: Reynal and Co., 1956), pp. viii–ix, 86.
20. Peter T. Conmy, "The Vigilance Committee of 1856," MS. in Bancroft Library, dated Sept. 1, 1938.
21. William Henry Ellison, *A Self-Governing Dominion: California, 1849–1860* (Berkeley and Los Angeles: University of California Press, 1950), pp. 247, 263, 266–67.
22. John W. Caughey, "Their Majesties the Mob," *PHR* 26 (1957): 221, 223, 230–31; Caughey, *Their Majesties the Mob* (Chicago: University of Chicago Press, 1960), p. 4.
23. John M. Myers, *San Francisco's Reign of Terror*, pp. 2–3, 70; Clifford M. Drury, *William Anderson Scott: "No Ordinary Man"* (Glendale, Calif.: A. H. Clark, 1967), pp. 186–87, 189, 199.
24. Walton Bean, *California: An Interpretive History* (New York: McGraw-Hill, 1968), pp. 137, 148.
25. Bradford Luckingham, "Associational Life on Urban Frontier: San Francisco, 1848–1856," p. 153.
26. See Richard Maxwell Brown, "The American Vigilante Tradition," in Hugh Davis Graham and Ted Robert Gurr, eds., *Violence in America: Historical and Comparative Perspectives* (New York: Bantam Books, 1969); and Richard Maxwell Brown, "Pivot of American Vigilantism: The San Francisco Vigilance Committee of 1856," in John A. Carroll, ed., *Reflections of Western Historians* (Tucson: University of Arizona Press, 1969). Both essays are conveniently reprinted in Brown, *Strain of Violence: Historical Studies of American Violence and Vigilantism*, pp. 95–143.
27. Brown, *Strain of Violence*, pp. 137–38.
28. *Ibid.*, p. 134.
29. David A. Williams, *David C. Broderick: A Political Portrait*, pp. 125, 129, 143. Warren A. Beck and David A. Williams, *California: A History of the Golden State* (Garden City: Doubleday, 1972), pp. 178–79, argues along the same lines.

30. Roger Olmsted, "San Francisco and the Vigilante Style," *American West* 7, no. 1 (1970): 6–10, 63–64; no. 2: 20–27, 60–62. The material is also in T. H. Watkins and R. R. Olmsted, *Mirror of the Dream: An Illustrated History of San Francisco* (San Francisco: Scrimshaw Press, 1976), pp. 55–94.
31. Starr, *Americans and the California Dream*, pp. 85–87, 93–94.
32. Roger Lotchin, *San Francisco, 1846–1856: From Hamlet to City*, pp. 17, 245–58, 268, 275, 381, 384.
33. Peter R. Decker, *Fortunes and Failures: White-Collar Mobility in Nineteenth Century San Francisco*, pp. 34, 37, 61–63, 72–73, 81, 85, 92, 129, 140.
34. R. A. Burchell, *The San Francisco Irish, 1848–1880*, pp. 14, 52, 54, 123, 129, 184.

Index

Library of Congress Cataloging in Publication Data

Senkewicz, Robert M., 1947–
Vigilantes in gold rush San Francisco.

Bibliography: p.
Includes index.
1. Frontier and pioneer life—California—San Francisco. 2. Vigilance committees—California—History—19th century. 3. San Francisco (Calif.)—History. 4. California—Gold discoveries. I. Title.
F869.S357S46 1985 979.4′6104 83-40284
ISBN 0-8047-1230-1